Theravāda Buddhism

The Library of Religious Beliefs and Practices
Edited by: John Hinnells, University of Manchester, and Ninian Smart, Universities of Lancaster and Santa Barbara

Already published:

The Ancient Egyptians: Their Religious Beliefs and Practices
A. Rosalie David

Jews: Their Religious Beliefs and Practices
Alan Unterman

The Sikhs: Their Religious Beliefs and Practices
W. Owen Cole and Piara Singh Sambhi

Zoroastrians: Their Religious Beliefs and Practices
Mary Boyce

This series provides pioneering and scholarly introductions to different religions in a readable form. It is concerned with the beliefs and practices of religions in their social, cultural and historical setting. Authors come from a variety of backgrounds and approach the study of religious beliefs and practices from their different points of view. Some focus mainly on questions of history, teachings, customs and ritual practices. Others consider, within the context of a specific religion or geographical region, the inter-relationships between religions; the interaction of religion and the arts; religion and social organization; the involvement of religion in political affairs; and, for ancient cultures, the interpretation of archaeological evidence. In this way the series brings out the multi-disciplinary nature of the study of religion. It is intended for students of religion, ideas, social sciences and history, and for the interested layperson. Books are in preparation on the British, the Hindus, the Mahayana Buddhists and the Muslims.

Theravāda Buddhism

A social history from ancient Benares to modern Colombo

Richard F. Gombrich

ROUTLEDGE

London and New York

For my parents

First published in 1988 by
Routledge & Kegan Paul Ltd

Reprinted in 1991 and 1994
by Routledge
11 New Fetter Lane,
London EC4P 4EE

Simultaneously published in the USA and Canada
by Routledge
29 West 35th Street, New York, NY 10001

Set in Garamond
by Witwell Ltd., Southport
and printed in Great Britain
by R. Clay & Co. Ltd.
Bungay, Suffolk

Library of Congress Cataloging in Publication Data
Gombrich, Richard Francis.
Theravāda Buddhism
(Library of religious beliefs and practices)
Bibliography: p.
Includes index.
1. Theravāda Buddhism. 2. Theravāda Buddhism- Sri Lanka.
3. Sri Lanka-Religion. I. Title.
II. Series.
BQ7185.G66 1988 294.3'91'09 87--13981

British Library CIP Data also available

ISBN 0-415-07585-8

Contents

Acknowledgments and recommendations for further reading

There are two great pleasures in working on Theravāda Buddhism: the primary sources and the secondary sources. To praise the Pali Canon and its commentaries would be an impertinence. I hope it may not be thought impertinent, however, to say what admirable books modern scholars have written on the subject matter of this one. Very often I have found I could do no better than attempt to summarize the conclusions of my learned and lucid predecessors. I only hope that what is essentially a presentation of their work has not been too inept to encourage the reader to go back to their fuller accounts. Here are the works I particularly have in mind; in brackets after each are the numbers of the chapters which most heavily rely on them.

Walpola Rahula: *What the Buddha taught* (3)
Walpola Rahula: *History of Buddhism in Ceylon: The Anuradhapura Period* (6)
Mohan Wijayaratna: *Le moine bouddhiste selon les textes du Theravâda* (4)
Michael Carrithers: *The Forest Monks of Sri Lanka: An Anthropological and Historical Study* (4)
R.A.L.H. Gunawardana: *Robe and Plough: Monasticism and Economic Interest in Early Medieval Sri Lanka* (6)

Kitsiri Malalgoda: *Buddhism in Sinhalese Society 1750–1900: A Study of Religious Revival and Change* (7)
Heinz Bechert: *Buddhismus, Staat und Gesellschaft in den Ländern des Theravada Buddhismus* (7)
Gananath Obeyesekere: 'Religious Symbolism and Political Change in Ceylon' (article) (7)

Naturally these works figure, with others, in the references (which constitute almost my only footnotes). But that does not convey my full debt to them. This is especially true of *What the Buddha taught* and of Malalgoda's book. The Ven. Dr Rahula has provided my basic understanding of Buddhism, so adequate acknowledgment through such academic apparatus is impossible. The first half of chapter 7 owes so much to Malalgoda that to signal every point I have learnt from him would look absurd. Since all these authors are, happily, alive and well as I write, I hope they will forgive me for depending more heavily on their work than the footnotes can indicate.

I am also grateful to my friend and teacher Gananath Obeyesekere for letting me use in chapter 8 some of the fruits of our joint researches.

Though I cannot here list the many other scholars to whom I am indebted for their publications, I must mention, as a kind of patron saint of our studies, T.W. Rhys Davids, who not only founded the Pali Text Society (in 1881) but also wrote so sensibly and so elegantly about Buddhism.

For their help in the form of criticism and advice I am most grateful to Steven Collins, Lance Cousins, David Gellner, Mohan Wijayaratna and Paul Williams, colleagues whose work I confidently expect to overtake much of my own.

I would also like to thank the staff of the Instituut voor Oosterse Talen of Utrecht University for the hospitality of their superb library.

Richard Gombrich,
Oxford, August 1985

CHAPTER ONE

Introduction

A. INTRODUCTORY INFORMATION

Buddhists consider that their religion has Three Jewels*: the Buddha, the Dhamma and the Sangha. They begin any ritual or religious ceremony by saying three times that they 'take refuge' in these Three Jewels, which are therefore also called the Three Refuges. Indeed, the taking of the Refuges is what defines a Buddhist.

When they take refuge in the Buddha, Buddhists are thinking first and foremost of Gotama Buddha. Buddha is a title, meaning 'Enlightened' or 'Awakened'. Gotama was the family name of a man who was born on the Nepalese side of the modern Indian-Nepali border, probably in the sixth century BCE, and died at the age of 80. According to later tradition, his personal name was Siddhattha. At the age of 35 he attained Enlightenment by realizing the Truth, the Dhamma. Outsiders see him as the founder of Buddhism; for Buddhists the matter is slightly more complicated. As they see it, the Truth is eternal, but not always realized. Time has no beginning or end but goes through vast cycles. Every now and again there arises in the world a religious genius, a Buddha, who has the infinite wisdom to comprehend the Truth and the infinite compassion to preach it to the suffering world, so that others too may attain

*When English terms translate Buddhist technical terms we shall normally capitalize them.

Enlightenment. Gotama is the most recent Teacher in the infinite series of Buddhas. He was human, not divine, and is no longer personally accessible to us.

(The last sentence would not be accepted by Mahāyāna Buddhists. In this book the terms Buddhism and Buddhist refer primarily to the Theravāda tradition. Not everything said is correct for all Buddhist traditions, e.g. those of Tibet and the Far East. About *all* Buddhists few valid generalizations are possible.)

Every Buddha realizes and preaches the Truth. But not all of them ensure that that Truth will long be available to men. By preaching a code of monastic discipline, Gotama Buddha founded an Order, a Sangha. This institution not only consists of those who have decided to devote their lives to striving for Enlightenment; it also preserves the memory of the Buddha's Teaching. Thus, in a metaphor central to Buddhism, the Buddha is the great physician, the Dhamma is the remedy he prescribes, the Sangha is the nurse who administers that remedy.

The word Dhamma is variously translated into English. In so far as it is what the Buddhas teach, the intellectual content of Buddhism, it is aptly translated 'Doctrine'. This doctrine both describes and prescribes, so it is both 'Truth' and 'Law'.

When a modern Buddhist takes refuge in the Sangha he is thinking primarily of monks. In Theravāda Buddhist countries – Sri Lanka, Burma and Thailand are the main ones – most villages contain monasteries housing at least one monk, a man with shaven head wearing yellow robes. However, the term Sangha is ambiguous. In early texts it was used to refer to all who had accepted certain fundamental Buddhist doctrines and signalled their acceptance by taking the Three Refuges. Another traditional reference is to all who have attained a certain degree of sanctity, so that they will be Enlightened within seven lifetimes at the most; they are technically called Stream Enterers. Probably this latter meaning, the 'ideal Sangha', and the first meaning originally referred to exactly the same people, the community of professed Buddhists. However, the commoner use of the term is, and has long been, to refer to the 'conventional Sangha', namely those ordained. Unless otherwise stated, that will be the use of 'Sangha' in this book. For some 1500 years the Order contained monks, nuns and novices, both male and female. But early in the present millennium the female ordination tradition was lost. In Theravāda countries today there are some women who lead cloistered lives and behave like nuns, but they are not strictly reckoned as members of the Sangha.

If Theravāda Buddhists want to refer to Buddhism not just as a doctrine but as a phenomenon in history, a whole religion, they usually call it the Sāsana, the Teaching. For example, where English speakers might talk of the welfare of Buddhism, they would talk of the welfare of the Sāsana. Gotama Buddha founded the present Sāsana.

Theravāda is the branch of Buddhism now preserved in Sri Lanka and parts of continental southeast Asia. (As will be explained (pp. 110–12), it is misleading to call it a sect; one could call it a denomination.) The term means 'Doctrine of the Elders'; the elders in question are the senior monks, who preserve tradition. The title thus claims conservatism. An adherent of Theravāda is called a Theravādin. Theravāda reached Ceylon from India in or very near 250 BCE. For more than a thousand years thereafter it existed mainly in Ceylon and southeast India. In the eleventh century it went from Ceylon to Burma; over the next two centuries it diffused into the areas which are now Thailand, Laos and Cambodia. In all Theravādin countries there are minority populations who are for the most part not Buddhists; Theravāda has been the religion of the majority community (Sinhalese, Burmese, Thai, etc.) and generally enjoyed state patronage and official status, except of course under colonial rule. In Sri Lanka, Burma and Thailand Theravāda Buddhism is today in some sense the established religion and enjoys widespread support and patronage. Information about Laos is hard to come by, but it seems that the communist government there has preserved the Sangha in some form. In Cambodia, on the other hand, the Khmer Rouges government of Pol Pot in the late 1970s massacred most of the monks and defrocked the rest, so that the Sāsana is virtually extinct. However, Theravāda is showing new life, not only in the western and developed world – Theravādin monasteries have been founded in several countries of western Europe, in North America and in Australia – but also in non-communist countries of Asia: Nepal, Malaysia, Singapore and Indonesia. Its arrival in these countries is, however, so recent that it is too soon to say whether it can strike roots and command popular support.

Hallmarks of Theravāda Buddhism are the use of Pali as its main sacred language and dependence on the Pali version of the Buddhist Canon as its sacred scripture. The Buddhist terms in this book are in Pali, unless otherwise stated. The word Pali originally meant '(canonical) text'; its use to designate the *language* of the Theravādin canonical texts seems not to antedate the eighteenth century. Pali is an ancient derivative of Sanskrit and quite close to it. Thus some words which may be more familiar to the reader in their Sanskrit forms turn up in this book with small phonetic changes: for Sanskrit *Dharma*, *karman* and *nirvāṇa* Pali has *Dhamma*, *kamma* and *nibbāna*. *Buddha* and *Sangha*, on the other hand, are the same in both languages. (However, in chapter 2 most Indian words are in Sanskrit, as appropriate to the subject matter.)

Pali literature is quite extensive, but very little of it is what we would call secular. So far as we know, it has all been composed by members of the Sangha. The Canon itself is voluminous. In Pali it is called the *Tipiṭaka*, which means that it consists of 'three baskets', i.e. three collections of texts: the *Vinaya Piṭaka*, which contains the *vinaya*, i.e. the rules or 'discipline' of the Sangha; the *Sutta Piṭaka*, which contains the Buddha's sermons and some religious poetry and other miscellaneous texts – this is far the largest 'basket'; and the *Abhidhamma Piṭaka*, which contains what is sometimes called 'systematic philosophy', a scholastic elaboration of doctrine, especially as regards the analysis of mind. Then there are the commentaries on the Canon, which probably consist largely of material compiled in ancient India, though in their present form they almost all come from Ceylon; and sub-commentaries and similar ancillary literature. Among this ancillary literature stands one monumental work, the *Visuddhi-magga*, *The Path to Purity*. It is a summary compendium of Theravādin doctrine, written in Ceylon in the early fifth century CE by Buddhaghosa, the monk who also put the most important commentaries in their final shape.

Perhaps the most notable Pali text which is quite independent of the Canon is the *Mahāvaṃsa*, *The Great Chronicle* of Buddhism in Ceylon. Other Theravādin countries emulated the *Mahāvaṃsa* and compiled chronicles of their own.

Not all the literature of Theravāda Buddhism is in Pali. In late mediaeval Ceylon some Buddhist works were composed in Sanskrit. Far more important, popular religious literature has everywhere been composed in the local languages. Much of it is translated or paraphrased from the Pali or otherwise depends closely on the Canon for its subject matter, but there is also a fair amount of apocryphal literature.

The traditional English name of the country with which the latter half of this book is concerned is Ceylon. A new constitution in 1972 changed the official name of the country to Sri Lanka. These words are of course in the Sinhala language, and 'Ceylon' is presumably a corruption of them, as 'Spain' is a corruption of 'España'. I have never understood therefore why 'Sri Lanka' should be used in English, let alone the barbarous adjective 'Sri Lankan' in place of 'Ceylonese'; in English we do not call Spain 'España'. However, I wish to offend no national susceptibilities, so I have tried to conform to the new usage and have called the country 'Ceylon' only when referring to periods before it officially shed that name. As will be explained below, the majority of the population of Sri Lanka have always been Sinhalese. Their language can also be called 'Sinhalese' but I have preferred to refer to it as Sinhala.

The names of Sinhalese monks, which they acquire at ordination, have two parts: the name of their village of origin, followed by a Pali given name. Modern bureaucracy often reduces the name of the village to an initial. Sinhalese tend to refer to monks by the village name, but not consistently; I have chosen the latter (Pali) name, shorn of honorifics, for bare reference, e.g. I refer to the Ven. Hikkaḍuve Sumangala as Sumangala.

Two final points of usage. When I write *vinaya* I refer to monastic discipline, whereas *Vinaya* refers to the text, the *Vinaya Piṭaka*. When I write *nikāya* in referring to a monastic ordination tradition (see p. 111) I am using the common noun, whereas Nikāya is being used as part of the proper names of such groups; neither has anything to do with the *Nikāya* which is a body of texts, a sub-division of the *Sutta Piṭaka*.

I must now turn to the theoretical issues raised by writing a social history of Buddhism. Any reader who is not interested in them and wishes to take my interpretive framework on trust can turn straight to p. 18.

B. A *SOCIAL* HISTORY OF BUDDHISM?

To attempt to write the social history of a religion is a problematic enterprise. Such an enterprise has never been undertaken outside the modern West; it smacks of a secularized society. Most people in the world do not regard religion as a fit subject for empirical study. What they want to know about a religion is whether the beliefs it inculcates are true or false, whether the conduct it recommends is right or wrong. Since religions other than one's own are wrong – or at least wrong for oneself – to study them would be an irrelevance or worse. Since one's own religion represents the truth, and truth is timeless, to imply that that truth has only been reached through historical circumstance and that belief in it may be similarly conditioned seems likewise sacrilegious, or at best foolish.

The classic formulation of this problem is that of Edward Gibbon:

> The theologian may indulge the pleasing task of describing Religion as she descended from Heaven, arrayed in her native

> purity. A more melancholy duty is imposed on the historian. He must discover the inevitable mixture of error and corruption which she contracted in a long residence upon earth, among a weak and degenerate race of beings.
>
> Our curiosity is naturally prompted to inquire by what means the Christian faith obtained so remarkable a victory over the established religions of the earth. To this inquiry, an obvious but satisfactory answer may be returned; that it was owing to the convincing evidence of the doctrine itself, and to the ruling providence of its great Author. But, as truth and reason seldom find so favourable a reception in the world, and as the wisdom of Providence frequently condescends to use the passions of the human heart, and the general circumstances of mankind, as instruments to execute its purpose; we may still be permitted, though with becoming submission, to ask not indeed what were the first, but what were the secondary causes of the rapid growth of the Christian church.[1]

Or the problem can be put in another way: if religion claims to explain the world, can we in the world explain religion?

This is not to say that religions necessarily lack historical awareness or concern. A religion which ascribes its origins to a human founder – like the three great world religions: Buddhism, Christianity and Islam – is intensely concerned with the biography of that founder, and above all with how he came to have access to the truth. A religion which sees itself as having a beginning in time also foresees its end (coterminous, perhaps, with the end of the world), though both beginning and end may be cyclically recurrent events in a timescale stretching beyond the limits of human imagination. Extending from a beginning to an already predicted end, the religion will thus have a course to run through history, and its adherents may chart its progress. Such religions tend to produce chronicles of their central institution, their church, for the health of that organization is the best measure of the health of the religion as a whole, an indicator whether it is duly proceeding towards apocalyptic climax or terminal decline. Since Hinduism is not a historical religion in this sense, for it has neither a historical founder nor a church, it is not surprising that for over a thousand years classical India produced no historiography. Historical writing in the Indian cultural area began (probably in the fourth century CE) in the Buddhist monasteries of Ceylon with chronicles of the Buddhist monastic order, the Sangha, in that island state.

To such church chronicles Christianity and the other monotheistic religions offer many parallels. Unlike Indian Buddhism, they are also rich in hagiography, the lives of individual saints whose example should inspire the faithful. (Hagiography is not unknown to Buddhism, but the character of the religion makes it lend itself less to personality cults.) In the West – I am talking of the pre-modern West – such historical religious literature sees God as the ultimate cause of all events, the motor behind history. (I ignore here the problematic role of the Devil; to include him would not affect my argument.) God is traditionally conceived to work through individuals. On the human plane, it is individual men and women whose characters and decisions influence the lives of others, and such influence is most commonly perceived as taking place through the conscious decision of the influenced. An individual who has great power to influence others in this way (as against power to coerce them) is said to be endowed with God's grace, charisma. If God has thus given someone the power to influence others – for example, to convert them – no further explanation of that influence can be required.

This is not what is meant by social history. A social historian works on the principle that historical events cannot be explained purely as the results, let alone the intended results, of conscious decisions taken by isolated individuals; this, however, leaves open the question whether they are the work of God (or some otherwise named transcendent, autonomous force).

Both of these points need to be amplified, the latter first. When religious people encounter an attempt to explain their beliefs or customs in social terms they often suspect that this is but a cover for an attempt either to prove them wrong (as may be done by a missionary from another religion) or to relativize all religious beliefs and values. Moreover, their suspicions are often justified. But they need not be so. To show the circumstances under which a belief or value comes to be held is *not* to invalidate it. Of this the history of science furnishes innumerable examples. We now know the speed of light. It could be discovered only after certain other advances had been made, advances both conceptual (most basically, that light is a thing which travels) and technical (so that its speed could be measured). What has been discovered is an objective fact: it was true even before anyone knew it and will still be true even if no one alive knows it. But that does not mean that we cannot write a history of how it came to be discovered or ask, for instance, who now knows it or does not know it or refuses to believe in it, and why.

Similarly, religions make various statements, such as 'The good go to heaven when they die' or 'There is a blissful state, the extinction of greed, hatred and delusion, which men can attain in this life', and to investigate how these statements came first to be made and who has believed or believes in them is not to impugn (or to support) their veracity. In the first and most successful popular western book about Buddhism, T. W. Rhys Davids begins by remarking that Buddhists 'far outnumber' Christians, immediately adding, 'From such summary statements, however, great misconceptions may possibly arise, quite apart from the fact that numbers are no test of truth, but rather the contrary.'[2] (I suspect that the last four words are a playful echo of Gibbon.) Not all the truth claims made by religions can be correct, because some of them conflict; but beyond that the empirical investigator has nothing to say and need pose no threat. My view is that, like ethical propositions, metaphysical propositions cannot be refuted (let alone confirmed) by empirical evidence, but that does not mean that they are meaningless or valueless. I hold that 'One should respect people's religious opinions' is a valid ethical proposition regardless of who holds it or why.

Nevertheless, a social account of religion cannot command general attention unless its author aims for a certain metaphysical neutrality. If his apparatus of causal explanation depends on a particular metaphysic, so that, for example, he explains all misfortunes such as famine, disease and war as merely the results of bad *karma* or God's punishment of sinners, he cannot command credence among those who do not accept the metaphysic. Worse, he cannot enter intellectual debate about his explanations and it is hard to see what criticism, let alone refutation, he would accept. His account may edify believers but it cannot contribute to general human understanding.

It is true that in so far as a religion (or any ideology) claims to explain human thought and action, the events of history, it is not amenable to being explained itself. But that 'in so far as' saves our subject. Marxist materialism is an extreme example of an ideology which claims to offer an ultimate explanation, so that in the last resort it shares no common ground with those who do not agree with that explanation or do not accept its ultimacy. Buddhism, on the other hand, makes no such grandiose claims. All that the Buddha claimed to explain was continued rebirth into this world of suffering. (It is not quite accurate to say that he explained suffering itself: that he took as axiomatic.) He stated quite explicitly that he had not explained other things; he regarded them as unimportant. Thus Buddhism seems to me to have no basic tenets which might conflict with explanations of its own history, even if it might regard them as a waste of time.

This book will thus be metaphysically neutral and look only for explanations which do not rest on religious assumptions. Thus, for example, I find 'charisma' a worthless concept: if we stay neutral about the operation of divine grace, to say that a man has charisma is just a way of saying that he easily influences people; it explains nothing. We should probably ask rather what it is in *their* circumstances which makes them open to his influence.

However, while I hope that my explanations are metaphysically neutral (agnostic), I do make a negative assumption: that one cannot explain everything. There is a widespread view that 'there is no such thing as chance'. Man searches for meaning in the world. 'When the bus crashed X was killed while Y, sitting next to him, didn't get so much as a scratch. There must be a reason for it.' I disagree. I accept the role of pure chance in human affairs. I also accept free will, because I consider that Karl Popper has shown determinism to be untenable.[3] If the bus driver chose to take an unnecessary risk, nothing made that choice inevitable.

This brings me to consider my second point, the role of the individual in religious history. Viewed as a historical phenomenon, a religion is a tradition. The customs and beliefs of a religious tradition are transmitted by institutions both formal and informal. While it is usually formal institutions which act to preserve orthodoxy and orthopraxy, in other words to prevent change, the main force of conservatism is the mere process of socialization. By and large, people hold to their ideas and customs because they have learnt them from their parents, etc., and the rewards for conformity outweigh the satisfactions to be derived from a change. While this is perhaps banal, it does show that it is for the most part change which the historian has to explain. So what is my view of innovation in religious history?

To admit that people's thoughts and actions are largely the product of their education and social circumstance is not to deny them free will or the ability to innovate. Clearly the Buddha was one of the greatest innovators of all time. Innovation itself, however, is not all that rare or remarkable. Every human being continually generates new meaningful sentences, but few of them seem worthy of permanent record. Even religious innovators abound, as a visit to a psychiatric hospital will unhappily confirm.

Even when an individual proposes changes, he is not merely reacting to a tradition but necessarily using the language of that tradition. If he fails to use the accepted code he cannot communicate. This means that the historian cannot hope to do justice to the new message unless he has mastered its medium, the code in which the message was conveyed. We can only understand what the Buddha's words meant to him and his contemporaries in so far as we understand the system of ideas he was arguing against, the language of his society. ('Language' here bears a broad, metaphorical sense; but it is difficult to reach that broad understanding without any knowledge of the relevant language in its narrow, literal sense.)

Thus innovation is never creation *ex nihilo*: it is a modification of tradition; it uses tradition as its raw material. But one can go further. I. A. Richards has shown that the poet can only work with the resources provided by his language, which embodies his cultural traditions; it is his language which inspires him.[4] My father, E.H. Gombrich, writing of artistic creativity, has stressed the role of feedback.[5] Feedback works at two levels. During the act of creation there is constant feedback between the creator and what he is making, as when a painter constantly reacts to what appears, by accident or design, on the canvas before him. Something analogous is true of the creator of new ideas: the formulation of his ideas gives him new food for thought; but this is a psychological matter likely to remain inaccessible to the social historian, especially when he is concerned with a figure of the remote past. However, feedback also works on the societal level: the individual innovator creates new conditions to which in turn he reacts. We shall see that the Buddha lived to become concerned with problems arising from that tangible result of his own innovations, the Sangha.

History is unlikely to remember innovations unless they have found acceptance either among many people or at least among the powerful. Most religions which have flourished have done so not merely through the cogency of their ideas but because at some point they have attracted powerful patronage. Whatever their emotional appeal to us, the religions of the oppressed mostly (not all: Christianity is an exception) remain in obscurity.

Wherein does the cogency of ideas consist? Or rather – since this is my real problem – what makes any religious innovation acceptable? Of course, religions consist not only of ideas: they also offer modes of feeling and patterns of behaviour – customs and institutions. Nevertheless, I am here considering religious innovation and change, and systems of action and feeling too must be communicated primarily through language and the ideas that language alone can convey. So to talk of the 'cogency of ideas' is a reasonable and convenient shorthand for religious innovation in general.

My answer is that the new ideas will seem cogent and may gain acceptance if they seem to offer solutions better than those already available to current problems. Such problems may be cognitive or ethical or social, they may be intellectual, emotional or practical. That religion offers a solution to a problem does not mean that that problem is necessarily religious in character or would not admit of a quite non-religious solution. If I am starving – a severe practical problem – I may take drastic steps to acquire food, for instance by stealing it, or take comfort in a religion which tells me to stop desiring to be fed or promises me a reward in heaven for a virtuous death; hence Marx's comment that religion is the opium of the people.

Religions tend to offer solutions in particular to two problems, the problem of suffering and the problem of human evil. Their answers to problems tend also to be of a very general, wide-ranging character, leaving particulars to be sorted out by more specialized systems of thought. This high level of generality often allows for much latitude in individual interpretation: the same doctrine or practice can satisfy various requirements because it is variously understood.

We cannot explain how new solutions arise in the minds of individual innovators; but they are motivated to search for new solutions by their problems, tensions or frustrations. And if their solutions seem good to others with similar problems, they may well adopt them.

My view of religious conservatism is a corollary of this view of innovation. Because of the pressures which arise merely from being a member of a social group, people accept the ideas and behaviour patterns of their socializers and peers so long as no better solutions present themselves. They may be acutely unhappy and frustrated, but stay that way until an innovator offers them something better than what they have already. Even then, they may not accept the innovation.

Human problems are infinitely varied, even though some, like death, are always with us, and others, like hunger or loneliness, occur with distressing frequency. So in saying that religious innovations must be seen as answers to problems I have not said anything very substantial about historical causation; even Marxists might accept this formulation, though they would probably dislike my individualist emphasis. So far I have merely presented a guideline for research, the heuristic strategy of looking at the 'problem situation' (Popper's term).[6] I do, however, disagree with dialectical materialism, and must briefly explain why.

The limitations of Marxist and Weberian views of religion

Unlike Marxists and Weberians, I do not think that there is necessarily a close relation between the religion and the economy of a social group. In this and the next two paragraphs I am using the names of Marx and Weber as a convenient shorthand for certain theories; my concern is to discuss those specific theories of causation in religious history, not to attack Marx or Weber (or their followers), so it does not matter if I have over-simplified the views actually held by those two great thinkers. The Marxist interpretation of history I take to be materialist: that the ecology, techniques and social relations of material (i.e. economic) production, which Marxists call 'the base' or 'the forces of production', determine the superstructure, the systems of social organization, custom, thought and sensibility we call culture – including religion. If it is claimed that Marx put forward a much weaker thesis which allowed also for the superstructure to influence the base (i.e. that Marx was not a strict materialist), I have to reply that in that case I cannot see the difference between Marx's and Weber's views of causation. Marxist materialism also holds that history progresses, in that all societies evolve through set stages from one kind of base to another.

Weber's theory I take to be that religion/ideology interacts with socio-economic conditions (in which the economic element still has causal primacy); this interaction results in an elective affinity between religious and social forms. Weber's position is extremely plausible. It has formed the backbone of almost all non-Marxist sociology of religion, and one might argue that were there no such affinity there could not be a sociology of religion. Plainly I do not take so negative a view, otherwise I could not have embarked on writing this book.

However, I do think that the theories of Marx and Weber suffer from defects. Firstly, Marxism, in particular, makes too little allowance for the social forces of inertia. Inertia, or conservatism, may cause cultural forms to persist, perhaps even for centuries, while material conditions ('the base') are changing. (Such inertia is more likely if change is gradual.) Weber built this conservatism into his general theory by holding tradition to be one of the three sources of 'legitimacy', i.e. a reason why people act as they do. Some Marxists admit the existence of time-lags, which they call 'contradictions'; if a social group has a religion or ideology which goes with an economic base other than the one actually present, they predict that the strain will cause them to change – sooner or later. But this leads one into the second difficulty: that by making the statements about how base and superstructure match less precise, one makes them untestable. The theory becomes untestable because of the various escape clauses, which do not specify, for instance, how long a 'contradiction' may last.

However, the greatest defect of materialist theories of religion seems to me to be the poverty of their conclusions. Certainly one can accept that unless a society produces a food surplus, i.e. more food than is needed to keep the producers alive and producing, it cannot support a priestly class, or indeed any non-producers. But this is so uninformative as to be very nearly a tautology. Even the concept of a surplus is distressingly imprecise, for the view of what constitutes a basic sufficiency of food itself varies widely; what determines that variation? At best one can say that economic conditions set certain limits, very wide limits, to religious possibilities. The basic problem, at least with the Marxist historiography of India, is that it sticks to an evolutionary scheme which allows for only about half a dozen types of society. But religion and all the other manifestations of human culture which Marxists assign to the superstructure are infinitely varied. We want to know more about them than whether they fit into one of half a dozen categories. For example, if Buddhism, Jainism and several other religions began at about the same place and time, we want to know what appealed to whom and why. It is just not very informative (whether or not it is true) to say that they emerged because agriculture had become sufficiently productive to allow the formation of a state and an exploiting landowner class, for such a change in the base has occurred many times in world history with widely varying results.

Even Max Weber's theory, in my opinion, is open to the same objection of barrenness. He scored one great success when he showed the historical association of Protestant puritanism (chiefly Calvinism) with the rise of capitalism in northwest Europe in the sixteenth and seventeenth centuries. However, were they Calvinists because they were capitalists, or vice versa? The answer seemed to be that the causality worked both ways: Calvinism was an ideology which supplied businessmen with a justification for their capitalist activity (as Marxists would hope); but equally Calvinism itself raised problems – the uncertainty whether one was of the elect – which led to attitudes and actions (this-worldly asceticism) which in effect made one a capitalist. In fact Weber showed that the latter could occur even where precedent and tradition were against it.

Following this line of thought, one is going to argue that the ideological differences between Buddhism and Jainism will lead their adherents into different social and economic situations. That does in fact seem to be a much easier case to argue than that they appealed to different economic classes in the first place, a proposition for which (so far as I know) there is no evidence. Thus the effects of a religion on economic and social conditions may turn out to be at least as interesting and important as the converse. But the superiority of Weberian to Marxist theory does not lie only in admitting two-way causation between base and superstructure (a move some modern Marxists, no longer strict materialists, are prepared to welcome), and thus approaching the idea of feedback. It lies even more in abandoning the idea of a linear progress, an inevitable evolution, which takes society through a fixed and finite number of stages. Thus the Weberian theory admits of far more variety in history and is more alive to the complexity of social events.

For me, however, it still admits too little variety, in so far as it still focuses on only two variables, religion and the economy. It is still the economy which must co-vary with religion, regardless of what is going on in other areas of society and culture. My view of the truth is less tidy.

I see different areas of human culture as having a certain autonomy, so that they do not necessarily move in step. Mathematics and music, economics and religious thought each have their own history, their own progress from problem to attempted solution to new problem. They may move at different speeds, but also in rather different ways, for some have closer connections with the social and material world than others. Thus, the progress of pure mathematics must depend almost entirely on the current problem situation in the field, hardly at all on material and social factors. Developments in music or the visual arts have more to do with the current state of those arts than with conditions elsewhere in society, though technology, for example, may also affect them. On the other hand, areas of human endeavour which grapple directly with society and its problems, like applied economics or perhaps short-story writing, are likely to be much more influenced by social circumstance. Religious ideas seem to me to come near this end of the pure/applied continuum: since they claim to be relevant to the whole of human life they are likely to be profoundly affected by life as currently lived around them. On the other hand, they too stand in a tradition, a tradition which is often self-conscious and highly organized. So they too respond to problems in their area – the religious thought of their time – as well as to material and social conditions.

Since I thus see human culture as composed of many strands, areas which are partly autonomous, I do not consider that finding a solution to a problem in one area need entail change in another. Even within religion, different areas can change at different speeds; for example, someone may find a solution to an intellectual problem he has about doctrine without this entailing any change in his behaviour. On the other hand, a small change in belief may entail vast unintended consequences (on which see below), such as persecution for heresy. A conscientious Roman Catholic, for example, who becomes convinced that during mass there is no transubstantiation, may consequently become a Protestant, which will probably entail massive changes in his entire religious and social life. This knock-on effect often occurs because religion is so much a matter of allegiance, of identity.

Religious affiliation as a badge of membership in a social group is a topic a social historian cannot ignore. Sometimes the social allegiance appears to be the true determinant of action and the religious language to be an obfuscation, the question of orthodoxy or orthopraxy a mere epiphenomenon. For example, when the Christian world split over whether the Holy Ghost proceeds from the Father and the Son or from the Father alone, the truth being (one supposes) impossible to ascertain, one readily asserts that the doctrinal controversy was the mere language used to express rivalries less abstrusely grounded. This kind of use of religion to express group loyalties will figure in the latter half of this book, for Buddhist and national interests have tended to be identified in the predominantly Theravādin countries. Even more important in this book is my own analysis of Buddhist identity, of what exactly is involved in being a Buddhist; the question seems to me crucial for a proper understanding of Buddhist theory, and will occupy the last part of this chapter.

Unintended consequences

I mentioned that I accept Karl Popper's arguments against determinism. I also accept what he calls 'methodological individualism', the principle that the subjects and agents of human history are individuals, not collective impersonal or superpersonal forces like 'the collective subconscious', 'the world spirit', or 'history' itself. But this is very far from saying that history is simply the product of human intentions. In the first place, obviously but not trivially, there are many great events – usually disasters – like earthquakes, epidemics, floods and droughts, which have no connection or only the remotest connection with human will or agency but exercise profound influence on history. (I have been greatly impressed by William H. McNeill's book, *Plagues and Peoples*, and use it below (pp. 58–9).)

Popper has stressed a less immediately obvious but even more important point: the part played in human affairs by the *unintended consequences* of our actions. 'We hardly ever produce in social life precisely the effect that we wish to produce, and we usually get things that we do not want into the bargain.'[7] Indeed, unintended –– but inevitable – consequences of one's actions may be the very opposite of what one wishes. If I go to a cocktail party, my entry makes the room more crowded, my conversation makes it noisier. The higher noise level feeds back so that my interlocutor and I have to raise our voices in order to hear each other, so giving another twist to the vicious circle. Popper himself gives the example that if I wish to sell my house my entry into the market will depress the prices (other things being equal); one can generalize this example to all small free markets: 'Whoever wants to sell something always depresses the market value of what he wants to sell; whoever wants to buy something raises the market value of what he wants to buy.'[8] These examples show that there are laws (or regularities, if one wants a more modest word) in the behaviour of human collectivities (such as cocktail party guests) and institutions (such as markets) which are quite independent of the wills of individuals; nor are these regularities themselves wills or intentions. Thus social events cannot all be reduced to matters of psychology.

The power of institutional traditions in Theravādin history can be illustrated by a matter I have already mentioned. The Order of nuns has died out. There are many women who lead nun-like lives and would evidently wish to be real nuns if that were possible. But the tradition of the Sangha, embodied in the *Vinaya Piṭaka*, says that a nun must undergo a double ordination, one by validly ordained monks and the other by validly ordained nuns. Since no validly ordained nuns remain in the Theravādin tradition, the Order of nuns can apparently not be revived. Or can it? There are still nuns in some Mahāyāna countries. The scriptures say nothing to prevent their officiating at a Theravādin ordination. In recent times some have accordingly suggested that Sri Lanka revive the Order of nuns by having postulants ordained by Mahāyānist nuns. There may well be individual lady aspirants who would welcome the idea. But if their ordination was not accepted by the wider society it would be useless, and evidently they judge that public opinion – notably that of the local (male) Sangha – is not yet amenable, since there is suspicion that the Mahāyāna tradition may be lax in discipline. It seems likely that the Order of nuns will soon be revived in Theravāda by *western* Theravādins, who do not have to bother about public opinion in their own societies, since that opinion is perfectly indifferent to this question.

This case illustrates two points: that innovation by an individual cannot succeed without public acceptance; and that a social situation often exists despite, not because of, people's wishes. I doubt whether anyone is actually pleased that there are no nuns in Sri Lanka, and many people are very sorry; but tradition dictates that there is no remedy. This is probably an unintended consequence of a rule which the Buddha laid down in quite other circumstances. It is hard to believe that were he alive today he would not permit the re-establishment of the nuns' Order.

To ascribe unwelcome happenings to malign volition, whether single or collective, human or divine, Popper calls 'the conspiracy theory of society'.[9] Unfortunately, popular perceptions of society are very often conspiracy theories. The Indian caste system and the British slump are ascribed to 'them', pointing at those who most benefit (or suffer least) from the situation, or at others whom one dislikes and distrusts. But it is utterly naive to ascribe the origin of the caste system to a brahmin conspiracy, even if individual brahmins exploit their advantage under the system once it is in place.

Words are no less liable than actions to entail unintended consequences. In their case our intentions face an additional hazard: the problem of communication. Every teacher has learnt by bitter experience how hard it is to convey a message fully and accurately. People simply will not hear what for their own reasons they are not disposed to hear. On the other hand, they will often hear or assimilate a distorted version of our message. Human messages are often filtered through institutions, such intermediaries as school, church or state bureaucracy, which give further opportunities for distortion. (One can even argue, at the risk of over-simplification, that the entire apparatus of the modern state is a massive example of unintended consequences, distorting the voiced wishes of individual citizens and giving them the opposite of what they want.) Indeed, it is so unusual in human affairs to achieve just what one intended that the historian should draw special attention to such a success and never take it for granted.

The entire history of Christianity may be a case in point. Did Jesus Christ envisage the Christian church or a Christian society? He seems to have expected a rapid end to the world and salvation for his band of followers. The Sermon on the Mount is not a charter for an enduring institution. But one cannot plausibly go to the extreme of claiming that Jesus had nothing to do with the historical phenomenon of Christianity – for example, by laying the entire responsibility for it on the shoulders of

St Paul. Christian Socialism in our times is not a phenomenon that Jesus could have foreseen or intended; but its attempt to apply the values he preached to politics is but one of the myriad unintended consequences which have flowed from his gospel.

Can the same be said of the Buddha's relation to Buddhism? Clearly to a large extent it can: the Buddha could not have foreseen or intended most of the consequences that have flowed from his preaching. On the other hand, he did found a rational institution, an institution consciously and carefully designed to a particular end. This institution was the Sangha, the monastic Order.

The Sangha

At the time of the Buddha, there were other holy men (and perhaps women) who had left society to look for salvation beyond its boundaries. Some were silent sages, some preached, some listened. The followers of a few eminent teachers had evidently organized to practise and preserve their teachings. One of these traditions, the Jain, is still flourishing in India; its great teacher Mahāvīra (whether he was the founder is disputed) was probably an older contemporary of the Buddha. When other men who had renounced all familial and other social ties – henceforth I shall refer to them simply as 'renouncers' – first began to follow the Buddha, they were acting in accord with an existent custom. Such an organized group began simply as the body of men who were trying to follow the path their teacher had mapped out to the goal he had defined; in its origin the institution did not necessarily have any instrumental character.

The Buddhist Order, the Sangha of monks (*bhikkhu-sangha*), was such a group too; but it was always more than that. The story goes that when the Buddha himself attained Enlightenment he was tempted to rest content; why should he give himself the trouble of preaching? It was only the entreaty of the greatest god which persuaded him to communicate his discovery of the truth to others. The founding and organization of the Sangha is a logical development: converts too were to spread the word. When the Buddha had acquired sixty full-time followers, mendicants like him (for that is the meaning of *bhikkhu*), he ordered them to disperse, saying,

> Go monks and travel for the welfare and happiness of the people, out of compassion for the world, for the benefit, welfare and happiness of gods and men. No two of you go the same way. Teach

> the Dhamma, monks ... and proclaim the pure holy life. There are beings with little passion in their natures who are languishing for lack of hearing the Dhamma; they will understand it.[10]

The duty laid on monks to preach naturally shaded over into a duty to preserve the Teachings. It has always been a live issue, both among Buddhists and among their critics, whether the life of a monk is selfish, even anti-social. Is it not selfish to renounce one's social responsibilities in order to seek one's own salvation? Certainly both brahmins in India and Confucians in China (to say nothing of Christian missionaries) have argued in this vein, and this was also one strand in the Mahāyāna criticism of earlier Buddhism. But the above story shows that concern for the happiness of all beings is the foundation of the Sangha's very existence.

That story occurs at the beginning of one half of the *Vinaya Piṭaka*, the *Khandhaka*. In the introduction to the other half, the *Sutta-vibhanga*, it is explained that the Buddha formulated the rules for monks so that 'the pure holy life', the practice of Buddhism, should not die out with the first generation of disciples. Whether or not the Buddha said exactly what is reported in that scripture, it is a fact that among all the bodies of renouncers it was only the Buddhists who invented monastic life. The Sangha was organized as a community quite unlike the Jains and other renouncers, uniquely well organized to preserve not only a way of life but also a body of scripture in an age before writing was known, or at least widely used. Indeed, one of the two Jain denominations, the Digambara, claims that the early Jains lost their scriptures; and none of the other contemporary sects seem to have preserved theirs. It is hard to believe that the Buddhist Sangha's development was not planned.

According to scriptural tradition, the Buddha had a definite view of the future. When he was persuaded, apparently against his better judgment, to permit the founding of an Order of nuns, he is said to have declared that now his teaching would only endure for five hundred years. If this story is true, he was too pessimistic. When several centuries had passed and Buddhism was still flourishing, the figure in the story had to be revised. The Theravādin view is that what was meant was five thousand years. By the Theravādin computation which seems to have been current for about the last thousand years, and which puts the Buddha rather earlier than modern scholars find plausible, the 2500th anniversary of the Buddha's Teaching occurred in 1956, so we are just over half way through.

What inquiries will the evidence support?

In the above paragraphs I have several times raised the question whether a story about the Buddha is true. This raises the problem of how reliable our sources are. All our earliest information about the Buddha and his teachings is contained in the collection of texts which is collectively known as the Canon. Since I have recently published elsewhere[11] an accessible account of the Canon's formation, and it is not of central relevance to our theme, I shall not repeat it here. Buddhists hold that the whole Canon is 'the word of the Buddha', but some of the canonical texts themselves state that they are by disciples, not by the Buddha himself, so even orthodox Buddhists do not take this blanket term literally. On the other hand, the first external evidence for the existence of Buddhist scriptural texts occurs in an Asokan inscription c.250 BCE. For this and other reasons, some western scholars have been extremely sceptical about the authenticity of the Canon, and consequently about how much we can know about the Buddha or his teachings.

My own position is this. In the precise *form* in which we have them, the Pali texts are undoubtedly much later than the Buddha; as will be further discussed below (p. 71), they were long preserved only orally and not written down till the first century BCE; moreover, their language may have been modified even long after that. On the other hand, I have the greatest difficulty in accepting that the main edifice is not the work of one genius. By 'the main edifice' I mean the *content* of the main body of sermons, the four *Nikāyas*, and of the main body of monastic rules. As happens in every field, scholars who want to impose their own ideas on the material have tried to exclude various texts as late interpolations. For instance, Mrs C.A.F. Rhys Davids, the widow of the author cited above and a Pali scholar in her own right, had a conspiracy theory that the Buddha's entire message had been reworked and distorted by soulless monks. She did not explain how such tinkering, even corporate tinkering, could have won the assent of the entire Buddhist community. I find (as Buddhists have always found) that the central part of the Canon (as I have just defined it) presents such originality, intelligence, grandeur and – most relevantly – coherence, that it is hard to see it as a composite work.

I accept the destructive results of modern critical scholarship which show that the traditional accounts of the Buddha's life are largely without even canonical foundation, so that we know next to nothing about the Buddha as a person, apart from his ideas. I admire the recent book by Michael Carrithers[12] in which he presents the Buddha almost entirely through those ideas. It is the ideas, after all, which have affected men's lives.

I consider extreme scepticism to be a faulty method. If we are too rigorous, we can doubt most of our knowledge about the past, certainly about ancient India, where the evidence is sparse and rarely dated. I am not urging that we should claim certainty when we do not have it, but that we should provisionally accept tradition till we have something to put in its place – all the while preserving a modest awareness of our uncertainty.

My position has an important corollary. The main aim of scholars of Indian religion, influenced by the ideals of western classical scholarship and also, perhaps, by Protestant fundamentalism, has been to try to restore original texts and to establish the original meanings intended by their authors. Naturally this is a valid aim. But it is not always possible to succeed in it; and there is no reason why it should be our only aim. We can also study what the texts have meant to later generations. The advantage of this investigation is that we have better evidence. Many scholars of Buddhism, both western and Hindu, have tried to prove that the Buddha himself did not preach the doctrine of no soul as it has been understood in the Theravādin tradition and will be briefly expounded below. This amounts to a claim that this great religious teacher has been completely misunderstood by his followers. If this could be demonstrated, it would be a fascinating example of unintended consequences. But the proponents of the theory have offered no account of how such a total misunderstanding could have arisen. I therefore think that modern scholarship should begin by examining the tradition itself, noting changes only as they are properly documented, and postpone the delights of delving beyond the evidence. To put the matter in the terms I have used above, the point of interest is not just what the Buddha said, but what his hearers have heard. How has his message been filtered through the institution he founded to preserve it, the Sangha?

Theravādin history: the uneven pace of change

Since this purports to be a social history of Theravāda Buddhism over a span of 2500 years, the uneven weighting of the different periods requires explanation. I share with Theravāda Buddhists (and most scholars) the view that their form of Buddhism is extremely conservative. Doctrinally, Theravāda seems to have undergone very little change or development since its origin in ancient India. While there have naturally been slight shifts in emphasis, the system of ideas we are dealing with throughout our history remains that expounded by the Buddha – at least, according to the Theravādin interpretation. To give due weight to Theravādin doctrine (which is in any case what westerners tend to assume religion is all about) I must therefore dwell on the doctrines expounded by the Buddha himself. The only 'church father' who stands out as an independent author is Buddhaghosa (fifth century CE), and even he is probably as unoriginal as he claims and aspires to be.

Religion is, as mentioned above, not only a matter of thinking and believing, but also of doing and feeling. If we turn to the history of Theravādin practice and sentiment, there is rather more change to record. Even here, however, Theravāda has been amazingly conservative, especially in Ceylon. Conservatism is the policy and pride of most religions, but change usually creeps in. A glance at the map shows – however much Sinhalese nationalists may wish to ignore the fact – that the island of Ceylon is in the Indian cultural area. At the same time it is an island on the exteme edge of that area. I attribute its cultural conservatism above all to this geographical situation. The religious changes which have swept India reached Ceylon late, weakly, or not at all. The archaism of the Tamil spoken in the Jaffna peninsula compared to that on the mainland less than 25 miles away is a striking parallel to Sinhalese religious conservatism. Brahmins and their culture have played hardly any role in Ceylon, far less than in the Hindu/Buddhist states of continental southeast Asia or in far-off Indonesia; for the last few centuries they have not even existed in Ceylon as a separate community. Although Ceylon has a Muslim minority, basically a trading community, the country never suffered Muslim invasion, let alone Muslim rule. The first foreigners to rule the Sinhalese were Christian colonial powers, in comparatively modern times. Even then, the Portuguese, who arrived in 1505, and the Dutch, who superseded them in 1658, held only limited coastal areas, so that the Buddhist culture could continue without radical interruption (though not without some serious problems and periods of decline) in the Kandyan kingdom, the Sinhalese state in the mountainous centre of the island. The first unavoidable confrontation between Sinhalese Buddhism and an alien religious tradition occurred only in the nineteenth century when Protestant missionaries, with the (initially reluctant) blessing of the British government, invaded Ceylon with their preaching and pamphlets.

A synoptic view of the history of Buddhism in Ceylon must therefore be very uneven in its chronological coverage. The confrontation with Christianity is the one great and sudden break in Sinhalese Buddhist history, far more significant than the vicissitudes which affected the fortunes of the Sangha during the previous two thousand years. For this reason I have devoted a substantial chapter to this nineteenth-century confrontation. The Christians withdrew, but both British colonial rule and the great worldwide changes which have followed it in recent years have set profound changes in motion in the culture of Sri Lanka. After the riots of July 1983, one has to conclude by asking whether Sinhalese civilization can survive those changes.

I have made plain that it is change which I think offers the challenge and opportunity to produce interesting explanations. I see three major points of change in the story I have to tell. The earliest, and greatest, is the Buddha's founding of the Sāsana. To do any justice to this story I must attempt to reconstruct the problem situation of his time, a difficult and controversial topic. That is why the next chapter has to be devoted to pre-Buddhist India. The most recent of the three changes, the accelerating change of the last 150 years, I have just discussed. The other great change in Theravādin history, it seems to me, came about when the religion migrated from India to Ceylon. It had to settle into a new social and cultural environment, a change which brought about a redefinition of what it is to be a Buddhist, a subtle change in Buddhist identity.

Buddhist identity

I have already warned the reader that the question of Buddhist identity will play an important part in my analysis. Indeed, if this book breaks new ground it will mainly be in my treatment of this question.

Let us return to the opening page of Rhys Davids' pioneering work. The sentence after the one I have quoted above reads:

> Before comparing the numbers of Christians and Buddhists, it is necessary to decide, not only what Christianity is, and what is Buddhism; but also, as regards the Buddhists, whether a firm belief in one religion should or should not, as far as statistics are concerned, be nullified by an equally firm believe in another.[13]

I agree.

'In my first book, *Precept and Practice*, I reported that a monk told me, 'Gods are nothing to do with religion.'[14] For Buddhists, gods are powerful beings who can grant worldly favours, much like powerful people. Gods form a superhuman power structure, and to discuss the existence or status of a particular god is much like discussing where power lies in strata of human society far above one's own. Buddhists deny the existence of a creator god, or any omnipotent or omniscient deity, or any being in the world who is not subject to decay and death. (Yes, even the gods die in the end.)

For Buddhists, religion is purely a matter of understanding and practising the Dhamma, understanding and practice which constitute progress towards salvation. They conceive salvation – or liberation, to use a more Indian term – as the total eradication of greed, hatred and delusion. To attain it is open to any human being, and it is ultimately the only thing worth attaining, for it is the only happiness which is not transient. A person who has attained it will live on so long as his body keeps going, but thereafter not be reborn. Thus he will never have to suffer or die again. For Buddhists, religion is what is relevant to this quest for salvation, and nothing else.

Being told that gods have nothing to do with religion made me aware that the adherents of different religions draw the line between what is religion and what is not at very different places. Building on this realization, I devoted the first chapter of *Precept and Practice* to pointing out that Buddhists who worshipped gods were not thereby being inconsistent, unorthodox or syncretistic. They would only be syncretistic if they attributed to their gods the power to save them, to grant them *nibbāna*. Rhys Davids wrote:

> many of the Ceylonese so-called Buddhists, for instance, take their oaths in court as Christians, and most of them believe also in devil-worship, and in the power of the stars. Their whole belief is not Buddhist; many of their ideas are altogether outside Buddhism; their minds do not run only on Buddhist lines.... Not one of the five hundred millions who offer flowers now and then on Buddhist shrines, who are more or less moulded by Buddhist teaching, is only or altogether a Buddhist.[15]

While I agree with Rhys Davids' facts (except that the last sentence is a slight exaggeration, certainly as far as concerns the Sangha), even he has misinterpreted them.

To begin with, what might we say about a typical modern British Christian? Surely many of his ideas, for example about the nature of matter, are 'altogether outside' Christianity. If one were to say that for a Christian elementary particles are a non-religious, secular matter, I would answer that the same is true of gods, devils and planetary influences so far as the Buddhist is concerned. But what about the common British belief in ghosts? I have it on the authority of a former Archbishop of Canterbury that such a belief is neither prohibited nor prescribed to Christians. It is a belief which forms no part of Christianity, though it is quite typical of the kinds of belief that anthropologists label 'religious', for belief in supernormal beings is the most widely used working definition of religion in cross-cultural inquiry.

My example of ghosts shows that not even all the beliefs someone holds about what they themselves regard as supernatural need form part of their religion. One does not normally call British Christians who believe in ghosts 'syncretistic'. Moreover, since most Christians hold all sorts of beliefs and values which do not derive from Christianity, one could say that 'their minds do not run only on Christian lines'. Theravāda Buddhists have a narrower view than Christians of what constitutes religion, so it is even more obvious in their case that they need systems of thought and action besides Buddhism to cope with life in the world.

The reader may be with me thus far, and yet object that while admittedly Christians have non-Christian ideas, at least they do not accept another religion as well as Christianity; Buddhists by contrast are said to worship 'Hindu' gods in Sri Lanka, while in the Far East, one reads, Japanese Buddhists are also Shintoists, and Chinese Buddhists were also Confucianists or Taoists, or even adherents of all three religions. Are not Hinduism, Shintoism, etc. 'religions'?

My answer to this is not to quibble about the use of words. If one wishes to call (for instance) a system of patterned interaction with superhuman beings[16] a religion, I am happy to go along with that – indeed, I find it a sensible use of the term. But I maintain that to understand Theravāda Buddhism in its social context one has to probe further into its self-definition, into the question of Buddhist identity.

I wish to distinguish two kinds of phenomena we call 'religion', and thus to show that in India and the countries culturally influenced by India it can be quite normal to have two religions at once – one of each kind. I think that my distinction is cross-culturally valid, but it is particularly easy to apply it to India because it has already been partially articulated within the culture. What I am about to propose may not be applicable to societies with a very low level of social organization, such as hunters and gatherers, but they are not my concern; my concern is to elucidate religion (notably the 'world religions') as it functions in complex societies.

One kind of phenomenon we can reasonably call religion is a soteriology. This is the kind of religion which particularly concerns the individual, his highest goals and his fate after death. It provides an answer to the question, 'What must I do to be saved?' Being an answer to a question, it is above all a doctrine. In India, such a religion is usually referred to as a 'path' (*mārga, panthā*) – a path to salvation, most commonly called 'release' (*mokṣa*). Since such a religion is primarily a matter of belief, adherence is defined by assent to its doctrine and entry into the membership is formalized by a declaration of faith. Adherence to the religion is not *purely* a matter of belief, since the doctrine usually prescribes certain types of action (such as making donations or meditation or prayer) and even certain modes of feeling (such as love of God or equanimity); but belief is the primary determinant. The main problem for which such a religion offers the individual a solution is perhaps to give a meaning and direction to life, especially when he confronts the certainty of his own death.

For the other kind of religion there is no handy label to juxtapose to 'soteriology', but as it is the religion of man in society we can call it 'communal religion'. It is the kind of religion characterized by the great sociologist Durkheim, who saw religion as society reacting to its own existence, a kind of inchoate sociological awareness. Inevitably, it is located in the minds and actions of individuals, but it leaves little room for individual initiative; primarily it is a pattern of action. It solemnizes what happens to people, both singly and corporately, in the course of their lives in society; so on the one hand it marks life crises (birth, puberty, marriage, death) and on the other hand it is used for events of communal importance, to bring rain or celebrate a victory. The commonest name for the patterned action which religion prescribes is ritual, but it shades over into etiquette and hygiene. The problem to which such religion primarily answers is the ordering of society; for this it provides rules which typically operate without regard for individual preferences or the individual conscience. Indeed, such rules, whether or not they are ascribed to a personal law-giver (human or divine), are felt to be grounded in reality and thus not susceptible to change by mere human decision. Such religions have a concept which ignores the distinction between fact and value, a concept like 'nature' or 'natural law'. When we say that baby-bashing is unnatural, we mean that it contravenes our idea of how parents should behave and what parents *are*. To use the expression of Clifford Geertz, such a concept provides both an image and a programme for society.[17]

Most 'communal religions' provide a class of full-time or part-time priests, professional intermediaries between men and the powers of the universe. (For soteriologies on the other hand, as St Peter explains to Tomlinson in Kipling's poem of that name, priests in the end do not count: 'For the race is run by one and one, and never by two and two.') It is often these professionals who act as guardians of orthopraxy. For though communal religions are usually ascribed to individuals rather than chosen – one is born into them, and perhaps made a full member of society by undergoing certain of their rites – it is possible to be thrown out of society, temporarily or permanently, for doing the wrong thing: it will be flagrantly improper actions, rather than wrong beliefs, which entail such punishment.

There is no law that in a given culture or society both these kinds of religion must exist, let alone that a given individual must have both. Many tribal societies, for example, have no soteriology, and many western societies today have hardly any communal religion, both ritual and shared social norms having withered away to leave little more than etiquette. Moreover, both kinds of religion may be supplied by what sees itself as a single system; this has tended to happen with Christianity, which sees itself primarily as a soteriology but also used to provide social norms. Just as the line between the religious and the secular is drawn at quite different places in different cultures, the boundary between my two types of religion may vary from place to place. Indeed, it may vary so much, or be so blurred in some cases, as not to be useful for world-wide cross-cultural analysis. This however would hardly worry me, because my division certainly describes Indian culture well and is a useful heuristic device in the study of Indian religion. We shall see that Hinduism, while it has spawned many soteriologies as well, is a fine example of a communal religion. The Hindu communal religion has been conceptualized and codified in brahminical law books (Skt: *dharma-śāstra*), but it has also been lived, in an infinite number of local variants, by millions of Hindus for three thousand years. My characterization is perfectly exemplified by a label I was delighted to see, after I had drafted the above paragraphs, in the ethnographic section of the Jaipur Museum: 'Marriage occupies the most important position among the sixteen sacred rites of India. After the performance of this rite, one gets into the householder's stage of life.' This articulates the central concern of communal religion: the orderly perpetuation of society. No soteriology would regard marriage as a more important rite than initiation.

Just as we westerners, under the influence of monotheistic creeds, tend to ideologize differences, India shows the opposite trend, a drift from belief to practice. People originally differentiated by their beliefs tend as time passes to stress their distinctive practices: what they wear, what they eat, whom and how they marry.

Let me now apply the distinction between soteriology and communal religion to Buddhist history. The Buddha preached a soteriology. He was not much interested in communal religion, which he regarded, as we shall see, as something to be left behind as one took to the quest for salvation. A detail neatly illustrates my point: only in the 1970s did the Theravāda Buddhists of Sri Lanka begin to evolve a specifically Buddhist marriage ritual; until then (and for most of them to this day) marriage, like most other life crises, was a purely secular occasion.

On the other hand, Buddhists have always lived in societies, most of them peasant societies based on rice-growing, which required communal religions. While some forms of Mahāyāna Buddhism did manage to evolve a communal religion from within themselves – of this the Newar Buddhism of Nepal is an excellent example – Theravāda, more conservative, preserved the Buddha's indifference to communal religion and his negative attitude to ritual, negative in so much as he considered it irrelevant to salvation.

The Buddha was so clear that his path was directed to leaving the world altogether, as an inherently unsatisfactory place, that for Buddhists communal religion necessarily includes any attempt to better one's lot in this life by recourse to magic or the intervention of gods. All this they define as 'worldly' as opposed to 'supra-mundane'. Therefore the communal religion of Theravādins also caters for the worldly concerns of individuals.

In India when the Buddha preached, and increasingly as time passed, the communal religion was self-consciously articulated by a learned hereditary priesthood. (This would remain true even if, as we suspect, few people fully practised what that priesthood prescribed.) Only those who joined the Sangha, the professional salvation-seekers, were required by the Buddha to renounce conformity to the norms of the wider society. When Buddhism arrived in Sri Lanka, on the other hand, it entered a society without an articulated or systematized communal religion. If there were any brahmins there, as the chronicle avers, they were émigrés some two thousand miles from the central area of brahmin culture, in north India. It seems that then, as ever since, the communal religion of Sri Lanka consisted of a pantheon and a ritual and social system composed of elements which had arrived from southern India; as the result of the arrival of Buddhism, some new elements were added – for instance, Buddhist priests were in a limited way substituted for brahmins – and the whole was coloured by Buddhist ethical values. These composite elements of Hindu provincial culture have never been seen by the Sinhalese

Buddhists as forming a single system, so naturally they have no collective name; they merely share the negative characteristic of being irrelevant to salvation and so, in the words of my informant, 'nothing to do with religion'.

In the cultures of continental southeast Asia to which Theravāda Buddhism later migrated, the religious structure, in the terms I have just proposed, has been much the same. Modern observers tell us of 'spirit cults' in these countries – *nat* cults in Burma, *phii* cults in Thailand – but these again seem only to be parts of a communal religion which has not been classified as a single system. In these countries too the communal religions abound in elements which are clearly related to elements in Indian popular culture – the use of spirit possession is a good example – though naturally the similarities decrease with increased physical distance from India. But all these phenomena are considered irrelevant to one's fate at death or to spiritual progress, and so 'have nothing to do with religion', i.e. with Buddhism.

All this has implications for Buddhist identity: what is it to be a Buddhist layman? The answer differs in different societies. One cannot be a Christian and have a non-Christian wedding, or a Hindu without having a Hindu wedding, but Theravāda Buddhists for most of history have certainly not had Buddhist weddings, and if they have lived in Hindu societies they have had Hindu weddings without any inconsistency or incongruity. The classical Indian concept – a norm of the communal religion – was that it was the duty of a layman to respect and even materially support all holy men, of whatever 'path', who presented themselves. The edicts of Asoka, the great Buddhist emperor of India (see below), show him both inculcating and practising this precept. A holy man, such as a Buddhist monk, could claim disciples as followers of his 'way', but that could not in practice preclude multiple allegiance, and the boundary between Buddhist and non-Buddhist laity must have been a hard one to trace.

In Sri Lanka, on the other hand, and later in Burma and Thailand, Buddhism was the only 'way' to salvation, so there was no such multiple allegiance. Moreover, there was equally little chance of indifference. For in all these countries Buddhism was adopted as their personal faith by the rulers, and court patronage developed into state patronage and so acquired great wealth, power and prestige, as well as a monopoly of education and spiritual life.

My view of the Buddha's message as a pure soteriology and my consequent analysis of Buddhist identity put me at odds with many modern interpreters of Buddhism, including some Buddhists. Firstly, I must explain that under the impact both of western ideas of ethnicity and of western scholarship, some Buddhists themselves have in modern times been affected by the misunderstandings which I aspire to dispel. Thus they have come to regard 'Buddhism' and 'Hinduism' as entities precisely on a par with the monotheistic religions (primarily Christianity and Islam), and consequently to regard 'Buddhist' and 'Hindu' as total and mutually exclusive identities. I am not laying the blame for the communal conflict in contemporary Sri Lanka all at the door of these misunderstandings, for I am well aware not only of the long history of identifying 'Buddhist' with 'Sinhalese' in Sri Lanka, but also that the tensions probably owe more to economic causes and the cynical machinations of politicians than to ideology. Nevertheless, those misunderstandings have influenced modern middle-class Buddhists in Sri Lanka (and elsewhere), especially those who learn about their subject from English-language sources.

Secondly, my interpretation puts me at odds with those who see the Buddha as a social reformer. Certainly, in consenting to preach and then in establishing an Order of monks to do likewise, he showed his great compassion and concern for mankind. Moreover, he was supremely kind and understanding towards everyone, so far as we can tell. But his concern was to reform individuals and help them to leave society forever, not to reform the world. Life in the world he regarded as suffering, and the problem to which he offered a solution was the otherwise inevitable rebirth into the world. Though it could well be argued that the Buddha made life in the world more worth living, that surely was an unintended consequence of his teaching. To present him as a sort of socialist is a serious anachronism. He never preached against social inequality, only declared its irrelevance to salvation. He neither tried to abolish the caste system nor to do away with slavery. While a famous sermon, the *Sāmañña-phala Sutta*, stresses the practical benefits for a slave in leaving his servitude and joining the Order,[18] in fact runaway slaves were not allowed to join the Order. Moreover, though in ancient India there was no caste or other form of social ranking within the Order itself, the Order soon came to own (lay) slaves.

To avoid any possible misunderstanding, I should add that the fact that the Buddha did not hold certain views or have certain concerns which we now think desirable should not, in my view, inhibit any modern Buddhist from holding those views or having those concerns. *My* concern is merely with historical accuracy. For example, if the followers of Dr Ambedkar, leader of India's untouchable community at Independence, propagate a

Buddhism which refuses to recognize the institution of untouchability, they have all my sympathy. While they are wrong if they claim to be saying no more than what the Buddha said, they can claim with some justice that Buddhist doctrine allows Buddhists to innovate in this way, and indeed that, were a Buddha alive today, he might do the same.

Such flexibility is certainly in the spirit of Gotama Buddha. In a famous extended simile, he compared his doctrine to a raft.[19] Just as one makes a raft to cross a river, but only a fool, having crossed, would carry the raft further, so his preaching was to take men across the ocean of rebirth; once they were across they could go their ways without clinging to his words.

Here too, the reference is unambiguously to seeking salvation, not to worldly affairs. But the message that the Buddha wished his followers to use their own judgement is clear from other texts as well. On his deathbed he is supposed to have said that the Sangha could rescind all the 'minor' rules. But after his death they decided that since they were not sure which rules were 'minor' they would rescind none. The story rings true, for it is hard to imagine that the Sangha would have fabricated a saying with such subversive potential for their tradition. However, that Indian veneration for the Teacher, the guru, which the Buddha himself seems to have deprecated, prevented change and preserved tradition. Not for nothing is Theravāda called 'the doctrine of the Elders'.

CHAPTER TWO

Gotama Buddha's problem situation

A. VEDIC CIVILIZATION

In the canonical account of his last days, the *Mahā Parinibbāna Sutta*, the Buddha says that he is 80 years old and left home at 29.[1] Tradition has it that six years passed between the Great Renunciation, as his leaving home is known, and his Enlightenment.

The Buddhist era begins at the Buddha's Enlightenment. Modern Theravādins date this in 544/3 BCE, but this tradition is of uncertain antiquity and all western scholars agree that it puts the Buddha too early. For a long time scholars favoured either 486 or 483 BCE as the year of Buddha's death, so that the Enlightenment would fall in 531 or 528 BCE. But the consensus now is that for this date too the evidence is flimsy and we really do not know the Buddha's exact dates.[2] It raises fewer problems if he is dated a bit later. So the best we can say is that he was probably Enlightened between 550 and 450, more likely later rather than earlier.

The Vedic tradition

Whatever the precise date in absolute terms, we feel more certain of the relative chronology. We know that the Buddha lived at about the end of what is called the Vedic period of Indian history. The word 'Vedic' derives from Sanskrit *veda*. 'Vedic' is in the first instance the generic term for the literature which survives from that period – though of course it was not written down till many centuries later. The language of this literature, an early form of Sanskrit, is also known as Vedic (or Vedic Sanskrit). Classical Sanskrit follows the rules codified by Pāṇini, who probably lived in the fifth century BCE – he may have been a contemporary of the Buddha. Vedic Sanskrit is far less homogeneous. The language of the later Vedic literature approaches classical Sanskrit. On the other hand, that of the oldest texts had become, by the time of the Buddha, largely unintelligible to all but scholars, and that has remained the situation to this day.

The word *veda* means 'knowledge' and refers in this case to sacred knowledge, knowledge about ultimate matters. In fact the Sanskrit term for Vedic literature is *śruti*, what has been 'heard'. The texts have been 'heard' by inspired sages. Ultimately they are not composed, by gods or men, but exist eternally, whether anyone is aware of them or not. Buddhists hold the same view, not of their texts but of the Dhamma: that its existence is independent of its being cognized; and the same view of 'objective knowledge' exists nowadays (see my remarks on the speed of light on p. 7 above), though naturally we do not draw all the same conclusions from this as the ancient Indians did. One important difference between our view and the Indian tradition is that we think that truths are constantly being discovered, whereas Indian religious traditions hold that everything important was realized by sages long ago and is gradually being forgotten, so that the best we can do is to preserve the truth and possibly to recover some lost fragments. The cosmologies of classical Hinduism, Buddhism and Jainism all envisage that time progresses through vast cycles: when things have declined to a point at which all sacred/important knowledge has been lost, there eventually comes another revelation or realization. But this cyclicity is on so vast a scale that it does not really touch us.

Brahmins are the class of men whose duty and function it is to preserve *śruti*. The whole brahminical ideology of society is based on this fact. Brahmins are a hereditary class (though in very early times they were perhaps not); it is possible to lose one's status as a brahmin by gross misconduct, and there are also many unsatisfactory brahmins who do not in fact study or teach the Vedas; but to learn them and hand them on is both the right and the duty of the sons of brahmins – sons, for it gradually became restricted to males.

Śruti is eternally true and infallible. It tells men what to do. Since it is the prerogative of brahmins to learn and interpret it, all authority (on ultimate matters) rests with them. At an early stage, brahmins made the easy transition from saying that the Vedas are authoritative to saying that whatever is authoritative is in the Veda. Again, this could not have happened if the language of the Vedas had been widely understood. Nor is it necessary – or even plausible – to posit a brahmin conspiracy to account for this change: it was a transition which occurred as an unintended consequence of constantly invoking the authority of a very large and only partially intelligible body of texts, to which in any case very few people had access.

Thus it came about in early India that the measure of orthodoxy was whether one accepted *śruti* and whether one accepted the authority (in ideological matters) of brahmins – because the two acceptances amounted to the same. Heterodox thinkers like the Buddha were rejecting both the Vedas as the depository of final truth and the position of brahmins as arbiters of truth, because either rejection necessarily involved the other.

The Vedic texts are our only evidence for the religious life of the period. Indeed, if we leave out of account the prehistoric Indus valley civilization (its major centres collapsed early in the second millennium BCE and even its later vestiges are irrelevant to our story), there is virtually no archaeological evidence concerning Indian religion before the third century BCE: from that century date the first inscriptions, the first images and the first identifiable religious shrine. Remains of earlier material culture are direct evidence for economic conditions, but beyond that all would be conjecture, were it not for the literary evidence.

Vedic literature (*śruti*) is internally stratified. Over-simplifying somewhat, one can say that there are three strata: the four *Saṃhitā* texts; the *Brāhmaṇas*; and the *Upaniṣads*. Each of these strata presupposes the existence of the previous ones, so although they are interconnected they follow each other in time – as their language also shows. The four *Saṃhitā* (as they are often called in Sanskrit) are also called the four Vedas. This ambiguity of the term Veda is confusing. The four Vedas are called the *Ṛg Veda*, *Sāma Veda*, *Yajur Veda* and *Atharva Veda*. To make matters worse, in some contexts there are said to be just three Vedas: the *Atharva Veda* is not counted. The contents of the three overlap, but they differ in function: the *Ṛg Veda* is a book of hymns, the *Sāma Veda* arranges excerpts from those hymns for chanting, the *Yajur Veda* rearranges them according to their use in the sacrificial ritual. One recension of the *Yajur Veda* intersperses the liturgical formulae with instructions for the ritual and myths and theological argument to justify it, a process carried further in the *Brāhmaṇas*. The *Upaniṣads* (or, strictly speaking, their contents) are also known as the *Vedānta*, 'the conclusion of the Veda' – with both senses of the English word 'conclusion'. They discuss the mystical equivalences which reveal the ritual's esoteric meaning.

Historians generally divide the Vedic age into halves. The earlier they date c. 1500–c. 1000 BCE. Much though not all of the *Ṛg Veda* is that old. The latter half of the Vedic age, c. 1000–c. 500 BCE, saw the completion of the *Ṛg Veda*, the formation of the other Vedas, and the creation of the *Brāhmaṇas* and the earliest *Upaniṣads*, notably the *Bṛhad Āraṇyaka* and the *Chāndogya Upaniṣads*. These are the texts to which the Buddha could have reacted, and when I mention the *Upaniṣads* in this chapter it is to these earliest ones that I refer.

The early Vedic period

The early Vedic period we shall dispose of with the utmost brevity because no more is relevant to Buddhism. Around the middle of the second millennium BCE people speaking an Indo-European language, Sanskrit, entered northwest India from what is now northern Iran and southern Russia. Sanskrit and the languages deriving from it are known as Indo-Aryan. The linguistic term has been used to refer to the speakers of the language. The Indo-Aryans probably came in several waves over several centuries and were very closely related to people who settled in Iran and even further west in that period. They were pastoralists; at first they were nomadic, but gradually settled during the period and even began agriculture, mainly growing barley. They seem often to have gone cattle-raiding. Those who led them in war were their 'kings'. They used the horse in war, but as they penetrated India cattle became central to their economy; they reckoned their wealth in cattle. In India cattle have been just as important for their labour as draught animals and for their dung as fuel as for their edible products.

It is important to bear in mind that the Indo-Aryans did not enter an uninhabited land. For nearly two millennia they and their culture gradually penetrated India, moving east and south from their original seat in the Punjab. They mixed with people who spoke Muṇḍa or Dravidian languages, who have left no traces of their culture beyond some archaeological remains; we know as little about them as we would about the Indo-Aryans if they had left no texts. In fact we cannot even be sure whether some of the archaeological finds belong to Indo-Aryans, autochthonous populations, or a mixture.

It is to be assumed – though this is not fashionable in Indian historiography – that the clash of cultures between Indo-Aryans and autochthones was responsible for many of the changes in Indo-Aryan society. We can also assume that many – perhaps most – of the indigenous population came to be assimilated into Indo-Aryan culture. This probably was furthered by interbreeding, but cultural diffusion does not depend on that. We know from more recent history that when brahminical culture encounters another Indian culture with a priestly class, those priests are assimilated to brahmins and in time come to be regarded as a brahmin sub-caste. Similar assimilation no doubt affected many other local institutions, customs and beliefs. It is against this background that we must see the endless variety of local cultures still observable in India today, a variety nevertheless half shrouded in a tattered cloak of conceptual unity.

Most Indians are not brahmins, but brahmins evolved in ancient times the only indigenous ideology of society, so that all Indians before the Muslim invasions and conversions, and very many to this day, have thought about their society in brahminical terms, using brahminical concepts. Thus Indian society is a product of interaction between brahminical ideology and the material with which it has to grapple. The central concept and idea of this ideology is that of *dharma*, the world as it ideally is, the world as it should behave if it is to conform to its true nature. The *authority* for *dharma* the brahmin law-givers say to be the Vedas; but its *content* they must have derived from actual custom. As Geertz says, religion is both image and programme, a model of and a model for.[3] Indeed, the law-books explicitly say that local custom is the source of *dharma* where it does not contradict scripture. But once the law-giver has articulated the custom, his formulation moves from being descriptive to being normative.

The brahminical ideology of *dharma* has been the main communal religion (see p. 26 above) of India. It forms a large part of what outsiders (and recently Indians themselves) have come to call Hinduism. Not the whole of it – which is why it is so hopeless to try to describe Hinduism as a single religion. Hinduism includes several soteriologies too. And the local interpretations of *dharma* vary considerably. Hindu culture is by no means coterminous with *dharma*.

Throughout India, the communal religion of most communities attaches importance to certain altered states of consciousness. To be specific, it uses possession. Possession is sometimes confused with shamanism; but in shamanism one's spirit travels while one's body remains unconscious, whereas in possession one's body is temporarily inhabited by another spirit, while what happens to one's own spirit at the time is left undetermined. This temporary loss of the sense of self is just like hysteria as clinically defined by Freud and Breuer. In India possession is mainly valued when it is practised (perhaps one should rather say 'undergone') by specialists; they become possessed by non-human spirits, interact with an audience, and solve problems for clients.

The onset of possession is usually marked by quivering in the limbs. An ancient word for 'brahmin', *vipra*, etymologically means 'quiverer'. Vedic religion centred on sacrifices to various deities and it seems that the priests would alter their states of consciousness by taking a substance called *soma*. The identity of *soma* was forgotten in the later Vedic period, but it may have been a hallucinogenic mushroom.[4] However that may be, officiating priests in early Vedic religion apparently courted altered states of consciousness with some symptoms like those of possession states.

Later brahminism, however, denied all value to possession states and they were screened out of brahminical religion. To be possessed is to lose one's self-awareness and self-control. Brahminism inculcated control. We shall see that this is an important point of continuity between brahminism and Buddhism, and one which sets both off against the religion which is most widely prevalent in Indian society now and probably has been since time immemorial.

Vedic religion centred on sacrifice, and sacrifice centred on fire. The domestic fire, the hearth, received offerings on every ritual occasion, perhaps daily. The same fire was used for practical purposes, notably cooking. The brahmins also conceived of digestion as 'cooking', in this case in the fire of the stomach. Fire was for the Indo-Aryans (as for other Indo-European-speaking peoples) a symbol of man's conquest of nature; control and maintenance of fire characterized civilized as against mere animal existence. Lévi-Strauss's distinction between the raw and the cooked[5] was apparently familiar in Vedic India.

In early Vedic society there were perhaps four main social statuses: priests, rulers, ordinary free people, slaves. Later, most social status in India became ascribed by birth, but we do not know to what extent this was already so in the early Vedic period. Maybe ordinary people could become priests, rulers or slaves according to circumstances. A slave may have been just what we would call a servant; we know of no market in human beings. Perhaps they were prisoners of war.

Later Vedic society

We must now consider later Vedic society. Again, we shall say no more about it than is necessary for an understanding of Buddhism.

After about the turn of the first millennium BCE, the Indo-Aryans and those who had adopted their culture became increasingly settled and agricultural, though stock-rearing remained important. They began to grow rice as well as barley, and to use ploughs. They had some iron but apparently used it almost exclusively for weapons, very little for tools. The centre of their culture shifted slowly to the Upper Gangetic plains (mainly modern Haryana and Western Uttar Pradesh, with adjacent parts of the Punjab and Rajasthan).

The tenth and last book of the *Ṛg Veda*, which is presumed also to be the latest, contains a famous hymn (X.90) called the *Puruṣa-sūkta* ('Hymn of the Cosmic Man'). A huge male figure is compared and assimilated to the universe, which he both pervades and transcends. Verse 12 of this hymn runs: 'His mouth was the brahmin, arms were made the royal, his two thighs that which is the *vaiśya*, from his feet was born the *śūdra*.' This requires explanation and comment.

The cosmic man is here equated with society. The most important point is that society is conceived as an organic whole, and this whole contains four classes of men, who by the nature of things are hierarchically ranked. The ranking goes from the top down and there can be no argument about who comes above whom. Earlier verses have also equated the cosmic man with the universe. By being his mouth, the brahmins are thus the mouthpiece of reality. They are the language which expresses that reality, for it is they who utter the Vedas.

The royal class comes from the Man's arms, which symbolize power and strength. The term for this class here is *rājanya*, which is derived from the word for 'king', *rājan*; later this class was more commonly designated by the synonymous term *kṣatriya*. The prerogative of this class was the legitimate use of force. So they were at the same time rulers and warriors. In early times, when such men just led marauding bands to raid cattle or repulse raiders, there was presumably no distinction between chiefs and warriors. India always preserved in its concept of kingship an archaic feature of this period: that kingship was in the first instance over men, not territory. When Vedic texts mention kings, they may have ruled no more than a village, though by the Buddha's day a few kings evidently commanded substantial resources. They collected tithes from the peasantry, payments in kind.

The early Vedic term which I rendered above as 'ordinary free people' is *viś*; the word *vaiśya* in the *Puruṣa-sūkta* derives from that. The function of the *vaiśya* is fertility, economic production, symbolized presumably by the loins. As we have seen, economic production began with stock-rearing and gradually shifted to agriculture. Brahminism always categorized these two activities together as the domain of the *vaiśya*. At this stage commerce was not envisaged as a separate function, so evidently it played no great part yet in economic life. The economy was not yet monetarized.

The function of the *śūdra* is classically defined as serving the other orders. The higher orders all had the right to use the Veda – no doubt a reminiscence of the more fluid society of earlier times – though in fact Vedic learning early become almost a brahmin monopoly, with a few *kṣatriya* exceptions. But the *śūdra* was not supposed even to hear the Veda, let alone learn it. Two societies contiguous to India, ancient Iran and ancient Tibet, seem to have divided society into four classes with complementary functions, so India may have been influenced by them. Later, artisans were usually classified as *śūdra*, but the earliest texts do not assign the *śūdras* this function.

These four ranked social groups are known in Sanskrit by the word *varṇa*, which primarily means 'colour'. The colours were apparently symbolic. Later texts associate white with the brahmin, red with the *kṣatriya*, yellow with the *vaiśya* and black with the *śūdra*. It has nothing to do with skin pigmentation or a colour bar.

The four *varṇa* were hereditary status groups. And the text listing them was authoritative: there were only four. So when Vedic society expanded and encountered people who were not in any *varṇa*, it could only enrol them in a *varṇa* by some legal fiction or deny them a place in human society as they conceived it. It is the latter solution which led to the classification of what we call outcastes. These people – who today comprise perhaps a fifth of the Indian population – were not allowed to participate in caste society except in certain degraded roles. They have had to live apart from the rest of the society, in their own settlements at the edge of the village.

From the point of view of the ideology, castes, the status groups one finds in India today, are sub-divisions of the *varṇas*, a complication caused (allegedly) by miscegenation. The external observer would prefer to say that the *varṇa* ideology is the brahminical attempt to make sense of caste. The language in which brahminism expresses the hierarchic ranking of society is that of purity: the higher group is 'purer' than the lower. Purity and pollution are ideological constructs; but by a metaphor which still speaks to us they did have connections with cleanliness. Excreta are polluting, and purity is commonly regained by bathing. Personal purity, which is a way of conceiving how to deal with ineluctable biological facts, was not the same as the social purity of a descent group, but the two were related. Thus a menstruating woman and a corpse are both impure, so those who professionally handle garments stained by menstrual blood or dispose of corpses are permanently impure, and their children inherit that impurity even before they begin to exercise their professions.

Religion in the later Vedic period

Though the distinction may be even older, it is in the second half of the Vedic age that we first hear of the formal distinction between rituals of public and of purely domestic significance. The latter a qualified person can perform for himself; after the Vedic age, only brahmins were held to be so qualified, but earlier the top three *varṇas* were probably entitled to perform them. (We know that in later times those not qualified to perform brahminical domestic rituals for themselves only import a brahmin to do so for a few essential ceremonies of the life-cycle.) It is the rituals of public importance with which the Vedic texts are mainly concerned. Strictly, they are not communal rituals, in that every ritual is instituted by an individual, and that individual will be the beneficiary. The rituals which I call 'of public importance' were mostly instituted by rulers, who had to employ brahmin priests for the purpose. No distinction was made between the public office and private person of a ruler (or indeed anyone else); so the welfare of a king's subjects was thought to depend on his personal welfare. He was thus responsible for the maintenance and good order of the world: adequate rainfall, physical security, the caste hierarchy, etc. This good order was to be ensured by sacrifices, and it was essential to pay brahmin priests to perform them. To be a true ruler, a king thus had to have a brahmin chaplain, a 'front man' as the Sanskrit word (*purohita*) has it; the priests, on the other hand, depended on the kings for their material support. The roles of king and priest were thus complementary; they typified the roles of institutor (*yajamāna*) and officiant (*yajan*) at the sacrifice. (Only brahmins could officiate, but any member of the top three *varṇa* could be a *yajamāna*.) This pair of complementary roles, patron and functionary, became the model for a wide range of social arrangements in traditional India.

The *saṃhitā* texts provide the words to be used at sacrifices; the

Brāhmaṇas give instructions for the ritual and myths to justify it; the *Upaniṣads* give further esoteric interpretations, to the point of concluding that to understand the meaning of a rite can be even better than performing it. (This last point of course endangers the position of brahmin priests; it is no surprise that some of the sages named in the early *Upaniṣads* are *kṣatriyas*, and one is even a woman.) The strata of Vedic literature are thus complementary in function, and this has led some modern scholars, notably the great French Vedicist Louis Renou, to argue for the unity of Vedic literature. It is good to be reminded that chanting hymns from the *Ṛg Veda*, building fire altars according to instructions in the *Brāhmaṇas* and pondering esoteric meanings are activities which can be carried out at the same time and even by the same people. Nevertheless, the religious climate and world view of the *Upaniṣads* is utterly different from that of the *Ṛg Veda*. The development of Vedic religion strikingly illustrates the point made in the previous chapter, that different areas within a religion, let alone within a culture, may change at quite different speeds. It is the action system, the ritual, which tends to change most slowly. Though most Vedic sacrifices are very rarely performed today (and some are quite obsolete) they have hardly changed – not surprisingly, for one might argue that changelessness is their *raison d'être*. The brahminical marriage service of today is the same as it was in classical times and in important respects as it was in Vedic times: the couple walk round the sacred fire and the priest utters Vedic prayers. Mythology changed during the Vedic period, but slowly, with gradual shifts in emphasis. At the other extreme, soteriological doctrine and religious sentiment underwent a radical transformation towards the end of the period.

In the *Ṛg Veda*, man is thought to be born and die only once. If he lives well (the conditions are not clearly specified) he will join his ancestors in heaven, where life is a pleasant continuation of life on earth (as in so many religions). In the *Brāhmaṇas* is mentioned for the first time the possibility of re-death. If the ancestral spirits are not fed, they may starve – hence the necessity for commemorative funeral feasts, at which the food fed to brahmins somehow serves to feed the ancestors, and for daily libations of water, which presumably thirsty ancestors may drink. The system of ideas underlying the rituals can only be pieced together deductively, but it seems that the dead do not all go to heaven, but some elsewhere, and that neither destination perhaps is permanent. A brahminical soteriology begins to emerge: a man who institutes a particular sacrifice, the *jyotiṣṭoma*, can thereby gain heaven. Sacrificial victims too, whether animals or plants, being destined for the gods, go straight to heaven. A fully-fledged soteriology first emerges only in the *Upaniṣads*; but before explaining that, we must say more about the sacrifice.

The early parts of the *Ṛg Veda* offer no evidence that at the beginning there was any elaborate theory of the sacrifice: it was a matter of giving things to the gods and getting sons, cattle and long life in return. Fire was the mediator between earth and heaven and took up the offerings. But already in the later hymns there are theories and questions about how it all works. These speculations try to tease out some basic principles, unifying ideas to make sense of the apparent multiplicity of phenomena. So many gods in turn are addressed as powerful; are they really all different?

Two basic ideas must here be mentioned. One is a metaphysical theory of language. We have mentioned that the Vedic poets thought of their inspiration as an external force which put into their minds and onto their lips the eternal, uncreated Vedas. On this view, which has survived from that day to this, the language of the Vedas, Sanskrit, corresponds profoundly to the nature of things. In fact, when philosophers later came to develop this idea systematically, Sanskrit words were held to be ontologically prior to their referents. The Vedas as language thus represent the essence of reality. This aspect of reality, like others, must have some kind of underlying unity; that unity is sometimes found in the syllable *Oṃ*,[6] which is said to encapsulate the entire Veda, sometimes in a more subtle principle, perhaps language not yet realized in utterance. (I say 'perhaps' because this theory was certainly important later, but it is not clear quite how early it was articulated.) This unifying principle or single essence behind the Vedas, therefore behind the Sanskrit language, therefore behind reality, was called *brahman*. The word *brāhmaṇa*, 'brahmin', derives from *brahman*. What we have said shows that the brahmin, by being the custodian of the Vedas, holds the key to reality, and the Sanskrit language is itself an indispensable guide to that reality. The use of Sanskrit is essential to brahminism, and a critic of brahminism was almost bound to be critical of the use of Sanskrit.

The second idea is the equivalence of the macrocosm and the microcosm, man and the world. This idea is developed in the most elaborate ways. The most important single text for it is the hymn already cited, that to/of the cosmic man, Puruṣa. A full commentary on this hymn would be little less than a whole history of Hindu theology. In figurative terms which are necessarily paradoxical but not obscure, the hymn states that Man is at the same time the world, more than the world, the sacrifice, and himself – for *puruṣa* is about the commonest word for 'man'. It is likely that in very ancient times there were real human sacrifices, for the *Brāhmaṇas* preserve elaborate prescriptions for performing them, but when one was last performed is pure guesswork.

The Cosmic Man, according to the *Puruṣa-sūkta*, created the world by means of a sacrifice in which he sacrificed himself – for nothing else was available. This cosmogonic sacrifice was then held to be proto-typical for all sacrifices, so that the actual victim was a substitute for man himself. From this theory arose the various elaborate and bizarre homologies which the texts propose between the parts of the universe, of the (object of) sacrifice, and of man, the sacrificer.

Again the search for a single underlying principle played a part in these speculations. The essence sought in man was what kept him alive and sentient. Various candidates were proposed, but a favoured one was breath. 'Breath' was probably the original meaning of the word *ātman* (as of our 'spirit'), which has become the most widely known of the Sanskrit words for the soul. If the essence of man was the *ātman* and the essence of the universe was *brahman*, the principle of macrocosm-microcosm equivalence led to the famous conclusion that *ātman=brahman*. As the *Chāndogya Upaniṣad* put it, 'Thou art that'; man is in essence the same as the essence of the world – not as it looks to you now, but as it can be understood by the wise. We shall see that the Buddha built on this principle of macrocosm-microcosm equivalence, though he stood the Upaniṣadic conclusion on its head.

The *Upaniṣads* propounded to initiates the doctrine that those who did not understand this truth of the unity underlying all phenomena were condemned to perpetual rebirth. (They did not claim that the phenomena of daily experience were unreal or illusory; that step came much later.) The worst aspect of rebirth, presumably, was that it involved re-death. Certainly, there is an emotional world of difference between the *Ṛg Veda*, where life seems to be something one cannot have enough of, and the *Upaniṣads*, which offer an escape from *saṃsāra*, 'keeping going', the endless round of rebirth and consequent suffering.

The solution lies in a gnosis, a realization of one's true nature. At death, the soul which realizes its identity with *brahman*, the ground of the universe, will merge into it and never again know the pain of individuation. The identification of one's *ātman* with *brahman* is 'at the same time the truth to be discovered and the end to be attained'.[7]

We have traced an intellectual route to this conclusion. But it seems likely that it was first reached by an experiential route. Mystical experiences of the oneness of things are attested from all over the world. I agree with those who think that some ancient Indian sages must have had such experiences. It is sure that they gradually systematized a quest for them by means of self-discipline. This methodical self-discipline took various forms, but all generally pass under the blanket term *yoga.*

Two aspects of yoga must concern us: mortification of the flesh and meditation. (Both, Eliade has pointed out, reverse the normal course of nature.) Mortification of the flesh, *tapas* in Sanskrit, was the time-honoured method of trying to obtain supernormal powers and supramundane goals. It has been practised in India from the earliest times to the present day. The ascetic subjected himself to extremes of heat (the basic meaning of *tapas*) and cold, hunger and thirst, and courted every kind of discomfort, notably by not washing. This remained the highroad to salvation in Jainism; it was the method the Buddha tried and found wanting. The Buddha criticized the practice of austerities for paying too much attention to the body and so distracting one from what really mattered; and indeed such asceticism was not associated for the most part with the quest for understanding or insight as the solution to life's problems. It has been associated more with another strand in Indian religious thought, the tradition that the root of all evil is passion, or even just emotion, so that salvation lies in eradicating all passion and no longer having any likes or dislikes.

The practice associated with gnostic soteriology is meditation. There is nothing said in Vedic literature about the *technique* of meditation. The Buddhist texts are probably the earliest we have on that subject. But the *Upaniṣads* do mention meditation. It is possible that they mean by it no more than what is meant in common English parlance, as when we say that someone is meditating on some topic, i.e. pondering it. The goal of meditation, after all, was to realize the truth of received teachings. But somewhat later Sanskrit texts on meditation probably reflect a much older tradition: these texts describe the means to gnosis as sitting quietly in a secluded place, withdrawing the senses from their objects and stilling all discursive thought. Such concentration was to lead to an *experience*, which, though described in metaphysical language as a saving truth, was (like all experiences) beyond what can be put into mere words.

I have intentionally made this account of meditation vague and general enough to cover almost all the Indian yogic traditions. These traditions combine elements from the two techniques: asceticism and meditation. Of the main religious traditions to have survived, only Jainism – especially of the Digambara variety – has continued to lay stress on actual mortification of the flesh; in the others, asceticism has been moderated to a demand for a simple life-style and indifference to worldly pleasures. For salvation, this indifference is to be cultivated to the point of stilling all emotion, at least in so far as it is directed toward worldly objects: this is expressed as indifference to pleasure and pain and freedom from desire and aversion. The earliest statement of this doctrine is in the *Bṛhad Āraṇyaka Upaniṣad*:[8] someone who has got rid of all desire '*is* brahman and goes to brahman' (at death). From this time on, while Indian soteriologies vary somewhat in the theoretical priority they assign to the emotional and intellectual aspects of salvation, they all assume that freedom from desire is the main prerequisite for gnosis. One could in fact arrange the religions (soteriologies) along a scale according to the relative importance they assign to asceticism and gnosis, in other words whether they emphasize the emotions or lack of understanding as the main barrier to salvation. Jainism, especially in the Digambara tradition, stands at the ascetic end, some brahminical/Vedāntic traditions at the gnostic end, and Buddhism dead in the middle.

Eliade has called the state at which the *yogin* aims by stopping sense perception 'enstasis': the meditator 'stands within' himself. This should be the polar opposite of ecstasy 'standing outside' oneself as the shaman does. We distinguished above between shamanism and possession; but it is certainly possible (and often done) to call the state of possession too an ecstatic trance. We shall see in the last chapter that to this day Buddhism preserves the tradition that enstasis and ecstasy are totally different and only enstasis is of soteriological value, yet we shall also see that to the outside investigator there are striking affinities between the two states which suggest that the rigidity of the distinction depends on cultural context.

The sacrifice was made for certain ends, but by what mechanism did those ends come about? In the early Vedic period, when the gods were conceived as powerful supermen, it was up to them to grant or withhold the benefits for which the sacrificer asked. But as brahminical speculation came to posit some principle beyond the gods, and the sacrifice was systematically homologized to the universe, its success could not depend on something so unpredictable as divine caprice. It was argued that the sacrifice must work; if it failed, that could only be due to defective performance. The more popular hypothesis to explain the rise of the theory that sacrifices must work is that it was a brahmin conspiracy to increase their fee income. Though I cannot disprove this, I am suspicious of conspiracy theories (see above, p. 17); it also seems strange for priests to invent a theory assigning all blame for what goes wrong to their own professional shortcomings. I prefer to find an intellectual reason for the new theory.

Admittedly, the new theory is not very impressive – even though it was to have a vast influence on Indian thought. Sacrifices are effective because of an omnipresent causal force, called 'the unseen' (*adṛṣṭa*). Later texts draw agricultural analogies: the act is the seed, the result the harvest. We shall see that this theory too is of vital importance to Buddhism.

In brahminical literature the fire sacrifice (*yajña*) very early became prototypical for any religious act; virtually any act of religious significance could (metaphorically) be called a sacrifice. For example, reciting the Veda was called 'the sacrifice to *brahman*'.

Another term for a religious act was *karman*. This represents a semantic narrowing, a specialization, rather than a broadening, because *karman* is derived from the verb 'to do' and basically means no more than 'act'. In brahminical literature, however, the word refers usually to *significant* acts, i.e. rituals. Thus the theory of the inevitable causal efficacy of the (properly performed) sacrifice could easily be transferred to all religiously prescribed acts, and, negatively, to proscribed acts as well: sins of omission or commission must entail bad consequences. It is likely that at its very inception this theory applied only to ritual acts, but already in the *Bṛhad Āraṇyaka Upaniṣad*, probably the earliest text to mention the *karman* theory, good *karman* includes moral qualities such as kindness and truthfulness. But for brahminism morality remained mainly extrinsic, like ritual: realized in action which derives its value from the social context. It was the Buddha who first completely ethicized the concept: in Hinduism ritual and moral obligations remain lumped together.

They remain together because of the particularistic nature of the Hindu universe, in which one man's moral meat is another man's poison: what is right for the brahmin is forbidden to the outcaste and vice versa. According to this view of the world, everything is in a category which has its own nature, and its duty is to conform to that ideal nature. It is the peculiar nature/duty (*sva-dharma*) of fire to burn, of rocks to be hard, of grass to grow, of cows to eat that grass and give milk. In exactly the same way, it is the duty of a potter to pot and of a brahmin to study and teach the Veda. This 'division of labour' (which is much more than that term implies nowadays) we have already encountered with the *varṇa* system. The division, however, is carried even into the individual life-cycle. The high-caste male is to pass through certain stages of life (the term is *āśrama*), for which different life-styles are prescribed. The classical system of ideally passing through four such stages is later than the Buddha, but the nucleus of the system is old and relevant. The most fundamental distinction within the system was between being a householder and not being one. The householder is the married man, economically and sexually active – in the neat phrase, he is involved in both production and reproduction. It is common sense that the continuance of society depends on such men and their wives. In brahminical terms, the householder is the institutor of sacrifice (*yajamāna*) and so maintains the universe. When this is compared to what has been said above about the ideological view of the king, it will be appreciated that the difference (from this point of view) between the king and the householder is merely one of degree: the king does his duty merely to ensure that all (high-caste) householders can continue to do theirs. In the religious context, the king is merely the householder writ large. We shall meet this point again.

For brahminism, therefore, the householder's life was the foundation of society, the pivot on which all rested. It should be preceded (at least for brahmins) by Vedic study, a period of chaste studentship called *brahmacarya*, literally '*brahman* activity'; and followed by retirement from worldly affairs and devoting oneself to religion, to improve one's fate after death.

All this, as it was conceived, was still life in the world of action, of *karman*. What motivated one to action? In the final analysis, desire for the results. As part of the householder's life of production and reproduction, desire was necessary; in its place, therefore, it was even laudable. Desire was part of the brahminical scheme of things. Desire kept one in the world, in society, and so ensured the continuance of that society.

It followed, however, from the above premises, that every *karman* had to bring results. If the results were not evident in this life, they would crop up in a future life. Thus *karman*, inasmuch as it was motivated action, ensured rebirth. So much for present *karman* with its future results. But in the present life there are also occurrences, often disagreeable ones, which do not seem to be the result of one's acts or desires. For these the theory of *karman* offers the untestable and irrefutable explanation that they must be the results of actions in former lives. *Karman* thus offers an explanation for the problem of suffering. It is probably its apparent explanatory power which has made the theory so widely accepted.

It would pose no logical problem of coherence to combine this theory of *karman* and rebirth with a cheerful acceptance, a glad readiness to go on living again and again. One can decide that on balance life offers more pleasure than pain. Indeed, our scant evidence suggests that the evaluation of life in the early Vedic period was not so negative; and much later, in mediaeval Hinduism, the axiom that life was suffering came to receive little attention. However, all classical Indian religions, from the *Upaniṣads* on, took it as axiomatic that never-ending rebirth was undesirable and one's aim was to get off the treadmill. Moreover, even rebirth in heaven was less desirable than such escape, for even life in heaven was not eternal. It could not be eternal, within the terms of the system, because all *karman* is finite and so can produce only finite results. In the end, even a heavenly being exhausts his stock of good *karman* as he goes on enjoying heavenly delights, and must be reborn in a less pleasant environment. The denizens of heaven are by definition gods, so this is to say that gods too have finite lives.

The best, therefore, that action in the world could bring you was temporary relief from life's problems. Doing your duty inevitably paid dividends, but those dividends needed perpetual replenishment. (Theologians found reasons why such replenishment did not take place in the heavens.) In our terms (pp. 25–6 above), the communal religion of *dharma* and *sva-dharma* was no soteriology, for it offered no final solution.

There were, accordingly, men (and possibly women) who wanted no part of this world, the social world with its ascribed status and prescribed duties. Brahminism came to describe such people as 'renouncers' (*saṃnyāsin*), and even assigned their way of life a place in the life-cycle, an option one could take up when one had fulfilled one's duties as a householder. Whether these full-time salvation-seekers really began in conscious reaction to the brahminical world or originated quite outside that world is a much debated question which I shall not pursue. What matters to us is that the institution of renunciation, even before it was formalized by brahminism, does make sense in terms of brahmin ideology. If life in society brings only rebirth, it is only life outside society which can bring escape from rebirth. Society with its web of obligations becomes an analogue for the entire cycle of *saṃsāra*, and on the other hand the homeless life with no social ties becomes an analogue for that release from rebirth for which it is conceived to be literally a preparation.

Seen in these terms, as Louis Dumont showed in his famous essay 'World Renunciation in Indian Religions',[9] the institution of renunciation sets up a whole set of binary oppositions, pairs of opposites. The renouncer leaves the organized space of home and settlement (village) for homelessness and the formless wilderness. He has no fire, the symbol and instrument of sacrifice. He may neither produce nor reproduce, for Desire is Death. He leaves the world of ascribed statuses, notably caste, for the casteless world of individual achievement – though the only kind of achievement valued is religious progress. He even tries to abandon ordinary perceptual and thought processes to attain altered states of consciousness.

This world, which rejected the traditional institutions of society, the Buddha joined when he made the Great Renunciation. Yet had Buddhism entirely stayed there, it would have no history.

B. THE SOCIAL CONDITIONS OF HIS DAY

The man who was to become the Buddha was born in Kapilavatthu, a town in what is now the Nepalese Terai, and spent his life in what is now Bihar and Eastern Uttar Pradesh. (The word Bihar is in fact the same as *vihāra*, the Buddhist word for 'monastery'.) Though this area is now intersected by the international boundary between India and Nepal, it is a geographical unit, the middle Gangetic plain. Nevertheless, the Buddha's birthplace is sufficiently far from anywhere mentioned in brahminical texts of that period to make one wonder whether Vedic civilization can have penetrated at all to where he was born and grew up. For instance, the brahminical kinship system was exogamous, whereas the Buddha's kin seem to have married their cross-cousins. It is even possible that the Buddha's mother tongue was not an Indo-Aryan language. Certainly, when he walked southeast into central Bihar, the scene of his Enlightenment, he encountered brahminical culture with the critical eye of someone who had not been brought up to take its presuppositions for granted.

The Buddha came from a community called (in Sanskrit) Śākyas; hence his commonest Sanskrit title, Śākyamuni, 'the Sage of the Śākyas'. This fact is of great historical importance, because according to the Buddha (or, strictly speaking, according to words attributed to him in the *Mahā Parinibbāna Sutta*)[10] he modelled the organization of his Sangha on that of such communities as his own. Historians usually call these communities 'tribes', but I am wary of that term, which corresponds to no word in Sanskrit or Pali. 'Tribe' evokes an isolated community with no socially structured inequality. The Śākyas seem not to have had a *varṇa* system but they did have servants. They were isolated to the extent that they were self-governing, and their polity was of a form not envisaged in brahminical theory. We deduce that the heads of households – maybe only those above a certain age or otherwise of a certain standing – met in council to discuss their problems and tried to reach unanimous decisions. Some historians call this an oligarchy, some a republic; certainly it was not a brahminical monarchy, and makes more than dubious the later story that the future Buddha's father was the local king. This polity presented the Buddha with a model of how a casteless society could function. In the Sangha he instituted no principle of rank but seniority, counted in that case from ordination; maybe age was the ranking principle in the Śākya council.

We have described above (pp. 36, 39) how the *varṇa* system spread by imposing its categories on analogous social groups in the societies with which it came into contact. Groups of men who exercised political power could only be of the *kṣatriya varṇa*. That is how the Buddha, speaking in brahminical terms – for there was no other language in which to describe society – came to describe himself as a *kṣatriya* when he met caste-proud brahmins. It does not prove that his father had ever heard of the term.

By ideology, of course, the *kṣatriya* ranks second, beneath the brahmin. Yet he is the man with the real physical power, on whom even the brahmin depends for his safety and physical welfare. The relations between brahmin and *kṣatriya* have always been somewhat ambiguous, since their power relations depend entirely on your point of view. That this ambivalence was very marked at the end of the Vedic period we can see from the early *Upaniṣads*, where kings are shown lording it over brahmins and even teaching them doctrines. (One cannot witness this ambivalence where foreign rule has stripped *kṣatriyas* of their real power.) It hardly seems a coincidence therefore that the Buddha and Mahāvīra, the two greatest religious leaders of the period, men who challenged everything the brahmins stood for, both claimed *kṣatriya* status – or had it claimed for them by their early followers.

What were the material conditions of the society in which the Buddha preached? The most obvious difference from the society described in the previous section is that that was entirely rural, a village-based society, whereas the Buddha spent much of his time in cities. Max Weber aptly begins his account of Buddhism with these words: 'Like Jainism, but even more clearly, Buddhism presents itself as the product of the time of urban development, of urban kingship and the city nobles.'[11] The Buddha talked to kings, Pasenadi of Kosala, Bimbisāra and his son Ajātasattu of Magadha, who ruled quite sizeable territories from their urban capitals.

Thus the Buddha's period saw not only urbanization, but the beginnings of what one might call states.

The period also saw the first use of money and the beginnings of organized trade.

Both urbanization and trade can only arise when there is an agricultural surplus. The contentious question is what produced this surplus. As the centre of civilization moved down the Ganges it came to an area of higher rainfall and hence greater agricultural potential: the area was fertile ground for rice. On the other hand, the more luxuriant vegetation may have been harder to clear than the scrub jungle further northwest. D.D. Kosambi accordingly argued[12] that the agricultural surplus was made possible by the use of iron plough shares and other tools. These came, he said, from the rich iron deposits in south Bihar; at the same time smelting techniques might have advanced to produce harder iron. There are indeed a few references to iron tools in texts of the period, though they cannot be very precisely dated and give no clue to the prevalence or quality of the iron. The problem is the lack of archaeological evidence. R.S. Sharma, a historian who wholeheartedly supports Kosambi's thesis, writes:

> literary references are not matched by archaeological discoveries of tools belonging to the age of the Buddha. In Eastern UP and Bihar there is evidence for the use of iron from c. 700 B.C. onwards but so far no ploughshare has been discovered, and iron tools for agriculture are not found in good numbers. Nevertheless this can be explained by ecological reasons. The acid, humid, warm alluvial soil of eastern UP and Bihar has proved to be highly corrosive.[13]

There also does not seem to have been great improvement in the quality of the iron used.

> Later when steel came into use it proved more lasting and serviceable. But in 600–300 B.C. most iron objects belonged to the wrought category. Even till recent times in Bihar ploughshares were made of semi-steel; after a few years' use they get heavily rusted.[14]

It may indeed be that we find so few iron tools of the period because they have all rusted away, but this does make iron a friable foundation on which to build a whole theory of cultural change.

It is worth remembering, as A. Ghosh points out,[15] that urbanization can occur without any iron. The Egyptians without iron cut granite blocks and built fortified cities. The cities of central America arose in a civilization which had no plough, no stockbreeding, no sailing boats and no wheeled transport, let alone iron.[16] In India, the Harappan civilization produced cities without using iron tools. Jungle can be cleared by burning; though Sharma objects that one still has to dig out the stumps, that is not impossible with, for example, copper-bronze tools.[17]

Sharma also argues that wet paddy cultivation was the agricultural base of the new economic surplus. Here he seems on less slippery ground because Buddhist canonical texts not only allude to wet rice production but show that irrigation techniques were well understood. Sharma suggests that transplantation, which greatly increases yield, began in the Buddha's day. But unfortunately this is a guess. Transplantation is described in a Jain text which 'may have existed before the third century B.C.'[18] – hardly convincing evidence for the Buddha's day. On the other hand, the techniques may have been in use much *earlier* than the Buddha. Again, we leave the summary to Sharma:

> In eastern India rice was undoubtedly produced before 1200 B.C.; ... around 1000 B.C. we get wet rice grains. It has been claimed that cultivated rice appeared in the Vindhyan region near Allahabad in the neolithic phase around 5000 B.C. In any case about 7000 B.C. we get charred rice grains from Sonpur [in central Bihar]. We do not know whether the cultivators used transplantation, but there is no doubt about the use of rice in this part of the country before its large-scale colonization since *c.* 600 B.C.[19]

The failure of archaeology to support the (plausible) view that the new wealth must have derived from technical advance goes beyond the problems of iron and rice transplantation. To quote Sharma again:

> It is argued that before 300 B.C. no visible change in the material life of the people can be detected on the basic of archaeological excavations. In a way it is correct because till *c.* 300 B.C. we do not find burnt bricks, ring wells, profuse [Northern Black Polished] sherds, numerous terracottas and coins, and too many iron agricultural tools. But what is more crucial for the understanding of the material life of the age of the Buddha is the very cropping up of a large number of settlements in the alluvium belt of the middle Gangetic basin ...[20]

So we gather from Sharma himself, though he never spells out this conclusion, that the main reason for the production of a surplus was probably not a technical discovery but simply the spread of population into a region with better ecological conditions for agriculture.

Towns and cities arise primarily as settlements of people whose main livelihood is not derived directly from agriculture – though to be sure they may also house absentee landlords. They are political and commercial centres. There can be no trade without an economic surplus; but though trade seems to be a necessary condition for the creation of towns, it is not a sufficient one. On the other hand, it is too easily forgotten that commerce itself depends on organization: on an infrastructure of communications and a certain level of legality and security, both products of stable political conditions.[21] For all its technical ignorance, meso-America had a 'well-developed power structure'.[22] The clay soil in this region quickly hardens when dry to make good roads (which become impassable for vehicles during the monsoon); there were no paved roads till Sher Shah built the Grand Trunk Road in the fifteenth century. It is kings who construct the roads along which vehicles can move and allow for land trade in larger quantities than a pedlar carries on his back. Moreover, security in the countryside of Bihar and neighbouring areas has rarely if ever been good; without the security provided by towns, large-scale trade is impossible.

The earliest coins found are dated to the late sixth century BCE[23] and they were widely used by the end of the fifth.[24] These early coins are all punch-marked, not inscribed. They have a high silver content, which must have come from outside the region, but not all historians agree with Ghosh that it must have come from outside India. It is unlikely that there was extensive foreign trade; some Buddhist texts talk of sea trade, but they are not among the earliest ones. The fact that an early brahminical law-book prohibits going to sea[25] betrays the possibility, but this text too is probably a bit later.

Does trade on such a scale depend on literacy? There is no evidence for writing in the Buddha's day. There are three references to writing in the *Vinaya Piṭaka*, in texts generally thought to date from the fourth century (if not later) in their present form; there is one extremely doubtful reference in an older text.[26] As stated above, no examples of writing survive from before the third century. Ghosh thinks that as Asoka's inscriptions use the same script over most of India 'it would be reasonable to allow one or two centuries for standardization'.[27] Thus although Romila Thapar states in the Pelican *History of India* that writing was used in the Buddha's day,[28] there is no evidence to support her. If it existed at all, we can be sure that its use was very limited, perhaps to accounting. Certainly there were no books: at this time, and for several centuries more, scriptures had to be preserved orally. We observe in passing that this would disprove Professor Goody's theory that 'the religions of conversion ... are all religions of the book'.[29]

The archaeological, as against the textual, evidence for cities at this time is astonishingly meagre, because building was in wood and mud. No public monument or public building which could go back to the time of the Buddha has been found, with the possible exception of a palace at Kauśambī. Towns had sacred spots called *caitya*, but apparently they carried no large edifices.[30] Even baked brick is found only sporadically and at a few sites.[31] No evidence has been found of city planning or public drainage till as late as the second century BCE.[32] Notwithstanding the claims of a few enthusiastic excavators, the earliest date it seems reasonable to assign to an Indian city (after the prehistoric Indus Valley civilization) is *c.*600 BCE: both Kauśambī and Ujjain may be that old.[33]

Kauśambī and Ujjain are only two of the score or so of towns mentioned in the Buddhist Canon.[34] The Pali sources have the Buddha spending most of his time (for instance, passing the rains retreats) at Rājagaha, Vesālī and Sāvatthī – all towns which continued to be prominent in Buddhist history. A text in the *Dīgha Nikāya*[35] list six 'great cities': Campā, Rājagaha, Sāvatthī, Sāketa, Kosambī = Kauśambī and Benares (= Varanasi).

Of these six, all but Sāketa were capitals of what the texts call 'large countries' (*mahā janapada*).[36] There is a canonical list of sixteen such 'large countries';[37] it seems to have been almost a technical term. We saw in the last chapter that Indian kings are conceived of in the first instance as ruling men rather than territory, a heritage perhaps of the nomadic past. Heesterman has shown that even when they settled down, the Hindu state was seen rather as a field of power centred on the king than as a firmly bounded tract of land.[38] From the brilliant person of the king, power radiated like rays from the sun, soaking up the taxes to form his economic base as the sun's rays soak up moisture from the earth.

The power of some of these suns increased with the greater resources at their command. Twice in early Indian history the sizes of kingdoms made critical increases, almost quantum leaps, which greatly affected Buddhist history. The first critical leap was the establishment of the 'large countries'; the second, we shall see, was the creation of the Mauryan empire two or three centuries later. At both junctures, the larger unit rarely destroyed the smaller, but rather subsumed it, fitting it into an overarching structure. Thus developed a complex graduation of lordship and overlordship. The power required to control the larger structure was no doubt initially acquired by force – just how, we do not know – but its retention must have depended also on an increasingly efficient and complex apparatus of government control.

Thus there arose two major new professions, both presumably urban-based: state officials and traders. The former must have been much the smaller and we do not know how it originally related to the *varṇa* system, which never acknowledged it; later, with the increasing use of writing, bureaucrats have tended to be brahmins. There have long been far too many brahmins for them all to gain a living as priests, and though the law-books allow them to follow various professions if 'in distress' they rather frown on agriculture, which an early authority says 'destroys the Veda'.[39]

Nor did the earliest form of the *varṇa* ideology (which was still current at the time of the Buddha) have a place for trade. That came to be assigned to the *vaiśya*. But in the Buddha's day the dominant strata of urban society were not catered for, not even recognized, by brahminism.

In fact, the brahmin law-givers of this period are explicitly hostile to towns. Gautama, probably the oldest (P.V. Kane dates him between 600 and 400 BCE), says that 'some prohibit Vedic recitation in a city',[40] which for brahmins amounts to saying 'Extra rurem nulla salus'. (His commentator says that so sweeping a view is not Gautama's: he means only those cities in which low people like *śūdras* predominate. But on this we may in turn comment that that qualification would make no practical difference.) Baudhāyana, whom Kane dates 500–200 BCE, puts it more graphically: 'His body veiled in dust, his face and eyes full of it, that the city-dweller, even if well restrained, should attain salvation is an impossibility.'[41] The countless particularistic rules of brahmin orthodoxy were formulated for village society.

To whom did the Buddha's message appeal?

There is some evidence that the Buddha's message appealed especially to town-dwellers and the new social classes. B.G. Gokhale has analysed[42] the social composition of the early Sangha, basing himself on two canonical collections of religious poems, the *Thera-* and *Therī-gāthā*, which are ascribed to monks and nuns respectively. It is the commentary on these texts which makes the ascriptions of authorship; in most cases it goes on to supply such biographical details as where the author was from and to which *varṇa* he or she belonged. The commentary which we have dates only from the fifth century CE, but we know that it rests on a far older tradition, so maybe its information is authentic. We thus have plausible information on a sample of over 300 monks and nuns. More than two-thirds of them came from large towns, and of these two-thirds 86 per cent from just four cities: Sāvatthī, Rājagaha, Kapilavatthu and Vesālī. As for *varṇa*, of 328 religious 134 (about 40 per cent) were brahmin, 75 *kṣatriya*, 98 *vaiśya* and 11 *śūdra*; 10 were outcastes. From various terms applied to their families we can further deduce that nearly half of them came from wealthy or powerful houses. Thus the brahmin recruits were not the traditional village priest but rather upper-class urbanites. If these figures have any foundation, they show that Buddhism, though it admitted anyone to the Sangha, was not primarily a religion of the downtrodden.

The canonical texts – without recourse to the commentaries – can also give us an idea of the social composition of the Buddha's lay support. The term which constantly recurs is *gahapati*, which literally means 'master of a house', i.e. 'householder'. To this day in Indian villages people think of the population very much in terms of family groups or 'houses', each one with its head. It is far easier to get from a villager an estimate of how many such units there are in an area than of the total number of human beings. It is from these 'householders' that such institutions as village councils have always recruited their membership. A household includes not only close kin but servants and other dependants. When ancient texts mention householders, they are referring to heads of families of the top three *varṇas*; the other families do not 'count' socially. Moreover, since brahmins and *kṣatriyas* can have formed only a small part of the population, the term must refer mainly to heads of families which brahminism classified as *vaiśya*. Indeed, the term *vaiśya* (Pali: *vessa*) is rare in Buddhist scripture; it occurs only when discussing brahmin classification, not as the natural designation for someone's primary social status. It is clear that the canonical *gahapati* is the head of a 'respectable' family – but not a brahmin, unless specifically said to be so.

Who were these people in terms of class or profession? In the Canon, most of them evidently own land, but they usually have labourers to do the physical work. Sometimes they are also in business. In fact, they illustrate how it is in the first instance wealth derived from agriculture which provides business capital. The average *gahapati* who gave material support to the Buddha and his Sangha thus seems to have been something like a gentleman farmer, perhaps with a town house. On the other hand, inscriptions in the western Deccan, where Buddhism flourished in the early centuries CE, use the term *gahapati* to refer to urban merchants.[43] We must distinguish between reference and meaning:

the meaning of *gahapati* is simple and unvarying, but the reference shifts with the social context.

We mentioned at the end of the last chapter that by the time of the Buddha there was already a whole milieu of renouncers, a kind of counter-culture with which brahminical ideology was struggling to come to terms. There constantly recurs in the early Buddhist texts a blanket expression for holy men: *samaṇa-brāhmaṇa.* These two types of holy men were antithetical. The term *samaṇa* seems to mean something like 'ascetic'. When Gotama became one by 'going forth', as the term was (i.e. leaving home), there were many kinds of such ascetics. Our knowledge of their practices is very patchy. But evidently most of them were rather extreme in their rejection of human culture. Typically they wore no clothes at all and eschewed all comforts. Some took vows to behave like cattle or like dogs.[44]

One ancient religion from this ascetic milieu, Jainism, survives to this day. In their desire to escape rebirth Jains hold that all *karman*, since it entails consequences, is undesirable; thus they arrive at the radical conclusion that the best course is to do nothing at all. The best solution is to remain motionless and starve to death. The Digambara Jain renouncers still go completely naked, after plucking their hair out by the roots to symbolize their rejection of all social roles. They may only eat with and from their hands and only once a day – at other times not even water may be ingested. They may not wash or clean their teeth. They carry homelessness to the point of being more or less constantly on the move: they normally do not spend two nights in the same place. Thus the path to salvation seems to have been conceived primarily as one of mortification (*tapas*), not meditation.

What impelled people to undertake such frightful austerities? What were the peculiar problems caused by the social changes outlined above? In particular, can one suggest why the religious movements of the time all took it as axiomatic that life as we normally experience it was something to be escaped from?

It has been customary to point out that rapid social change tends to upset people. This is no doubt true, though not very informative. Professor Ghosh has provided a more precise and interesting summary of how urbanization may engender a spiritual malaise: the movement from village to town to city entails a more complex division of labour and professional specialization; social organization less in terms of kinship groups and more in terms of goal-oriented associations; less stringent control over the individual and greater dependence on impersonal institutions of control (bureaucracy, police, etc.); greater individual freedom and mobility and hence some disintegration of the traditional culture and social order.[45] We may add that these factors operate more rapidly as one climbs the social scale: some city slum neighbourhoods are more like village communities than the wealthier districts can ever be. We know too little about the Buddha's social environment to apply every factor Ghosh has listed to that time, but the general picture is familiar: a move away from the closed community towards a more open society, an increase in the individual's power to choose and hence doubt about choosing rightly.

Some Marxist historians have suggested that the increased awareness of life's misery naturally reflects the new class structure, in which non-productive classes exploit the labour of the primary producers. I find this theory humane but unconvincing as an account of Buddhism, if only because the evidence suggests, as shown above, that Buddhism appealed mainly to the better-off.

There is, however, another factor which may have made reflective people gloomier about life. So far as I know, it has not previously been suggested in a Buddhist or Indological context, and I hasten to add that I am not putting it forward as a total explanation for the axiom that life is suffering, but merely as a possible contributory cause, in conjunction with Ghosh's list and doubtless others not yet thought of. But reading McNeill's *Plagues and Peoples* persuaded me that one should consider problems of public health and mortality.

As the centre of civilization moved down the Ganges it encountered a warmer, wetter climate. Here flourished many parasites carrying diseases to mankind.

> Today the Ganges region sustains cholera, malaria, and dengue fever together with a great variety of multi-celled parasites, as well as the more universal diseases of cities and civilization that are familiar in cooler climes. What disease organisms may have circulated in ancient times cannot be said for sure, but the climate of the Ganges Valley certainly must have permitted a rich array of parasites to arise as soon as dense populations came into existence.[46]

Diseases were endemic here which were absent from the northwest of India where the Indo-Aryans had first settled; they must have afflicted the newcomers, who had built up no resistance to them, and so slowed the pace of advance. The difficulty that the northern Chinese of the Yellow

River flood plain had in populating the Yangtze Valley further south furnishes a striking ecological parallel.[47] Wet paddy cultivation is also a less healthy occupation than stockrearing. The growth of towns in the Gangetic basin showed that the worst initial obstacles had been overcome. However, we can be sure that concentration of population heightened disease incidence and indeed mortality, for this consequence has everywhere followed urbanization. This is both because of the hygienic problems that arise, notably that it is hard to get uncontaminated water, and because concentrations of population sustain disease-bearing parasites which die out where hosts are few; in the long run these parasites become endemic, resistance develops by natural selection and the diseases become childhood afflictions from which most patients recover; but this balance takes several generations to develop and at first mortality is bound to be much higher than in the surrounding countryside.[48]

This connection between cities and morbidity was not unknown to ancient India: the classical medical work the *Caraka Saṃhitā* mentions it.[49] It is quite possible that in the Buddha's environment disease and sudden death had actually become much more frequent. Maybe it is no accident that the early Buddhists were fond of medical metaphors, describing the Buddha as the great physician, etc. (see p. 2). It has even been surmised[50] that the very format of the first sermon and its Four Noble Truths follows a medical model: diagnosing the complaint, finding its cause, finding what would eliminate the cause, prescribing the medicine to achieve that elimination.

We must now turn to the content of the Buddha's message. But first I must briefly revert to a theme in my Introduction. Readers may justly object that the reason why the Buddha said that life is suffering is that it is simply true. I am not concerned to dispute that. But this view had not been current in India earlier and there are many times and places at which it has not been held or at least not emphasized. The task I have set myself is to explain why it became acceptable when it did.

CHAPTER THREE

The Buddha's Dhamma

The Buddha preached his first sermon, thus 'setting in motion the wheel of the Law', in the deer park of Sarnath, just outside Benares.[1] Its opening statement establishes Buddhism as the religion of 'the middle way'. The man who has left home must avoid two extremes: attachment to the pleasures of the senses and attachment to mortifications. The former is low and vulgar, the second is painful, and neither does any good. The Buddha has realized a middle way which leads to calm, understanding and *nibbāna*.

It was the Buddha's own experience, according to the Canon, which led him to this position. After leaving home and the life of sensual pleasures, he had become the disciple successively of two spiritual teachers. They had taught him meditative techniques that had taken him into ecstatic trances without bringing the understanding he was looking for. He had then gone off with five like-minded ascetics and practised extreme asceticism, till he realized that he was in danger of dying for lack of food without being nearer to a solution.[2] So he began to eat, in moderation, at which backsliding his colleagues left him in disgust. Then he found the answer.

At first he was in a state of bliss and felt disinclined to take the trouble to preach, for he doubted whether his message would be appreciated. The heavens were alarmed at this and the greatest god, Brahmā, the personification of the brahminical monistic principle, came down to entreat him personally. He agreed to preach, and thought of beginning with his former teachers, but then discovered (by supernormal means) that they had died. So he resolved to preach to his five former fellows. On his way to see them he met another ascetic, to whom he announced his Enlightenment. 'May it be so,' said the ascetic, and passed on his way. When the five saw him arriving they agreed to give him the cold shoulder, but then found themselves unable to stick to their agreement. It is at this point, the text says, that he uttered the first sermon.

Of course we do not really know what the Buddha said in his first sermon – no one was there with shorthand or a tape recorder – and it has even been convincingly demonstrated[3] that the language of the text as we have it is in the main a set of formulae, expressions which are by no means self-explanatory but *refer* to already established doctrines. Nevertheless, the compilers of the Canon put in the first sermon what they knew to be the very essence of the Buddha's Enlightenment. That Buddhism is 'the Middle Way' became its Leitmotiv. The term has been variously applied. Mahāyāna applied it to ontology, making Buddhism the middle way between affirmation and denial of existence. The whole context, however, and the presence in the first sentence of the word *pabbajita*, 'the man who has left home', show that the main reference is to practice, and more precisely to the practice of those people who were about to become the Sangha. This middle way between indulgence and asceticism is the principle informing all the Sangha's rules of life. We shall explore this in more detail in the next chapter. Here we need only remind the reader how the 'middle' was defined in its historical context. The life of attachment to the pleasures of the senses is perhaps a common-sense concept. But this common sense came to be ideologized as an ideal by brahminism, in that sensual pleasure is one of the ideals of the householder, to be pursued till it conflicts with higher ideals of duty or interest. The Buddha calls this way of life *gamma*. While this word came normally to mean 'vulgar', and it is certainly appropriate to see that meaning in this text too, I find it no mere coincidence that literally (etymologically) it means 'of the village': the village was at that time and place the opposite both of the city which brahminism viewed with such suspicion and of the wilderness in which the ascetics led their wandering life. Elsewhere in the Canon *gāma-dhamma*, 'the way of the village', is a term for sexual intercourse.[4] Of the ascetic extreme we have said enough. So decisively did the Buddha reject it that in the Buddhist tradition the word *tapas* (see above pp. 44 and 57), when used to apply to Buddhist practice, refers to meditation and/or 'reasoned moral self-discipline'.[5]

After enunciating the middle way, the Buddha tersely revealed the content of his liberating insight. He had realized Four Noble Truths: suffering; the origin of suffering; the abolition of suffering; and the path leading to that abolition of suffering. Unfortunately *dukkha*, the word we translate 'suffering', lacks a close English equivalent: it is the opposite of well-being and so more general than suffering. The meaning of the First Noble Truth is that life is unsatisfactory. The origin of suffering the Buddha declared to be 'thirst', which is a metaphor for desire. In other words, frustration arises only when you want something. Accordingly, suffering can be abolished by eradicating desire; the Third Noble Truth not only draws this logical corollary but also states that such eradication is possible. The Fourth Noble Truth tells you how to do it, in a formula called the Noble Eightfold Path. This Path came to be more simply expressed as a necessary progress through three stages: morality, meditation and wisdom. Each stage is usually considered a prerequisite for the next: only a moral person can meditate successfully and meditation in turn is the necessary training for wisdom. The content of this wisdom, which is called 'seeing things as they are', is the Four Noble Truths. But one must pass beyond a merely intellectual understanding: Enlightenment consists in fully internalizing that understanding, *realizing* it in the fullest sense, and so silencing the passions.

The Buddha often stressed that it was his own realization, his experience of the deathless state of *nibbāna*, which entitled him to teach, for he was teaching not a mere theory but a practice which he knew to work. He criticized brahmins for teaching what they had not themselves experienced.[6] The Dhamma, while it is certainly the Truth, also has a prescriptive force: 'the Truth which is to be realized *and* what should be done to realize it'. Progressing towards that realization is a skill, and as that progress is a series of mental events a good mental state is called 'skilful' (*kusala*). This is why the Buddha habitually used the words 'skilful' and 'unskilful' where we would naturally say 'moral' and 'immoral' or 'virtuous' and 'vicious'.

In identifying desire – which may be positive or negative – as the origin of suffering, the Buddha seems to stand in the tradition (predominant in the ascetic milieu) which considered the emotions and appetites as the obstacle to liberation and the root of all evil. Yet the matter is not so simple, for liberation here consists in a realization of the true nature of reality. There is a more complex formulation of the content of the Buddha's Enlightenment.[7] It is known as the Chain of Dependent Origination (*paṭicca-samuppāda*), and in it desire in turn derives from ignorance, which stands at the beginning of the sequence – though not as an absolute beginning in itself. This gnostic formulation must relate to the Upaniṣadic analysis of man's predicament. Wherever we look in Buddhist doctrine, desire and ignorance intertwine, inseparable, as the basic problem, the enemy within. The three 'roots of evil' are greed (or lust), hatred and delusion. In his third sermon,[8] the Buddha explained that we and the objects of our perceptions are all on fire, ablaze with greed, hatred and delusion. If we only realize this, we become disenchanted with everything and are freed. Here again, greed and hatred are desire, delusion is another term for ignorance, failing to 'see things as they are'. *Nibbāna* means 'blowing out'. What must be blown out is the triple fire of greed, hatred and delusion.

Endless misunderstanding has been caused by western writers who have assumed that *nibbāna* is the 'blowing out' of the person or soul. This is WRONG. In fact it is a Buddhist heresy. The texts are plain: one must extinguish the fires of greed, hatred and delusion.

The confusion has arisen because of the Buddha's teaching that beings have no soul, no abiding essence. This 'no-soul doctrine' (*anatta-vāda*) he expounded in his second sermon.[9] He analysed the individual into five constituents, which we may translate as body, feelings (of pleasure or pain), perception, volitions (including unconscious and inherited drives) and consciousness. Each in turn is not the self, for it is impermanent and so ultimately unsatisfactory. We must remember that eternal immutability was essential to the brahminical concept of the soul. Since this analysis of the person into physical and mental components is meant to be exhaustive, it shows that there is no soul or self as a separate entity. All such terms as soul, self, individual, etc. are mere conventional terms, and the same is true of the names of beings. In due course this doctrine of essence-lessness came to be applied to everything, not just living beings, and Buddhism took an extreme nominalist position, ultimately to the point of paradox. But the Buddha, as he clearly stated on other occasions, was interested in saving men, not in philosophy, and his first concern was the essence-lessness of individuals.

The underlying paradigm of the 'no-soul doctrine' seems to be that life cannot be satisfactory because it ends in death. All phenomenal existence is said to have three interlocking characteristics: impermanence, suffering and lack of soul or essence. This is simply a matter to be realized. There can be no question of getting rid of a soul because one has never had one. Even here the two interpretations of the origin of our problems, the emotionalist and the intellectualist, are intertwined. For if one realizes that one has no self, one cannot be selfish, so all desire falls away.

Nibbāna is not a 'thing' but the experience of being without greed, hatred and delusion. The poems of Enlightened monks and nuns describe it as blissfully peaceful and cool. That such an experience is logically possible was demonstrated by the Buddha's analysis; that it is attainable was shown by his example.

Buddhist meditation takes two forms. The first, concentration, is to achieve 'one-pointedness' and hence perfect stillness of mind. This is not unlike the meditation of the Hindu *yogin* and it is in this kind of meditation that the Buddha was trained by his two teachers. But for Buddhists it is only a propaideutic, because their aim is to achieve the clarity which 'sees things as they are' – impermanent, unsatisfactory, without essence. Hence they cultivate awareness. This form of meditation is distinctively and quintessentially Buddhist. By being aware of his own physique, feelings, states of mind and thoughts[10] the Buddhist will cease to identify with them as his 'self', to introject a sense of ego into what are but transient phenomena, constantly coming into being and passing away.

This awareness, aiming at detachment, is to be practised at the most mundane level and under all circumstances. In everyday life such awareness means a calm and controlled deportment, a lack of emotional display. In religious experience it means that the Buddha was diametrically opposed to that total loss of normal awareness which we call possession, the state which, so far as we can tell, has always been the hallmark of religious performance in the local cults of south Asian villagers. This opposition to possession Buddhism shared with the brahminism and probably all the other soteriologies of the day; all set themselves against such vulgar lack of self-control in favour of what they considered more 'civilized' standards. Though awareness is primarily a cognitive activity, it has an ethical facet too: attention, carefulness, conscientiousness, diligence. We shall return to these qualities in the next section.

Unselfishness and carefulness are cardinal Buddhist values; so are the four 'divine' states of mind: kindness, compassion, sympathetic joy and equanimity. (Buddhaghosa compared the four to the feelings a mother has for four sons: 'a child, an invalid, one in the flush of youth, and one busy with his own affairs'.[11]) The Buddha preached to the world out of his great compassion (*karuṇā*), and Buddhists extol kindness, which must, however, be selfless and disinterested. The *Metta Sutta*,[12] an ancient poem in the Canon, may well be the most widely used Pali text in Theravādin practice; it is a meditation on kindness in which one attempts to suffuse the world with the thought 'May all beings be happy.'

The positive values of kindness and unselfishness characterize Buddhism better than do the moral precepts for the laity, which are expressed negatively. Though usually called 'precepts', they are really undertakings, expressed in the first person. They are five: not to take life, steal, be unchaste (which is defined according to one's situation), lie, or take intoxicants, inasmuch as they lead to carelessness and hence to breaking the first four undertakings. Certain more specific abstentions may be added at prescribed times. Positively, the Buddhist's first duty is to be generous, and the primary – though by no means the only – object of his generosity is to be the Sangha. Generosity, keeping the moral undertakings, cultivating one's mind: these three[13] summarize the Buddhist path to a good rebirth and ultimately to release from all rebirth.

So far we have touched on doctrines which are more or less distinctive to Buddhism – and they are indeed central. The Buddha's view of the arena in which all this suffering and struggle to escape from suffering take place is at first glance not so very different from other cosmologies of the time. The world is layered, with heavens above us and hells below; as one goes up it, power, longevity and general well-being increase. But no situation is permanent: as explained on p. 48, even the gods must die. One's situation is determined by the quality of one's past acts, one's *kamma*. In the Buddhist view, the world (and life in the world, *saṃsāra*) can have no beginning, because nothing exists without a cause – this is the cosmic application of the doctrine of Dependent Origination. There can thus be no creator god, as he himself would require a cause. In any case, an omnipotent god would be otiose, as *kamma* explains suffering. We act from desire (as brahminism says) and hence we keep on acting and dying. This is why for Buddhists death and desire are but two sides of the same coin, and the world, including all but the highest, suprasensory, heavens is called the realm of Desire and said to be presided over by Māra, the personification of Death.

The Dhamma in its context: answers to brahminism

Since this is a social history it would be out of place to attempt here any further exposition of Buddhist doctrine, a topic already admirably expounded in many books. I shall merely suggest how these doctrines relate to others of that time and what may have made them appear convincing.

The most important point is that two rival analyses of life's problems were already on offer. I have dubbed them the intellectualist – which locates the nub of the problem in our lack of true understanding – and the emotionalist – which blames our lack of self-control. The Buddha wonderfully combined the two. You cannot see things straight because you are blinded by passion, and you allow your emotions to run you because you do not see things as they are. If one wanted to argue with this, it is not easy to see how one would begin – though of course many have tried. The main point, however, is that in outline this position must be acceptable to both emotionalists and intellectualists. This versatility has proved itself to have great value for survival.

The false view which feeds the emotions is that there is an eternal self. While this view has of course been very widely held, the particular version of the view against which the Buddha argued was the brahminical view found in the *Upaniṣads*, the *Vedānta*. It has not been sufficiently commented on that the Buddha preserves the brahminical doctrine of macrocosm–microcosm equivalence – but in a negative sense. For the *Vedānta*, the one identification which ultimately mattered was between the essence of the individual and the essence of the world: 'Thou art that.'[14] The Buddha denied the essence of the individual and correspondingly denied an essence to the world: no creator or omnipotent god, no underlying unity to phenomena.

The unenlightened are on fire with three fires. Fire in Buddhism is a negative symbol, standing for the home one has left and the passions one is trying to leave. We shall see below (p. 79) that the number three is no coincidence: the orthodox brahmin was supposed to maintain always the *three* fires required for major sacrifices, and the Buddha juxtaposed his fires to those.

However, the most important step that the Buddha took was to turn the doctrine of *karman* on its head. He ethicized it completely, made morality intrinsic, and so denied all soteriological value to ritual and all ultimate value to social distinctions. In place of a highly particularistic view of duty he propounded a simple and universal ethical dualism of right and wrong.

Some of these steps had already been taken by Jainism, and perhaps by other teachers among the renouncers. All these renouncers denied that the brahmins had through the Veda any privileged access to knowledge or understanding. They also denied, as a corollary, that sacrifice could produce results. The Jains and the Buddhists particularly criticized animal sacrifice, which they considered to be murderous cruelty; but their objections to sacrifice had deeper doctrinal roots, and extended to all brahminical ritual. (Perhaps one should simply say that it extended to all ritual whatsoever, but the ritual available for criticism was brahminical.)

We know from the Buddhist Canon that one of the Buddha's contemporaries, Pūraṇa Kassapa, denied all moral causation.[15] He said that whether you killed everything in sight or did nothing but acts of charity made not the slightest difference to your fate. This radical opposition to the theory of *karman* the Buddha heartily condemned: for him, it was axiomatic that moral behaviour was the foundation of spiritual progress. In fact, he regarded acceptance of the workings of *kamma* as the beginnings of wisdom; without it, one could not even enter on the path to deliverance (and thus become a member of the ideal Sangha – see p. 2 above). But he preached a very un-brahminical version of it.

His great innovation was to say that the moral quality of an act lies in the intention behind it. He put it succinctly: 'It is intention that I call *kamma*.'[16] It is easy to overlook the boldness, even audacity, of this statement. It is a linguistic sleight of hand, for *karman* in Sanskrit means precisely 'action', which in normal language is quite another thing than intention.

This single move overturns brahminical, caste-bound ethics. For the intention of a brahmin cannot plausibly be claimed to be ethically of quite a different kind from the intention of an outcaste. Intention can only be virtuous or wicked. The very term *sva-dharma*, the Sanskrit word meaning one's own particularistic duty, is absent from the Buddhist Canon. Continuing his revaluation of brahminical terms, the Buddha took the term 'pure' or 'purifying', the term appropriate to good ritual action, and gave it the meaning of 'virtuous' or 'meritorious'. It is this 'purifying action' (*puñña kamma*) which brings the good Buddhist rewards in this and future lives. But since acting is really mental, doing a good act is actually purifying one's state of mind. In meditation, such purification is undertaken directly, without any accompanying action. Thus there is a logical continuum between the moral actions of a man in the world and the meditations of a recluse. This shows why the Buddhists claim morality to be a prerequisite for meditation. The system is all of a piece.

This internalization of *karman* perhaps solved a difficulty. As explained in chapter 2, *karman* was a part of communal religion. It concerned life in this world and could only bring you worldly (including heavenly) rewards, not release from the whole system. The Jains, for example, have rigorously followed this reasoning: since one aims to escape from the world and all action brings worldly results, all action is undesirable; moral action is less bad than immoral action, but still undesirable. Here again, the Buddha wanted to steer a middle course, since good action was the foundation of his system. Is it necessary to be reborn to reap the results of good actions? No: the solution is this translation of the currency of good actions into the more fluid concept of mental purity. The virtuous man's thoughts approach ever nearer to the experience of *nibbāna*. As he turns to meditation and realization of the Dhamma, the language of *kamma* becomes inappropriate, but the goodness, far from being a hindrance, will all bear fruit in enabling him to see his way to the final goal.

Since ethical value lies in intention, the individual is autonomous and the final authority is what we would call his conscience. As a general rule, a monk could not be disciplined for an offence he did not admit. Similarly, the moral rules laid down for the laity (which also apply, *a fortiori*, to the Sangha) are, as we have seen, formulated as personal undertakings: the Buddhist layman declares, 'I undertake to abstain from taking life' and so forth, and thus articulates personal conscience. At least in theory, even the recitation of the words is useless and pointless unless one is consciously subscribing to their meaning.

The point of ritual lies in doing, not in intending. Thus ritual is ethically neutral for the Buddhist. It has no moral and hence no soteriological value. It is not normally forbidden, unless it involves an immoral act such as killing, but it is certainly not commended. We shall see that the Buddha continued his programme of putting new meanings to old words by asking his followers to substitute moral for ritual practices. One of the Three Fetters which tie men to continued existence in this world was declared to be infatuation with ritualistic observances, clinging to the letter rather than the spirit of actions.

This doctrine subverts brahminism from every angle. Buddhism denies the authority of the priesthood, their monopoly of sacred knowledge, their claim to mediate the divine, their very *raison d'être* as society's ritual specialists. The status that really matters is religious status, which is achieved by personal effort. Ascribed status, the caste hierarchy, is something that exists in the world, a fact of life, but of no spiritual significance. The true brahmin, said the Buddha, was the man with such universalistic values as gentleness and honesty, the true outcaste the man with the corresponding vices. 'Not by birth is one a brahmin or an outcaste, but by deeds (*kamma*).'[17]

This position, familiar from other religious traditions, is not that of a social revolutionary. Christians in mediaeval Europe did not deny the existence of the aristocracy, but said that their souls were just like the souls of plebeians; the virtuous but lowborn man could then be called 'one of nature's aristocrats' or 'a true gentleman', using the social term as a metaphor for a moral status but according the latter a higher value ultimately, i.e. in the eyes of God. The Buddha abolished secular status within the Sangha: there, he said, the four *varṇa* lose their identity as rivers do when they reach the sea, and men become simply sons and daughters of the Sākya.[18] But he never suggested that the rivers, or the *varṇa*, had not existed in the first place.

If *kamma* is completely ethicized, the whole universe becomes an ethical arena, because everywhere all beings are placed according to their deserts. If this is generalized into a view of the world, as it has been in Theravādin cultures, it means that ultimately power (including the power to enjoy oneself) and goodness are always perfectly correlated, both increasing as one proceeds (literally) up the universe. Gods are more powerful than human beings, but since they owe their position to their virtue they may be expected to exercise that power justly. Human beings, in turn, are better and also better off than animals, let alone demons. Moreover, even demons are only rationally punitive: they can be the instruments to give people their just deserts, but if they try to do more, like an over-zealous policeman, they will themselves be punished for it. This picture of a universe under control is from one angle reassuring; but in its belief that there is really no undeserved suffering it can also be harsh. It is not surprising that people have sought to mitigate this harshness through various ingenious escape clauses or simple inconsistencies (see part A of chapter 5 below).

Although the Buddha did not attempt to deny the facts of social life around him, the ethic of intention has radical implications for the social order, and some of these implications have indeed been drawn. If violence is always wrong, this calls into question the traditional role performance of the *kṣatriya*, the legitimate use of force.

So the ideological consequence of the Buddha's view of *kamma* has been influential in Theravādin societies. If acts are good or bad regardless of who does them, social role-playing is morally irrelevant. (Cosmic role-playing too: cruel demons deserve to stay in hell.) We have seen that in the brahminical view the *kṣatriya* is entitled to use force; it is of his essence to make war. And it is the function of the king to protect society internally too, by punishing criminals. It is open to Buddhists to argue, as has so often been done in other traditions, that ends may justify means and so violence can be justified, for example when the intention behind it is to protect society. There have been many Buddhist polities and societies which have fought wars and administered justice. But they have often been queasy about the moral basis for such acts. Of this the Emperor Asoka, perhaps the first ruler to declare himself a Buddhist, will furnish us with an example.

But it seems to me that traditional Theravāda has viewed *raison d'état* with distaste. There is a story about a former life of the Buddha which has been extremely popular; it has alternative titles: the *Temiya Jātaka* or the *Mūgapakkha Jātaka.*[19] In this bizarre story, the future Buddha is born as a king's long-awaited heir apparent. When he is a month old he is taken to sit on the lap of his doting father while he is on his judgment seat sentencing criminals to violent punishments, including death. There is no suggestion that these sentences are improper: the king is only doing his duty. As future Buddhas are in full possession of their faculties from birth, the baby prince understands what is going on. It reminds him that in a former life he too was a king and found it his duty to pronounce death sentences, and that as a consequence he had to undergo torment in hell for eighty thousand years. Determined to escape a repetition of that fate, he decides to pretend he is a cretinous deaf-mute, as the only way of avoiding the succession. He does not look like a defective child, so his father employs the most extravagant stratagems to make him react. His resolve remains such that no amount of pain or temptation to pleasure can provoke him into a response. Finally, when he has grown up, his father gives up and decides to have him destroyed; he orders a man to take him to the cemetery, kill him and bury him. While the man is digging the grave, the future Buddha speaks (for the first time in his life) and preaches to him. The man then calls the future Buddha's parents and he preaches to them. The whole city comes out to hear him. All are converted and settle down to lead a religious life there in the wilderness. The state is abandoned; the only people left in the city are the drunks.

This story seems to me to take one line of Buddhist thinking to its logical conclusion. We shall see, however, that the Buddha did not himself go so far. His specific criticism of social roles is directed almost exclusively at the brahmins; he was not explicitly critical of the exercise of royal or *kṣatriya* power. As we shall see, he had to reach accommodation with kings. But there was no need for him to accept any of the brahmins' social pretensions.

The brahmins located all authority in ultimate matters in the Vedas; since only they had access to the Vedas, in practice that meant that authority lay with them. Seen in a historical light, the Buddha's antithetical position was really somewhat analogous. Authority, he said, lay in the Dhamma; even he was only authoritative in so far as he had realized that Truth. 'He who sees me sees the Dhamma,' he said, 'and he who sees the Dhamma sees me.'[20] And on his deathbed he said to the monks: 'Some of you may think that you have no teacher any more. But when I am gone the Dhamma and the Rule I have taught are to be your teacher.'[21] In theory, therefore, the Buddha's word was the authority, though his relation to the truth he preached was not very different from the relation of the seers who pronounced the Veda to that eternal verity. In practice, however, people only had access to the Buddha's word through the Sangha, who both preserved it and interpreted it.

This was the almost inevitable result of an oral culture. To find out what the Buddha had said, you had to ask a monk, and a learned monk at that. So a layman or novice would have received the scripture along with its exegesis, and had little or no chance to inquire into it for himself. Even after the Canon was first written down, in the first century BCE, manuscripts must have been rare and more or less confined to a few monasteries. Printing was invented in China and first used for the reproduction of Buddhist texts – the oldest dated printed text is a Chinese version of the Mahāyānist *Diamond Sūtra* dated 868 CE. However, the Theravādin tradition did not exploit the invention: the Pali Canon was not printed till the late nineteenth century. This virtual restriction of texts to the Sangha had a profound influence on its history. The Theravādin Sangha was empirically the sole locus of authority on the Dhamma, just as only brahmins knew and could teach the Veda.

There was, however, an important difference. Brahmins were normally prepared only to teach other brahmins and a few other males high in the caste hierarchy. They not only preserved their scriptures in Sanskrit but used that language for all learned discourse. Sanskrit by the time of the Buddha was evidently not intelligible to people who had not studied it; the general spoken language (at least in that part of India) had diverged from Sanskrit considerably. The core texts, the *saṃhitā*, were in a language now so archaic that it presented difficulties even to the learned, as we learn from a brahminical text of the period.[22] By contrast, the Buddha intended his teaching to be accessible to all. He was not a teacher to keep anything concealed in his fist – we would say, up his sleeve. He told his monks always to preach in the local language.[23] (This led to Buddhists' becoming the greatest translators of the ancient world.) He rejected the use of Sanskrit and the brahmin style of chanting the scriptures, for that would have ritualized preaching, drawing attention away from content to form.[24] His teaching was exoteric, and he did all he could to democratize access to it.

The Buddha's doctrine of *kamma*, we have shown, gave the central role to the individual conscience. Yet we must understand even this doctrine, radical innovation though it was, within its historical context. A canonical text which has been very popular in the modern West for its apparently individualist message is the *Kālāma Sutta*.[25] In it the Buddha preaches that everyone is to make up his own mind about religious doctrine; one is not to take a teaching on trust but to test it on the touchstone of one's own experience. This is indeed a remarkable sermon. But a careful reading will show that the Buddha is confident, to say the least, that following his advice will lead his audience to accept his teaching. His appeal is that of the new man who finds himself at variance with accepted authority; it contains no implication that his own understanding of the truth might be either defective or valid only subjectively. To use the formulation of Steven Collins[26]: the Buddha is saying not 'Make your own truth' but 'Make the Truth your own'.

Buddhism as religious individualism

We have now sketched on the one hand the social conditions in which the Buddha taught and on the other the character of his teaching. We shall now attempt to relate the two, and in particular to suggest why his teaching appealed to the wealthier and more urban sectors of society.

The Buddha's Dhamma represents a strong form of what has been called 'religious individualism'. Steven Lukes has written [27]:

> *Religious individualism* may be defined as the view that the individual believer does not need intermediaries, that he has the primary responsibility for his own spiritual destiny, that he has the right and the duty to come to his own relationship with his God in his own way and by his own effort.... It is both a religious doctrine and, by implication, a view of the nature of religion; and it points to two further and important ideas: spiritual equality and religious self-scrutiny.

Since Lukes was writing with the West in mind, we must substitute for 'come to his own relationship with his God' a more general expression such as 'work out his own salvation'. With this change, the opening definition of religious individualism is much like my characterization of a soteriology. Buddhism well exemplifies in its doctrine of *kamma* the idea of spiritual equality and in its emphasis on awareness the idea of religious self-scrutiny.

Religious individualism in the West is associated with the Protestant Reformation and subsequent developments in Christianity. A.L. Basham has well written: 'Allowing for many obvious differences, it may well be that the appeal of Buddhism to the merchants of ancient India was very similar to that of Protestant reform movements to the merchants of 16th century Europe.'[28] Before exploring the similarities, we must say a word about the differences.

The crucial difference is that while both radical Protestants and the Buddha reject the pretensions of the clergy as religious intermediaries, the Protestants wished to find salvation while remaining in the world as laymen, whereas the early Buddhists assumed that to attain salvation it was necessary to leave the social world behind. We have explained the context which fashioned the Buddhist view; we should add that since for them the main soteriological activity was meditation, leaving the world was virtually a practical necessity. Meditation requires peace and privacy; no privacy is available in a traditional Indian social environment.

The Buddha did not consider it impossible for a layman to attain Enlightenment. A very few cases are recorded in the Canon, among them that of the Buddha's own father. A later Pali text says that lay life is not livable for an Enlightened person, so if a layman becomes Enlightened he (or she) will either enter the Sangha or die within the day[29] – as the Buddha's father did. On the other hand, there are plenty of canonical cases of laymen and laywomen who are said to have made spiritual progress. (This progress was measured in three stages short of Enlightenment.) Moreover, there are also a few cases of laymen who lived religious lives very like those of monks without actually joining the Sangha. They took Ten Precepts, the same ten as are undertaken by novices; this meant that they lived in complete chastity and renounced all economic activity, like monks. One such man, Ugga, even preached.[30]

But these few lay religious virtuosi, as Weber would have called them, do not invalidate the generalization that the Buddha expected those seriously interested in attaining salvation to become monks or nuns, that meditation was considered to be normally impossible for laity, and that much of the Buddha's teaching was only given to the Sangha. An extremely significant text concerns the death of the Buddha's greatest lay patron, the financier Anāthapiṇḍika. When this very wealthy and very devoted follower lay on his deathbed, Sāriputta, one of the Buddha's chief disciples, came and preached to him what appears to us an utterly basic short sermon on detachment. When Anāthapiṇḍika complained that he had never heard such a sermon before, Sāriputta said that such sermons were not preached to the laity because they would not mean anything to them.[31] Elsewhere[32] the Buddha says that monks have a duty to show laymen the way to heaven; note that he does not say the way to *nibbāna*.

Thus the Protestant assumption that all men share the same religious goal is not wholly applicable to Buddhism (until we come to modern times). The actual application of such religious egalitarianism in practice probably depends on widespread literacy and universal access to texts (not quite the same thing but clearly connected). The Protestant revolution coincided with the discovery of printing in Europe and the multiplication of Bibles. In the same way, the rise of what we shall call 'Protestant Buddhism' in nineteenth-century Ceylon (see ch. 7) depended on the spread of literacy and the printing of texts; not till then was it easy for laymen to have direct access to the scriptures.

The Buddha's recorded sermons to the laity deal mainly with morality. While morality is indeed, as we have seen, the foundation of all spiritual progress, he who does not proceed to the 'religious self-scrutiny' which was mainly reserved for the Sangha could expect no better result than a good rebirth, in heaven or in a pleasant position on earth – a result predicted also by other contemporary religions. His Dhamma and Discipline, the Buddha said, had just one flavour; as the sea tastes only of salt, they taste only of liberation.[33] (The figure may be an allusion to the early Upaniṣadic passage in which the dictum 'Thou art that' first occurs: there *brahman* is said to pervade the world just like the salt flavour in a dish of salt water.[34]) But just as a farmer knows the quality of his land and prefers to sow paddy where the soil is fertile, the Buddha sorts his audiences into three categories. The most fertile are the monks and nuns, the next best the lay disciples, and the worst the ascetics and brahmins committed to non-Buddhist views.[35]

This passage confronts us with the question who exactly the Buddha's lay disciples were: how did a person become so defined? From this passage we may deduce that it was any lay person who listened to the Buddha preaching, or indeed to any Buddhist sermon. This must have been rather a fluid social category. The term we translate 'lay disciple' or 'Buddhist layman' is *upāsaka* (feminine: *upāsikā*). As is equally true of the word *upaniṣad*, the etymological meaning is to do with 'sitting down by' someone – as we would say, sitting at their feet. The implication is giving respectful attention while someone teaches. The verb can also be shorn of this specificity and come to refer just to the attitude of respect or reverence.

From the doctrinal point of view, a lay disciple is someone who has declared his or her reverence for the Buddha and his Dhamma and Sangha by taking the Three Refuges (see p. 1); this, at least, is what became institutionalized in Buddhist societies, where religious affiliation became rather a clear-cut matter. But we have explained above that in traditional India, with its separation between communal religion and soteriology, the matter of religious affiliation and identity is not so simple.

In contemporary Theravādin societies we can observe that in actual usage the term *upāsaka* is not applied to *any* Buddhist but generally reserved for people who spend much time and energy on Buddhist activities, whether in private religious practices or in organizing activity to support the Sangha. Society is so constructed that such people are typically not much engaged in the business of earning a living, either because they are wealthy (e.g. married to rich husbands) or because they are elderly and have retired; I suspect that this has always been much the pattern. In another context, the term for a lay Buddhist is a 'donor' (*dāyaka*), someone who gives material support, usually food, to the Sangha. In Buddhist society a *dāyaka* will naturally normally be a Buddhist – though even in contemporary Colombo there are both Hindu and Muslim *dāyakas* – but in ancient India it was the duty of the householder to feed anyone who came to his door, just as it was the duty of a king to protect all holy men in his realm.

Thus I would venture an imaginative reconstruction. When a Buddhist monk came to the door of a householder for alms, he was given food and respectfully received; both were more likely if the household was urban and/or well-to-do. He may then have preached a simple sermon (typically on the virtue of generosity) to which a polite householder might respond by expressing his faith in the Buddha and his teachings. Such a response did not imply exclusive allegiance. Whether from then on the householder (or his wife) ranked as Buddhist depended on choice and context. At one extreme, he or she was never heard of again by the Buddhist community; at the other, he sought out the company of monks, began to neglect his ritual and other worldly duties, and in due course applied for ordination into the Sangha. In between must have been many who maintained a Buddhist identity by paying special honour to monks and nuns and regularly contributing to their upkeep, maybe by taking food to one of the monasteries which soon grew up in towns, while at the same time continuing to practise the local communal religion, marking life crises with traditional (not necessarily brahminical) rituals, observing Hindu festivals and propitiating deities for favours. In these latter practices they could continue to employ priests, whether a village shaman or a brahmin learned in the pan-Indian Vedic tradition, but only for worldly ends; they well understood that no priest could save them.

Of course, the Buddhist layman was encouraged to undertake certain moral vows. The Five Precepts (see above, p. 65) were for always. They were in fact almost the same as the five rules for the Jain layman; only the fifth was different. The fifth Jain rule is to eschew possessions. The prohibition on intoxicants was common to all religions we know of at the time, but the Buddhist emphasis on awareness (*appamāda* – see below) is distinctive. On certain days called *uposatha* days, the quarter days of the lunar month, the Buddhist laity were further encouraged to take Eight Precepts. For a night and a day they undertook complete chastity, not to eat solid food after midday, not to adorn themselves or witness entertainments, not to use luxurious beds. This list of abstentions is almost the same as that undertaken by novices on entering the Sangha; novices have just one additional rule, not to use money. Their list, confusingly, is called the Ten Precepts, because it splits up the seventh of the eight into two. It is also possible to take the Ten Precepts while remaining a layman, like Ugga, though it is not very common. That too is a permanent commitment. But while taking the Refuges and the Precepts expressed and reinforced one's own commitment, it did not necessarily raise the question in the wider society of whether one was a Buddhist, since there was no state apparatus to impose that category.

It is important to be aware of the differences between the Buddha and such Protestant leaders as Calvin. It is not that the Buddha was not a radical religious reformer. In one respect at least he was more radical even than Calvin. Both privatized religion, making salvation a matter for the individual alone. But the Calvinist hoped for public evidence that he was saved, evidence to be provided by his social standing. The Buddha, on the other hand, held salvation to be an experience so intimate that it should not be demonstrated or even normally mentioned to others. Buddhist gnosis, the attainment of *nibbāna*, is self-authenticating, a *certitudo salutis* (assurance of salvation) which is of no concern to society – from the saint's point of view. But this radicalism was reserved for the renouncer.

We turn now to the similarity between the Buddha's appeal and message to the laity and that of the Puritans. The European case may be more complex; but Buddhism certainly stands at the point when the old world of village life, of face-to-face relations conducted largely with lifelong acquaintances, was giving way to a more transient and varied experience of life. In an increasingly impersonal world, in which one had to do business with strangers, it may have helped both parties to a transaction to feel that the trader subscribed to a straightforward ethic of right and wrong and believed that a law of the universe would see to it that he was punished for cheating even if he evaded human detection. This universal moral law, replacing the certainty of censure by the community, perhaps helped to create that *prima facie* assumption that the trader was not wholly untrustworthy which is a prerequisite for flourishing trade. It may also have helped to create confidence in the honesty of bureaucrats and officials.

More specifically, since Buddhism was attached neither to community nor to locality, neither to shrine nor to hearth, but resided in the hearts of its adherents, it was readily transportable. It suited people who moved around, whether changing residence from village to town or travelling on business. Hence it spread along trade routes. It is striking that though monks were not normally allowed to travel during the rainy season, an exception is made[36] for the monk who is in a caravan or on a ship – presumably accompanying Buddhist merchants.

Moreover, Buddhism – like mercantile wealth –– was not ascribed but achieved. We have shown that it appealed largely to new men who did not fit well into the four-*varṇa* system of brahmin ideology. It seems to me of crucial importance that the Buddha was able to show that what brahmins believed to be ingrained in nature was nothing but a convention. He could show this because he could compare cultures. I have suggested above that he began with this advantage because he came from the very margin of Vedic civilization. But he was addressing audiences among whom were men who had acquired the same perception when they had travelled on business. Disputing with a young brahmin, the Buddha points out that in the far north-west and other distant countries there are only two *varṇa*, master and slave (or servant), and it happens that masters become slaves and slaves masters.[37]

The Buddha drew the full conclusions from this perception that elsewhere social status was achieved. He was more concerned to deflate brahmins than to build up a sociological theory of his own; he poked fun at the *Hymn of the Cosmic Man* (whom the brahmins of the day evidently identified with Brahmā): 'Brahmins say that they are the children of Brahmā, born from his mouth; and yet brahmin ladies, one notices, menstruate, get pregnant, give birth and give suck.'[38] He went on to say that *kṣatriyas* are superior to brahmins. It is hard to say in what spirit he made this statement, for the whole of the main text on the topic seems to me to be satirical (we return to it below). However, the Buddhist tradition does seem to have drawn the conclusion that social status is a matter of power. Another canonical text[39] records a discussion on caste after the Buddha's death between the monk Mahā Kaccāna and a king, in which the elder gets the king to agree that the four *varṇa* are equal, because any member of any of them who is rich can have members of any of them working for him.

An ethic for the socially mobile

The tone and content of the Buddha's moral teaching[40] were equally of a kind to appeal to businessmen. The ethic is founded on prudential considerations. Immorality entails five disadvantages: poverty, a bad reputation, social diffidence, anxiety on one's deathbed and a bad rebirth. As a corollary, moral behaviour brings five benefits, from wealth in this life to a good rebirth in the next.[41] This is just an extension of our adage that honesty is the best policy.

The ethic of intention is not prominent here, though also not contradicted. However, it is interesting to note that the Buddhist ethic, like the soteriology, does seem to be all of a piece. The King of Kosala is said[42] to have asked the Buddha one day whether there was one thing which could accomplish the ends of both this world and the next. Yes, said the Buddha: diligence. Diligence can win you longevity, health, beauty, heaven, birth in a good family and pleasures of the senses. The modern salutation 'Take care' would have met with the Buddha's approval. The word here rendered as 'diligence', *appamāda*, could also be translated 'attentiveness'; in psychological terms it is that *awareness* which was the most distinctive contribution of Buddhism to Indian (or the world's) soteriological practice. In economic terms it is realized as thrift, a thoroughly bourgeois value. The Buddha never suggests that the layman should eschew property; in fact, he commends wealth which is righteously acquired by one's own efforts. With it a man can properly care for his dependants and friends, guard against such catastrophes as kings and thieves, give their due tithe to guests, kin living and dead, the king and the gods, and make to religious wanderers and brahmins offerings which will lead him to heaven.[43] If his wealth should then diminish, a man has no regrets because he has used it well; but in another text the Buddha reassuringly says that the wealth of a man who uses it thus may be expected to increase.[44]

The Puritans promoted thrift to the extent of discouraging consumption. Here again, Buddhism's two-status system makes an important difference: the monk and nun are to consume no more than necessary (how much is necessary will be discussed in the next chapter) but the laity are not enjoined to refrain from pleasure altogether, only to be sober and prudent. In the best known sermon on lay ethics, the *Advice to Sigāla*,[45] the Buddha says that six outlets for wealth are to be avoided: drinking, being out late on the streets, visiting fairs, gambling, keeping bad company and laziness. Half of one's wealth should be used for one's business, a quarter consumed and a quarter saved against an emergency. These figures suggest a high rate of re-investment. If one wonders where religious donations and offerings are to come from, the commentary explains that they are part of consumption. We should remember that, other things being equal, such donations do buy a place in heaven.

While expenditure on communal religion is included in the lay budget, the Buddha constantly slips new ethical wine into the old brahminical bottles: pretending to interpret traditional ritual, he in fact abolishes it. In the same *Advice to Sigāla* he comes on Sigāla, a householder, worshipping the six directions – the four cardinal points, nadir and zenith. Sigāla explains that he promised his dying father always to worship the six directions. That is not how to do it, says the Buddha: the east stands for parents, the south for teachers, the west for wives and children, the north for friends and companions, the nadir for slaves and servants and the zenith for renouncers and brahmins. Some points in the ensuing amplification are noteworthy. The husband has a duty to provide his wife with adornment. She, for her part, must look after his earnings and be skilful and hard-working (another text[46] refers specifically to working with wool and cotton). Duties towards servants are: to assign work according to their strength; to provide food and wages; to look after them when they are ill; to give them a share of rare delicacies; and to give them holidays. The servants are to reciprocate by rising before their master and retiring after him, taking only what he gives them, doing good work and speaking well of him. To religious wanderers and brahmins the householder is to be friendly in thought, word and deed, keeping open house for them and supplying their temporal wants; again we notice the lack of exclusivity: the layman is to welcome holy men of all persuasions.

Another text conveys much the same message by punning on the names of the three ritual fires of the brahmin sacrificer. The layman is to abandon the three bad fires of passion, hatred and delusion but tend the three good fires, which are punningly identified as parents; wives, children and servants; renouncers and brahmins.[47]

The Canon even contains sermons preached by the Buddha to the Sangha's greatest lay patron, Anāthapiṇḍika, on economic success. In one,[48] the Buddha says that lay life has four forms of happiness: economic security; having enough for consumption; freedom from debt; leading a righteous life.

I know of no sermon which places the Buddha's teaching in its social context better than the *Subha Sutta*. Subha, a young brahmin, asks the Buddha whether a householder is not better than a renouncer (*pabbajita*), to which the Buddha replies that he condemns bad conduct and commends good whether the doer is householder or renouncer. Subha persists: brahmins say that the householder has great responsibilities and an arena for action (*kamma*) which allows him to gain great results, whereas the renouncer has a limited arena for action and correspondingly limited results. The Buddha again declines to generalize. Whether a way of life is full of cares and responsibilities or comparatively free of them, he says, it may go wrong and bring meagre results or go well and bring great results. He then supplies a simile. The life of the householder is hard work like agriculture, that of the renouncer easy like trade. But either may go well or badly.[49]

In its affinity with trade I see Buddhism (and Protestantism) as an ideological parallel to monetization. Weber talked of the demystification (*Entzauberung*) of the world; I take a major aspect of that to be that one no longer ascribes value to things on the basis of tradition, regarding them as *sui generis*, but is prepared to question their value by comparing them on a linear scale. In brief, demystification involves substituting quantity for quality in one's judgments.

I find a remarkable instance of this kind of demystification in a post-canonical Pali text, *The Questions of Milinda*. As background I must explain the pan-Indian belief in the 'act of truth'. An 'act of truth' is a statement which enables one to cause something normally impossible – a miracle – to happen. The statement is of a very particular kind: it is a true assertion that one has always excelled in one's social role – in Hindu terms, that one is a paragon in performing one's particularistic duties (*sva-dharma*), the duties of one's station. Thus for example Sītā's true statement that she is a paragon of conjugal chastity and has remained faithful to Rāma through every trial enables her to walk through fire unscathed.

In *The Questions of Milinda* a courtesan called Bindumatī is able to make the Ganges flow backwards by an act of truth. She can truly say that she has always given service for cash, regardless of who is paying, whether he be noble or slave, high caste or low.[50]

This is the rational ethic of the tradesman: 'You're as good as the colour of your money.' In economic life, cash is the common denominator, the great universalizer. The Buddha's concept of *kamma* is the precise equivalent in the ethical sphere: no matter who you say you are, you're as good as the quality of your *kamma*.

The Buddha on kings and politics

We have said enough about the Buddha's attitude to merchants and the relation of his teaching to economics. We must end this chapter with some remarks on his attitude to kings and the relation of his teaching to politics. On this topic I disagree with some recent scholarship: I do not think that the Buddha took a serious interest in politics or intended his teaching to have political consequences. But I do think that his perception that societal status depends on man-made conventions had some consequences, which however he probably neither foresaw nor intended.

Misunderstandings have arisen, in my view, because of a failure to differentiate two strands in the canonical material on kingship. One strand deals with real kings, the other with fantasy – though the fantasy is created to make important points.

In the Canon the Buddha meets and talks to several kings, some of them frequently. There is nothing historically improbable about this. Sometimes they asked his advice but often not; and on occasion they even gave *him* advice for his own good, as when King Bimbisāra advised him that kings would not take kindly to seeing soldiers desert by joining the Sangha[51] (see p. 116 below). When King Pasenadi, another important patron, instituted a vast Vedic sacrifice with great slaughter of cattle, the text records[52] that the Buddha deplored it but not that he remonstrated with the king or tried to stop it. (An ancient Jain text,[53] by contrast, tells of Jain ascetics actively interfering to spoil a brahminical animal sacrifice, an intervention which leads first to acrimony and then to violence.) I find it most significant that kings occur in a standard list of disasters (cited above, p. 78), bracketed with thieves.[54] Again, the recurrent list of kinds of 'bestial talk' forbidden to monks begins: 'Talk of kings, of robbers, of ministers of state; of war, of terrors, of battles. . .'[55] The theory may be that kings are protectors, but the reality is that they are predators.

We have already mentioned the moral problem about the use of violence. Violence was legitimate both in foreign and in home affairs;

Buddhist texts mention the many horrible tortures used in capital punishment. The brahminical term for such legitimate force was 'the stick' (*daṇḍa*). One of the most famous Buddhist aphorisms was the verse: 'All tremble at the stick, all fear death. Judging others by your own standard, do not kill or cause to kill.'[56] This has a general application, but is capable also of having a particular reference.

In the canonical collection of Long Sermons (*Dīgha Nikāya*), on the other hand, are three striking sermons which have kingship as a central theme. One, the *Cakkavatti-sīhanāda Sutta*,[57] concerns an idealized world ruler called a *cakkavatti* (the concept was common). In the Buddha's day there were no very large kingdoms in India, so it has been argued that texts about great emperors must be as late as the Mauryan empire, even that the picture of the ideal world ruler must be modelled on the Buddhist emperor Asoka. I disagree. The representation of one's own king as a world-ruler of untrammelled power is a commonplace of the ideology informing Vedic ritual. It was an institutionalized fantasy. In fact, many things said about the *cakkavatti* in the sermon are as fantastically idealized as the extent of his rule. He is a mythical being. If one thing was modelled on another, it must have been the scripture that inspired Asoka, not vice versa. (This does not mean that I feel certain that the text goes back to the Buddha, even though that is my working hypothesis – see p.20.)

It will be best slightly to postpone discussion of this text so that we can take the three sermons in the order in which they occur in the Canon. We begin with the *Kūṭadanta Sutta*.[58] The king described in this text is not called a *cakkavatti* but has the name Great-realm, which is but one of many clues that the Buddha tells the story as an intentionally transparent fiction – in fact, after he has told it he presents it as a story of one of his own former lives.

The Brahmin Kūṭadanta (Crooked-teeth) has heard a rumour that the Buddha knows how to perform a great sacrifice; he himself does not, and wishes to learn. He so far demeans himself as to go and ask the Buddha, a non-brahmin, to instruct him. The Buddha tells him a fable of how a great king was instructed by his chaplain in the performance of a great sacrifice. The chaplain told the king that there was much lawlessness and civil disorder in his kingdom; property was insecure. The king should deal with this not by taxation, nor by attempting to suppress it by force, but by improving the lot of the people directly.

The king should supply seed and feed to those who are working at agriculture and animal husbandry; he should supply capital to those who are working at commerce; he should organize food and wages for those working in his own service. Then those people will be keen on their jobs, and will not harass the countryside. The king will acquire a great pile. The country will be secure, free from public enemies. People will be happy, and dancing their children in their laps they will live, I think, with open doors.'[59]

The king took this advice, and only after taking these measures performed a sacrifice in the traditional sense – though in his sacrifice of course no animals were killed. At the end of the story the Buddha admitted, when challenged, that he himself had been the chaplain.

It does not detract from the beauty of this famous passage to point out that it is above all, or at least in the first instance, the interests of the propertied classes which are being advocated. The first thing the chaplain deprecates is the raising of extra taxes; he then goes on to recommend (and the Buddha adds that there occurred) the supply of capital to businessmen.

Like the *Advice to Sigāla*, discussed above, this text starts by pretending to interpret a current ritual. If we compare the two texts we shall see an even more important similarity. The king is to treat his subjects much as the layman is to treat his servants; in both cases this is not only right but sensible and will make one rich. The king here appears as the ideal Buddhist layman writ large. But his greater power does give him greater responsibilities.

How seriously was this parable intended or received? The Buddha is not talking to a king but to a village brahmin, saying how much better it would be if the king did something practical instead of instituting these absurd sacrifices. There is no suggestion that any king is going to hear of the advice, let alone act on it. Not surprisingly, we know of no Indian monarch who supplied capital to businessmen – not even Asoka claimed to have done that.

The *Cakkavatti-sīhanāda Sutta* is partly set in the future. A long and colourful myth tells how the world goes through vast cycles in which it gets alternately worse and better: moral decline causes the human life-span to shorten, till men only live to ten years old and kill each other off, a catastrophe which causes the few survivors to repent. At the end of the sermon we meet the next Buddha, Metteyya. Since he occurs in no other sermon, this casts doubt on the sermon's authenticity. Another suspicious feature is that the myth is set in an inappropriate frame. Most of the

Buddha's sermons are presented as preached in answer to a question or in some other appropriate context; but this one has a beginning and an ending in which the Buddha is talking to monks about something totally different. Either the whole text is apocryphal or at least it has been tampered with. The Theravādin tradition itself, however, does not doubt that the text is authentic, so it is grist to our mill.

From the rest of what we know of him, we cannot think that the Buddha believed that one day people would literally be no more than ten years old and go hunting each other like wild beasts. This casts doubt back on the seriousness of the first half of the myth, in which a mythical emperor of the world retires and instructs his son in the principles of good rule. These are mainly to protect and respect everyone according to the Dhamma and periodically to seek the advice of self-controlled holy men. But in the midst of this piety comes the sentence: 'You should provide wealth, my son, to anyone in your kingdom who is poor.'[60] We recollect the *Kūṭadanta Sutta.*

But this text takes the story and the argument further. After a while the son neglects his father's advice. Admonished, he restores the protection of the righteous, but fails to give wealth to the poor. This omission proves crucial. Theft begins when poverty forces a man to steal. Brought before the king, he explains his predicament, and the king gives him money. When other people hear of this they decide that theft is lucrative and follow the thief's example. To remedy this the king has thieves executed instead; but this only starts a vicious circle of violence and from then on things spiral downwards.

This text states that stealing and violence originate in poverty and that poverty is the king's responsibility; punishment becomes necessary only because of the king's earlier failure to prevent poverty. This humane theory, which ascribes the origin of crime to economic conditions rather than to vice, is not typical of Indian thinking on such matters, which tends to conspiracy theories. Buddhism tends to find its causes for human events in human psychology. This text, however, shows awareness of social developments as unintended consequences of human omissions or commissions. The first theft results from the king's omissions, the imitative thefts from his attempts to repair that omission. My personal feeling, which is no more than a guess, is that this idea is so bold and original that it is probably the Buddha's; maybe the text is composite and the latter part and the frame were cobbled on later. Whether the idea is the Buddha's or not, we should note how it follows on from the idea already expressed in the *Kūṭadanta Sutta*, that the king should provide wealth to his subjects.

Our final text, the *Aggañña Sutta*,[61] is full of interest but we must confine ourselves to what it says about kings. The context is that two brahmins who have recently entered the Sangha tell the Buddha that other brahmins are reviling them and consider them to have lost caste. (For the Buddhists, the Sangha is beyond caste; for brahmins, the fact that monks accept food from anyone makes them outcastes.) The Buddha's reply seems to me to be an extended satire on brahminical ideas, full of parody and puns. We have told above of his poking fun at the *Hymn of the Cosmic Man*; later in the text he so etymologizes the word meaning 'reciter of the Veda' as to make it mean 'non-meditator' instead. This is all joking.

The title of the text has been translated 'Knowledge of Origins'. It refers to an aetiological myth which is the sermon's centrepiece. The Buddha claims (satirically, in my view) to explain how the world began – in this cycle, for of course it has no absolute beginning. Radiant beings, undifferentiated by sex or social status, flit around above the cosmogonic waters. In due course their idleness and greed lead them into trouble and they start living on earth. Then a being steals rice from another. Apprehended, he promises not to do it again, but he does; this is the origin of lying. Others then beat him up; this is the origin of punishment, legitimated force. They then decide to choose one of their number to keep order in return for a share of the produce. He is called 'The Great Elect' and is the first king and the first *kṣatriya*; indeed, that is the point of origin for the whole *varṇa* system. The Buddha then uses this myth to claim (again, I think, tongue in cheek) that *kṣatriyas* should rank above brahmins.

As a debunking job I think the sermon is serious: its main aim is to show that the caste system is nothing but a human convention. (This already argues against taking too seriously the claim that one *varṇa* is really better than another.) I cannot here go into all the reasons why I think that the positive statements in the myth are satirical and not meant to be taken literally. But one should note that the reasons here given for the origin of crime are quite different from those given in the previous *sutta*: with greed and idleness as the causes we are back to the simplistic view of human evil.

Along with the divine basis of the caste system, this sermon debunks the divine right of kings. This is certainly another interesting point of similarity between the Buddha's Dhamma and Protestantism. It is another facet of their 'demystification' of the world. Some scholars suggest that the Buddha propounded his social contract theory because of his observation of tribes like his own Śākyas or because of a memory of early Vedic practice. Given the whole context and flow of the sermon, I am sceptical of such a naturalistic explanation. In some of the Buddhist stories preserved in the *Jātaka* collection kings look vulnerable; they are liable to ejection by their indignant subjects if they fail in their duty, typically by failing to make it rain. That, however, is not a contractual view of kingship. The story of 'The Great Elect' is well known to Theravādin tradition, but I am not aware that it had any effect on the practice of politics and I doubt whether the Buddha ever thought that it could or should. Buddhism produced no parallel to the execution of Charles I; and the reason for that is yet again the reservation of its higher practice to monks and nuns.

CHAPTER FOUR

The Sangha's discipline

The history of Theravāda Buddhism seen from the point of view taken by the tradition itself (what anthropologists call the 'emic' view) is the history of the Sangha. This virtual identification of the fortunes of a religion with those of its professionals is alien to most religious traditions, even to some strands within Buddhism itself – not least to many educated Buddhists today. But in our view it constitutes the very core of Theravāda Buddhism. In this it is very Indian. Our view of early Indian religion and culture is mainly a brahmin view, because it is brahmins who composed and preserved texts. Similarly, Theravādin tradition is the product of texts composed by, and indeed largely for, monks and nuns. We shall show in chapter 6 that in the Theravādin societies of Ceylon and southeast Asia the Sangha, though remaining unlike brahmins in other ways, played a part analogous to brahmins as the cultural specialists of their society. Though one must not push the comparison between Buddhism and brahminism too far, to look for a lay tradition of Theravāda Buddhism is a misunderstanding of the same kind as looking for a low-caste tradition of brahminism: were it a lay tradition it would not be Theravāda, 'the doctrine of the elders', i.e. of the fully trained members of the Sangha.

To explain the phenomenon in these terms is not, however, to deny its coherence, its logic in terms of Buddhism itself. We have shown above that the Buddha, evidently influenced by his cultural environment, took it almost for granted that the vast majority of those who were serious about taking his way to salvation would join the Sangha; that though the conventional Sangha of those in robes and the ideal Sangha of those who were assured of Enlightenment in no more than seven lives might not be coterminous, the overlap was great and of prime importance.

In doctrinal terms, the path to salvation was spelled out in terms of morality, meditation and wisdom; the meditation and wisdom constituted a self-cultivation which would normally be the province only of the Sangha. We shall have more to say of lay practice in the next chapter. Doctrinally, the lay Buddhist was offered a set of noble ideals, ethical values which can no doubt stand comparison with those of any religion. For the adherent of any religion in the world, however, the problem is just how to apply his lofty ideals to the problems of day-to-day living. The Five Precepts tell one what not to do, but as advice for positive action they are – necessarily – vague.

General principles of the vinaya

Once society has attained a certain degree of complexity, to give a detailed handbook for living which foresees every contingency is clearly impossible. But if life is radically standardized and simplified, such a guide may be attempted. This is what is generally done by the rules of monastic orders, and this is what the *Vinaya Piṭaka* attempts to do for the Sangha, the world's oldest monastic order. It provides a complete way of life, a rule of conduct, for monks, nuns and novices; the general principles are never lost sight of, and they provide a means of generating a host of detailed, particular prescriptions.

The *vinaya* is a remarkable achievement. On the one hand, no one could accuse it of losing sight of the wood for the trees: the Buddha is constantly reminding his hearers that it is the spirit that counts. On the other hand, if, while keeping this spirit in mind, you continue to follow these instructions to the letter, you are implicitly assured of a satisfying life. Not of *nibbāna* itself, for to attain that you will have to add to the monk's pure conduct the practice of meditation and the total understanding and absorption of the doctrine which constitute wisdom. But this monastic way of life will give you a perfect springboard for those higher attainments.

The key to this life is that victory over craving which results in 'being content with little'. This is the attitude which must be cultivated, the attitude which lies at the heart of the simple life. In practice, the simple life is based on owning the minimum of property (we shall discuss what that means) and also on that drastic simplification which results from cutting the normal social ties to family and community. The Buddha told his monks to live as 'islands to themselves, their own resorts';[1] they were to be self-reliant, depending on no external resource. In this sense, we may say that living the life of the monk just as the *vinaya* prescribes it is very close, as close as it is possible to get, to acting out in daily life the spiritual goal of attaining *nibbāna*. As Carrithers puts it, commenting on the life and statements of a modern Sinhalese hermit monk: 'In this view ... the monk's way of life is more than merely a means to an end: it is very nearly the end in itself.'[2]

This explains why the present chapter goes into some detail about how exactly members of the Sangha are supposed to live. For in my understanding of the Theravādin tradition, this is the very heart of Buddhism: a painstaking practicality training a sensibility to understand suffering and thus to escape from it.

That practicality is embodied in a monk's *sīla* – the term I have been translating as 'morality', the prerequisite for meditation, wisdom and Enlightenment. To quote Carrithers again: the monk's 'inner life begins properly with his command of *sīla*, and this moral purity is rooted in his careful observance of rules, both great and small, which govern his every deed. *Sīla* is both inward and outward ..., two aspects of the same reality.'[3]

The Sangha, then, is conceived as an association of self-reliant individuals. But Buddhism's built-in dual character is of paramount importance in understanding this, its central institution. For Buddhism the supreme values are wisdom and compassion. Wisdom is Enlightenment; but to understand suffering in oneself is to understand it equally in all living beings and to wish them as well as one wishes oneself. That is why wisdom and compassion are considered inseparable in every Buddhist tradition. Their compatibility, even mutual reinforcement, at the highest level of attainment does not, however, solve all practical problems for those toiling on the lower reaches of the path: often progressing oneself and helping others to progress seem to conflict. (Every university teacher experiences the conflicting demands of teaching and research.) We shall see how this tension plays itself out in the later history of the Theravādin Sangha.

The duality is, however, already inherent in its constitution. For his own good the monk is to practise poverty and chastity; but in place of obedience he tries to preserve the Buddha's message, embodied in the scriptures, for the good of the world. While each individual monk is supposed to be seeking his own Enlightenment – the wisdom ideal – he is also to contribute to an atmosphere in which his fellow-monks can do likewise. Nor should he totally ignore the laity; if he does not teach them, recruitment to the Sangha will cease and Buddhism will die out, to the detriment of future generations. We shall explore relations with the laity at the end of the chapter. Here we wish to emphasize that the Sangha has always seen itself as a community – that is indeed what the name means. In fact, the monk does not just belong to the Sangha (which we spell with a capital), the totality – which came to be known as 'the Sangha of the four directions'; what is of practical importance to him most of the time is that he finds himself in a particular community, a *sangha*, a body of men who meet regularly and in their face-to-face relations have some of the qualities of a family.

Historically this again represents a kind of middle way between brahminism and Jainism. The brahmin is embedded in the society into which he is born: the Buddhist would call it community at the expense of individuality. Though the Jains too developed a Sangha, their religious heroes are first and foremost solitary renunciates, usually referred to as *muni*, the 'silent sage' of the ascetic tradition: individuality at the expense of community. The Buddhist tradition attempts to keep both in balance.

Thus the very rules of the *vinaya* have a dual rationale. For the individual, we have seen, the Sangha is to institutionalize the Middle Way between the spiritually unprofitable extremes of indulgence and needless discomfort. But the *Vinaya* itself gives more prominence to the community rationale. Whenever the Buddha is represented as disapproving of something, he says that it is not conducive to increasing the number of believers.[4] He then pronounces a rule, for which he gives a stock list of ten reasons.[5] They can be summarized as the protection and convenience of the Sangha, the moral purity of its members, increase in the number of believers and the good of non-believers. This, we might say, epitomizes the Buddhist view (at least in the Theravādin tradition) of how Buddhism relates to society. Nor is this empty rhetoric: the occasions for promulgating rules are frequently lay dissatisfaction. In fact the scriptures represent the process of forming the *Vinaya* as a continuous process of meeting exigencies, of solving problems as they arise, often as unintended consequences of previous rulings. (It is particularly interesting to observe the many cases where a new rule is shown to lead to a new problem, which is then solved by its modification.) The Canon attributes each ruling to the Buddha himself. Can this be so?

Dating and development of the rules

Modern scholars have tended to argue that the *vinaya* developed over as much as two or three centuries. The *Vinaya Piṭaka* has been assigned by one eminent contemporary scholar to the third century BCE.[6] In my opinion it can hardly be that late, for it is full of references to *realia* and yet betrays no acquaintance with states larger than the kingdoms of the Buddha's day. However, even if my argument – admittedly not conclusive – that it must therefore pre-date the Mauryan empire (probably founded in 324 BCE) is accepted, this still leaves a century for the *Vinaya* to develop.

In one respect modern scepticism seems on strong ground. The *Vinaya Piṭaka*, like the rest of the Canon, has survived in several recensions. All claim the authority of the First Council, but they differ in details and in arrangement. One can argue that where a version of the *Vinaya* has something which is not in the others, it must have been added after the monks using that version had split off to form their own sect (for precise details on such sect formation see pp. 110–12 below). Moreover, we can be fairly sure that most of the early splits which led to these separate recensions date from the third century BCE; only the first one, that of the *Mahāsānghikas*, may be a bit older. The recensions of the *Vinaya* which are probably oldest, other than the Pali, survive only in Chinese translation. They have not been translated from the Chinese, so that they are still not directly accessible to those, like me, who do not know Chinese. However, the contents of the various recensions of one of the two main parts of the *Vinaya*, the *Khandhaka* (see below), have been summarized by Frauwallner.[7] He argues that this book was composed about a century after the Buddha's death, perhaps in connection with the Second Council (see p. 128 below).

Though I necessarily speak with little authority, since I cannot myself check the evidence, I gather that the divergences between the Pali *Vinaya* and the versions surviving in Chinese are not so great that they would affect any of my arguments. Moreover, I must add that I have the strong impression, from the little contact I have had with those Chinese texts through other scholars, that they are not always very close or reliable translations. In particular, where the Pali has a difficulty the Chinese version tends to omit it. This means that we can by no means be sure that the appearance of something in the Pali text but not in the others proves that it was added after the Pali tradition separated from the rest (which happened during Asoka's reign: see chapter 5, part B). Besides, we shall see that the *Khandhaka* is unlikely to be the earliest part of the *Vinaya Piṭaka.*[8]

For the present, I cannot see that any subsequent scholarship has disproved what Rhys Davids and Oldenberg wrote about the construction and chronology of the *Vinaya* in 1880.[9] They dated its completion to c.350 BCE[10]. But in accepting even this degree of scepticism of the Buddhists' own claim that the text goes back to the First Council, held just after the Buddha's death, I am going by a hunch: the tradition has not yet been proved to be *substantially* incorrect, only to be impossible if taken to apply literally to every detail. The language of the Buddha's pronouncements is completely stereotyped, and many of the case histories read as if they had been compiled *ex post facto*, but none of this suffices to prove that the claim of the Buddha's authority for the rulings is fictitious where – as in most cases – the rulings are recorded in every recension of the text. The fabrication, if it is one, has been very carefully and thoroughly executed, for not only does the *Vinaya Piṭaka* display a great internal consistency, it can also be cross-checked in many places with the *Sutta Piṭaka.*

Oddly enough, the most basic of all *vinaya* texts is not, as it stands, a part of the Canon, though it has canonical status. I refer to the *pātimokkha*, the list of rules of personal conduct which all monks and nuns are to recite once a fortnight. (On this recitation see more below.) Half of the *Vinaya Piṭaka*, called the *Sutta-vibhanga*, consists of a commentary[11] on this code, which is embedded in it. The second major portion, the *Khandhaka*, deals mainly with the rules of community life – though it is not really possible to draw a line between what concerns the individual and what the community: for example, the *pātimokkha* is the individual code, but it must be rehearsed communally, and the rules for that rehearsal are in the *Khandhaka*. In trying to reconstruct the development of the *vinaya* it is tempting to assume a steady movement from rigour to laxity. But it seems impossible to stratify parts of the *Vinaya Piṭaka* on this principle. A monastery has a lay attendant called a *kappiya-kāraka*, which means 'suitable-maker'; he is someone who accepts gifts which monks are not allowed to accept, such as money, and uses them on their behalf: in modern parlance, he 'launders' them. While the word *kappiya-kāraka* does not appear in the *pātimokkha*, the practice which it represents certainly does. There is a long rule quite early in the code[12] which begins as follows: a layman may send a monk, via a messenger, the cost of a robe. The monk is to say, 'We don't accept the cost of a robe but we accept a robe at the time when it is permissible.' The messenger may then say, 'Have you anyone to look after you?' If he wants the robe, the monk should point out a monastery servant (*ārāmika*) or lay disciple (*upāsaka*) who looks after him, who can accept and use the purchase price.

This institutionalization of 'laundering' is a far call from the primitive simplicity which may be the product of our romantic imaginations. Or even of the Buddha's? He is recorded as having said that in the good old days – which presumably means earlier in his career – monks lived in forests, subsisted on alms and wore cast-off rags, and were perfectly content, whereas nowadays it is monks who 'receive the four requisites in abundance' who win respect. (The 'four requisites' are material comforts – see below.) So we come to two important conclusions. First, that the ever-lamented 'corruption of the Sangha' began, by the Buddha's own account, during his lifetime. Second, that the *Vinaya* as it stands is of a piece, and if we refuse to believe its own account of the Sangha's development – as of course we can – we are left with no certain knowledge of the subject. I agree with Wijayaratna[13] that while on the one hand 'it is probable that some rules were framed and arranged later, after the Buddha's death,' on the other, 'Whether or not such and such a precept was established by the Buddha himself, the important thing for us is the sense and interpretation given to it by Theravādin monachism.'

The middle way between discomfort and indulgence

As Wijayaratna goes on to show in his book, the general sense of the *vinaya*, in harmony with the opening words of the First Sermon, is that neither comfort nor discomfort should become an issue to distract one from the quest for Enlightenment. What the Buddha stressed was the monk's subjective state of satisfaction. One day the King of Kosala congratulated the Buddha: some renunciates, he said, he found haggard, ill-favoured and unsavoury, but the Buddha's monks were satisfied, healthy and cheerful. The practice of meditation requires a certain amount of solitude, but even the life of solitude is not to be taken too literally: true solitude, said the Buddha, is to be found not in the physical condition but in freeing oneself from anxiety about past and future and living free from desire.[14]

'If a comfort does not become an obstacle to the life of renunciation, monastic Buddhism does not consider it unsuitable for "renouncers". On the contrary, in several cases the Buddha indicated that discomfort is an obstacle on the path of internal progress.'[15] What exactly did this mean in practice?

There are two standard lists of the possessions permitted to the Buddhist monk. In one formulation, he is allowed four 'requisites': clothing (three robes), begging bowl, dwelling and medicine. The other list has eight items: three robes, begging bowl, razor, needle, belt and water-strainer. When the Sangha attracted the generosity of the faithful, property beyond these lists had to belong to the Sangha as a corporate body, not to any individual. But we shall see that this tended to degenerate into a legal fiction; and there have also been explicit modifications of this pristine rigour.

To this day, however, every member of the Sangha is supposed to reflect each evening that he/she has used the four requisites only to supply the basic necessities to maintain health, not with any greed or luxury.

When a monk is ordained, he is told at the end of the ceremony that he has four 'resorts' (*nissaya*), i.e. things to depend on: eating food got by begging; wearing rags from dustheaps; living at the foot of a tree; using fermented cattle urine as medicine. Anything more comfortable is to be regarded as an extra, not to be relied on.[16] These four means of subsistence were perhaps typical of the wandering renouncers of the time. But the Buddha did not insist on such asceticism. The first schism, albeit a temporary one, is said to have occurred when a wicked monk proposed to the Buddha that five practices be made compulsory:[17] subsisting on alms; vegetarianism; wearing only rags; living only in the jungle; living only at the foot of a tree. The Buddha's answer implied that except for staying outdoors in the rainy season all of these practices were allowed, but he refused to make them compulsory. The fact that the ordinand is not to be warned of the four *nissaya* in advance points in the same direction: he is not to be put off by giving him the impression that his life will necessarily be devoid of creature comforts.

A list of ascetic options in what one ate or wore or where one lived came to be classified in late texts as thirteen *dhutanga* (a purely technical term of obscure meaning). Nine of them are already listed – though not so labelled – in a canonical sermon.[18] But what the Buddha has to say about them is that they can be undertaken for all sorts of bad reasons, such as showing off; they are only worth while if they are undertaken to cultivate 'being content with little'. And that can be cultivated without stereotyped asceticism. However, the *dhutanga* represent a limit to what the Theravādin tradition will sanction by way of mortifying the flesh. The list does not include vegetarianism (though that too is permitted) but includes the other four practices suggested for imposition by the wicked monk, as well as such similar rigours as eating only once a day, living in a cemetery, and never lying down but sleeping seated. Some of the practices are mutually exclusive, and the tradition, so far as we can tell from modern practice, has been for a monk of ascetic temperament to take to them one at a time. These ascetic options thus remain open, but with the proviso that the monk practising them must not draw attention to the fact. Several are presumably not available to nuns, as they (for their own protection) are not allowed to go round alone.

Not surprisingly, the tendency to be too ascetic has been less of a problem in the history of the Sangha than the opposite. By comparison with other renouncers, such as Jains, who aim to own nothing at all, even the more ascetic Buddhists live in comfort. Moreover, being assured of food, clothing and shelter must have seemed an enviable lot to the poorest members of their society. Periodic claims that the Sangha has been infiltrated by men and women only interested in a comfortable life are all too plausible. The Sangha's tendency to luxurious living, exemplified especially in property ownership, has led again and again to demands for its 'purification'.

It is worth asking why this should be. The Indian renouncer is supposed to be outside the social system, just as the liberation he is seeking is outside the world. But there is always an element of ambiguity: *outside* easily shades into *above*. The state of *nibbāna* is wholly other, nothing to do with cosmic topography; yet there is always a tendency to represent it as above the highest heaven. The position of the ascetic is analogous. He is usually addressed by some such secular title as 'lord' or even more: in northern India to this day an ascetic is a 'great king' (*mahārāj*). In traditional Sinhala the Buddha is always referred to as 'Lord Buddha' or 'Great King Buddha'. Monks too are always 'lords'. We shall see below how this ambivalence between being beyond society and being at its head developed in Sinhalese culture.

This is not a purely structural question, the ambiguity of a spatial metaphor. Respect for freedom from material wants is a universal Indian value. This value produces the following dynamic. The more a monk demonstrates his indifference to worldly comforts, the more he impresses the laity and comes to be regarded as worthy of their material support. Indifference to comforts thus causes them to be provided. This presents a golden opportunity for the hypocrite and explains why monks who practise austerities are not allowed to advertise the fact.

Monks are not allowed to refuse gifts which are properly made to the whole Sangha, though they may deflect them from their own use. To refuse them would deprive the lay donor of a chance to earn merit (see next chapter).

This difficulty provides a fine example of the unintended nature of social consequences, as neat as our case of the man who lowers the price of that which he wishes to sell (p. 16). On the other hand, this unintended result of asceticism has no *inevitable* consequences for the ascetics themselves. They retain free will, and the steadfast among them will not be corrupted by popular favour. Others, however, do become corrupted as the enjoyment of comforts begins to affect their own values, so that they come to prize those rewards and to respect those monks who evidently have them. Probably the most valued and at the same time the most insidious of those rewards is fame. It follows that those who deviate from the Buddha's standard of 'contentment with little' are likely to become more widely known than those who preserve his ideals. Scandal and luxury are more easily visible than modesty and frugality. Thus persistent complaints of the corruption of the Sangha cannot prove that the Sangha has been preponderantly corrupt; they only show persistent awareness of the ideal.

We have shown how, inasmuch as the renouncer defined his condition as the antithesis of the brahminal norm, the essence of that condition was homelessness. Steven Collins has shown[19] how the idea of homelessness permeates early Buddhism: literally leaving home and the fire of the hearth, one has to extinguish the fires of greed, hate and delusion till, with the internalization of the no-soul doctrine, one is not at home even in oneself. To this day, Jain renouncers are supposed to keep moving and have no fixed abode for nine months of the year. Homelessness is a central issue in the Indian tradition of renunciation.

Like their Jain counterparts, Buddhist monks were enjoined to stay in one place for three months of the rainy season. I consider the parallel significant. The *Vinaya Piṭaka* has the Buddha promulgate the general rule for the rains retreat as the result of public criticism that by walking round during the monsoon monks are harming 'living beings with one sense' and destroying lots of little creatures.[20] Living beings with one sense are plants; Jains consider all matter to have some kind of life and categorize it by the number of sense organs it has. It is Jains, not Buddhists, who normally worry about the welfare of new grass or accidentally treading on beetles; but evidently the Buddha wished to avoid unfavourable comparison with these competitors.[21]

Monks were not allowed at the end of the rains retreat to stay where they were: they were supposed to resume their wanderings,[22] in conformity with the Buddha's original injunction to spread out and preach. However, there was never at any stage, so far as we know, a rule that one had to keep moving. Here again the middle way: between the brahminical householder's fixity and the Jain's perpetual motion. According to the *Vinaya Piṭaka*,[23] King Bimbisāra of Magadha presented the Buddha with a place to stay at Rājagaha, a bamboo grove, only a few months after the Enlightenment. It was neither too near nor too far from the town, accessible, not too crowded by day, quiet by night – a happy medium in every way. Strictly speaking, the gift was made to 'the universal Sangha with the Buddha at its head'. This donation was the model for many which followed, till there were monasteries in the four main cities of the region (Rājagaha, Vesālī, Sāvatthī and Kosambī) and on the routes between them;[24] and according to tradition the Buddha spent almost every rainy season in one of them. Initially monks were not allowed to reside in buildings, but when a big businessman of Rājagaha wanted to have some put up for the Sangha, the Buddha allowed it.[25] So it is that we find in the *pātimokkha* various rules about the permitted size and location of monastic buildings.[26] Buildings lead naturally to furniture, notably beds: when the King of Kosala's grandmother died he gave her furniture to the Sangha, but as monks are not allowed high or luxurious beds the Buddha had the feet taken off the sofas and the horsehair stuffing taken out of the divans.[27]

All these communal possessions required organization and looking after. There were the usual rules of boarding houses: leave this place as you would like to find it.[28] More significantly, monasteries had to appoint officials[29] to assign rooms, look after stores, and organize the acceptance of meals from the laity.

None of this, however, amounts to the complete abandonment of the wandering life, as was to happen in Sri Lanka. Monks still had no rights to the use of property in one monastery rather than another. Even nuns were enjoined to change residence at the end of the rains retreat,[30] and all but the old and infirm were encouraged to travel.[31] Their duty, after all, was to spread the word; they were not allowed to refuse an invitation to preach, even during the rains retreat.[32] Evidently the typical monastery would contain both regular residents and visitors. This is just what Holmes Welch[33] describes in his picture of how Chinese Buddhist monasteries functioned only fifty years ago, and though Chinese Buddhist monasticism lost some of the original Indian features, in this respect I think Welch may be describing an uninterrupted tradition. Bunnag's picture of contemporary Thai monasteries is very similar in this respect.[34]

After what has been said of the Buddha's appeal to the bourgeoisie and his emphasis on such virtues as thrift and diligence, it will come as no surprise that he strongly emphasized decorum for the Sangha. In a society which (though not unaware of hypocrisy) hardly differentiates between character and behaviour,[35] correct deportment is not a trivial consideration. Indeed, although many monks fail to live up to the ideal, it would be difficult to exaggerate the importance traditional Sinhalese Buddhists still ascribe to what we might dismiss as the monk's 'public image': he is to present a picture of calm control, walking with slow, measured steps, his eyes cast down on the road ahead of him, always quiet and making as few involuntary movements as possible.[36] The long last section of the *pātimokkha* consists of such rules of decorum, listing improprieties to be avoided when eating, preaching, or otherwise appearing in public.

Very much in character is the Buddha's attitude to washing. The *vinaya* does not explicitly enjoin it, but the many references show that it was frequent. We might assume this to be rational and normal. But while brahmins bathed frequently, under ritual prescription, the advanced Jain ascetic is forbidden ever to bathe or brush his teeth, both because he eschews comfort and for fear of killing bugs.

Renouncers differentiated themselves from householders, who looked after their hair, either by shaving it all off or by not tending it and allowing it to grow into a matted tangle. The Buddha naturally took the cleaner alternative: members of the Sangha all have their heads shaved on admission and go shaven thereafter. They do not, like some Jains, pluck it out by the roots – hence the razor in their equipment. Removing the hair makes a person's sex much less obvious, the more so if they are also dressed in shapeless garments; if the eyebrows too are shaved, as they are in some ordination traditions, the individual is startlingly transformed in the eyes of his acquaintances and seems depersonalized – till his new appearance becomes familiar. To this day, a well-turned-out monk has a shiny pate.

Considerations of decorum no doubt combined with those of comfort to establish the *vinaya* tradition that monks (and *a fortiori* nuns) should be properly dressed. The Buddha frowned on nudity. Nuns were not allowed even to bathe naked;[37] monks were not to be naked except when in a bathroom or actually covered by water, and when naked they may do each other services (e.g. passing the scrubber) but not interact in any other way.[38] The specific reason the *Vinaya* gives for forbidding nudity is that otherwise people would take monks for members of other, more ascetic sects.[39] The Buddha was always anxious to differentiate his Sangha from such extremists; they retaliated by calling the Buddhist monks nothing but 'shaven-headed householders'.[40] When some monks were stripped of their robes by highway robbers and continued their journey naked they were indeed taken for naked sectarians, which caused the Buddha to allow extra robes to be accepted in such emergencies.[41]

At the time, it was not customary for renouncers to accept gifts of clothing: they either went naked or somehow provided for themselves. For the first twenty years, according to the Canon, the Buddha and his followers wore robes made of such cast-off rags as they could find among refuse or in cemeteries.[42] But one day when the Buddha was ill his doctor offered him a robe, and from then on monks were allowed to accept cloth from the laity,[43] though they had to cut it up[44] and stitch it together again, presumably to reduce its value. As Wijayaratna remarks,[45] it may well be that as the Sangha grew it became extremely hard to find enough discarded cloth to clothe them all.

For Buddhist monks wear rather a lot of clothes by tropical standards. The monk has three robes. Nuns have two extra pieces of clothing. Both monks and nuns have a further cloth for wear when bathing outside in the monsoon.[46] The reason given for the 'three robes' is that they were what the Buddha found he needed to keep warm on a cold night.[47] However, decorum is also important. Except under certain special circumstances a monk or nun must never appear in public less than fully dressed in all the robes,[48] and there are detailed instructions on how they are to be worn.[49] Moreover, one must never wear a torn robe, which is why every monk and nun is to possess a needle and thread.

Robes were the monk's most valuable private property. He was not allowed to decorate his robes,[50] and was restricted to one set at a time.[51] On the other hand, he was allowed to exchange his robes; the Buddha exchanged his with Mahā Kassapa.[52] He was also allowed to give them to his old parents if they were in need.[53] This illustrates that they really were his property, not just objects for his use – the very thin edge of what was to prove a very long wedge. Any spare robes, on the other hand, belonged to the whole community, which in practice meant the monastery, and special officers were in charge of them.[54]

At the end of the rains retreat the laity offer the material for a robe to their local monastery.[55] This material has to be new, or at least in good condition. The local *sangha* cut it up and stitch it together again and then offer it to one of their number – the theory is that he should be one who has kept the rules of the retreat. There is a special name for this robe:

kaṭhina. The *Vinaya Piṭaka* and the entire Theravādin tradition contain only a very small number of monastic ceremonies, and this is the only one of them in which the laity are integrally involved. Not only has the *kaṭhina* festival survived from canonical times till today: it is the only Buddhist festival which is celebrated in virtually identical form in every Theravādin country.

In what must have been a striking departure from standard ascetic practice, monks were allowed to wear simple sandals, though not normally in the monastery.[56] (To go barefoot indoors is the universal Indian custom.) Conversely, unless ill they were not allowed umbrellas except within the monastery;[57] umbrellas are a sign of social dignity in India. Brahmins proverbially carry umbrellas. So far as I know, the prohibition on monks' doing so has long been a dead letter; in Sri Lanka there is a traditional kind of umbrella peculiar to monks, made of huge leaves of the talipot palm, while today they are manufactured of cloth dyed a monastic yellow.

Again in contradistinction to extreme ascetics, members of the Sangha had always to eat their food from alms-bowls, which were to be made of earthenware or non-precious metals,[58] and it was compulsory to possess one's own.[59]

The middle way in food was not to eat after midday; the Buddha explained that this was good for the health.[60] This practice is often conventionally referred to as eating only once a day, but to take that literally is one of the ascetic options (*dhutanga*), not the norm. My experience in contemporary Sri Lanka is that most monks have two meals, breakfast and lunch;[61] so long as the lunch is over by noon the discipline has not been infringed. Around six in the evening monks consume a snack which is called 'medicine', using the term from the canonical list of four requisites; this 'medicine' amounts to a drink and often also a little of some kind of food which requires no mastication. This view of 'medicine' goes back to the *Vinaya Piṭaka*, for the Buddha there[62] permits the use of clarified butter, fresh butter, sesame oil, honey and molasses as medicine, and their consumption – like that of other medicine – at any time. The original rigorous prescription of fermented cow's urine as the only medicine seems never to have been enforced, and indeed the Buddha's concern for the proper care of the sick is a recurrent feature of the *Vinaya*. Again, it is notable that to this day Digambara Jain ascetics may only ingest medicine along with their single daily meal.

How were the Sangha to come by their food? The most important principle was that they were forbidden to get it for themselves: no monk may consume any food he has not received from someone else.[63] (But a partial exception was made for fruit.) Total dependence on lay support is thus ensured: on the one hand, a monk may not live as a solitary hermit in the forest; on the other, he may not grow his own food. This rigorous interpretation of the general precept 'not to take what is not given' Buddhist monks shared with Jain renouncers. Another important principle is that a monk is to be indifferent to the quality of his food; he is not allowed to express any preference.[64] The corollary of this, in the Buddhist view, is that he is not a vegetarian: if he is given meat, he is to eat it.[65] However, this is not taken to extremes: certain meats, such as human flesh, are forbidden.[66] Moreover, in accordance with the principle that any Buddhist must avoid taking life, a monk must refuse to eat an animal which has been killed especially for him.[67] Clearly, once the laity learn of this rule they will not slaughter an animal to feed the Sangha. In practice (though the *Vinaya* says nothing of this) it is also feasible for a monk to let it be known that he would prefer not to eat meat.

The Sangha began by begging their food, though the term 'begging' is perhaps misleading. Members of the Sangha are to walk silently from door to door, asking for nothing, receiving in their bowls any scraps or leftovers that the laity may care to give them.[68] They do not even thank for the food, since it is they who are doing the favour by giving the laity a chance to earn merit; but they may say a few edifying words. These words usually take the form of informing the donor of the merit gained. Already in the Canon the Buddha tells a donor that he has thereby ensured his rebirth in heaven.[69] However, as we have seen, the Buddha refused to make the alms-round compulsory.[70] From the earliest days, there was no bar to accepting lay invitations to come for a meal. Though the first such recorded invitations were addressed to the Buddha himself and his entourage,[71] when the rules were elaborated the invitations were supposed (unless there was a famine) to be addressed impersonally to the Sangha in general; it is then the responsibility of a monastery officer to decide who should go.[72] This system is still largely in operation in the Sangha today: specific individuals may also be invited, but such invitations are less meritorious, and not customary on solemn occasions.

What was originally prohibited was to store food[73] or to cook it,[74] both practices being associated with the life of the householder, not that of the renouncer. The Buddha is said to have made exceptions to these rules during a famine,[75] when people brought food supplies to the monastery. The rules prohibiting monks from cooking and storing food are widely observed in the letter, but often by having lay servants handle and prepare food within the monasteries. Infringements of the rules can often be justified by invoking practical difficulties. Once laity are allowed to bring food to the monks – and the monastic regulations could hardly stop them – one can see that the line between receiving food *ad hoc*, the original intention, and arranging meals on a more regular basis becomes hard to draw.

Of course, what must seem to us today to violate the original spirit of the discipline is that monks should have servants at all. But in ancient India this was not so evident. To some extent, servants were taken for granted. Pupils acted as servants to their teachers, and it was assumed that an important monk like the Buddha would normally have another monk acting as his personal attendant. One could then draw the line by saying that it is all very well for one member of the Sangha to attend on another, but lay servants are different. In practice, however, what is to stop a lay devotee from devoting himself to personal attendance on the Sangha? Should one, then, draw the line by saying that he must not be hired or paid for the purpose? But this too can hardly be enforced in practice if it is rich lay devotees who wish to do the hiring and paying. They may even be donating the services of their own slaves.

Thus it is that the issue of whether the Sangha may have servants or slaves is little discussed in the *Vinaya*. Originally, before there were monastic establishments, there can have been no lay servants. But they gradually arrive on the scene and are taken almost for granted. For an ordinary servant there was a euphemistic term, *ārāmika* – literally just a person connected with a monastery. The *Vinaya* story[76] is that once a saintly monk was clearing a mountain slope to make a cave to live in, and the king promised to give him a man, an *ārāmika*, to help him. He asked the Buddha whether this would be in order and the Buddha agreed. However, the king for a long time forgot to do anything about it; then later, to atone for his negligence, he assigned the monk five hundred servants, who constituted a whole village. While this story seems absurd as it stands, it does illustrate how royal patronage must have shaped the Sangha's development. Throughout the history of Sri Lanka until very recently the richest monasteries have owned not only vast tracts of real estate but also the labour of its inhabitants, and probably only the king owned land on such a scale as to make such huge donations as whole villages possible.

As his very name indicates, it is the *kappiya-kāraka*, the 'legitimizer', who seems to be the gateway to laxity. We have seen above that such a figure already appears, albeit not under that name, in the *pātimokkha*, and that he might be a monastery servant or just a pious layman – a professional or an amateur, as it were. The *kappiya-kāraka* seems always to have had this ambiguous status. In modern societies he is not exactly a servant but a lay person, usually of some social standing, who is constantly in touch with the local monastery; he is not a full-time or salaried official, but rather a part-time lay trustee of monastic temporalities. It seems, however, that in the huge monastic establishments of ancient cities he was often a full-time attendant, a sort of bailiff.

On entering the Order as a novice one takes Ten Precepts, of which the final one is not to accept gold or silver. This prohibition is repeated in the *pātimokkha*,[77] along with another on buying and selling,[78] which is to include barter of a commercial character. On the occasion of a celebrated controversy which is said to have occurred a hundred years after the Buddha's death, a certain community of monks was accepting cash donations; they were censured by the majority.[79] The Theravādin tradition takes the strongest possible line against monks' accepting money: if somehow they have acquired it they are to get rid of it immediately, if necessary throwing it away.[80] At the same time, other episodes in the *Vinaya* make it clear that laymen did give cash to such 'legitimizers'. The price of a robe in the rule quoted above was presumably cash. Elsewhere in the *Vinaya*[81] the Buddha says,

> There are men of faith who deposit gold in the hands of *kappiya-kārakas*, saying, 'With this give the reverend what is permissible (*kappiya*).' Monks, I allow you to consent to what is permissible from that source. But in no way, I say, is gold or silver to be consented to or sought.

The last sentence echoes the wording of the *pātimokkha* rule forbidding the acceptance of money – or causing others to accept it.

This is not necessarily hypocrisy. If a layman spontaneously gives an attendant money to spend on a monk, the monk has willed nothing wrong. But evidently in practice the line between allowing and not allowing money to be collected or solicited for one by a proxy is a thin one.

An amusing line of text shows both that the 'legitimizers' must have been thoroughly institutionalized before the *Vinaya Piṭaka* was closed and that they were not an unmixed blessing. The prohibition on monks' cooking for themselves was rescinded, as mentioned above, during a famine, when 'the legitimizers took most of the food and gave little to the monks'.[82] The monks had a servant problem.[83]

The Sangha were enjoined to withdraw from the productive economy not in the sense that all labour was forbidden to them (though some was – for example, digging or even causing another to dig[84]) but that they were not allowed to earn. It is this, as well as the requirements of decorum, which made it one of the four offences in the gravest category to pretend supernormal powers one did not possess: such claims would be used for material ends. It was also an offence, though less serious, when one did in fact possess them to tell a layman.[85] (Like all Indians, Buddhists assume that progress towards self-control, whether by meditation or by austerities, brings with it as an inevitable by-product certain powers, such as flight.) The same thinking lies behind the general principle that monks are not to talk about or make a display of their religious progress,[86] whether in frugality or in meditation.

The disbarring offences and enforcement of chastity

The gravest category of offence is called *pārājika*. The traditional Buddhist etymology of the term is 'entailing defeat'; more likely it originally meant 'to be set aside', i.e. excluded from the Sangha. Anyone guilty of any of the four *pārājika* offences (eight for nuns) was deemed *ipso facto* to be no longer a monk[87] (or nun); that is the theory, but in practice some mechanism for giving force to the expulsion has often been required. The four offences, in the traditional order, are having sexual intercourse, taking something not given (above a trifling value), intentionally killing or causing to kill (as by inciting to suicide) a human being, and falsely claiming miraculous powers. For nuns were added: touching a man between shoulder and knee; allowing men various forms of physical contact; condoning or concealing another nun's *pārājika* offence; persisting in taking the side of a suspended monk.[88] Though these look more varied, the case histories establishing the last two also concern sexual offences.

No idea is more central to our concept of monasticism than sexual abstinence, so it is not surprising that the Buddha condemned sexual desire and activity both literally and metaphorically. Like the English words 'passion' and 'desire', the word *kāma* can refer to desires for objects in general or for sex in particular; and the Buddha condemned *kāma* in all its forms.[89] The only opinion, as against word or deed, for which a monk could be condemned was if, after three admonitions, he persisted in the view that there was nothing wrong with *kāma*.[90]

On the other hand, it is noteworthy that the Buddha did not hold the view, so widespread in traditional India and elsewhere, that sexual desire is the woman's fault and sexual intercourse the result of female temptation of the male. One brief text[91] reports that the King of Kosala was unhappy when news was brought to him that his wife had borne a daughter; the Buddha encouraged him with a little verse saying that some women are better than men. (From the modern feminist point of view he slightly spoilt this fine sentiment by adding that they may bear fine sons!) More substantial is his sermon which describes sexual desire of men for women and of women for men in identical terms.[92] He did not regard women as socially equal to men even within the Sangha, but he exhorted men to respect them: a monk should regard a woman, according to her age, as a mother, a sister or a daughter.[93]

Hierarchies of age and sex

While the Buddha had a keen eye for what was merely social convention, so that he saw men of all *varṇas* and classes as essentially equal, there were two social hierarchies he never questioned: age and sex. Even here, all were equal in their capacity for Enlightenment. One novice is supposed[94] to have become Enlightened at the tender age of seven (the minimum for joining the Sangha); and indeed the Buddha is supposed to have said that generally those who joined the Sangha late in life were less satisfactory.[95] A great many nuns have left testimony that they attained Enlightenment;[96] and the tradition that no woman could become a Buddha is not in the Canon. But when it came to social relations, even within the Sangha, age and male gender had precedence. (There is a slight difference, in that age was reckoned from ordination, not birth, so it was really seniority, whereas gender is of course absolute.) It is the senior monk who is to preside at the *pātimokkha* ceremony (see below) and generally has precedence in ecclesiastical affairs. Nuns, on the other hand, were subject not only to their own hierarchy of seniority, but also to monks. They had to receive double ordination, from both nuns and monks, and were always subject to masculine supervision: any nun, no matter how long ordained, ranked below the most junior monk.[97]

Apart from the precedence accorded to age and sex, monastic hierarchy was minimal. The functions of the office-holders concerned only temporalities and did not give them any precedence in religious matters – and this has generally continued to be the case even where the office of abbot, i.e. head of a monastery, has become institutionalized. But the relation of teacher and pupil is crucial. Every novice and junior monk becomes the personal responsibility of a preceptor, who is to teach him every aspect of what he needs to know. In this respect, of course, Buddhism is like all Indian traditions: no culture, perhaps, has so emphasized the teacher's responsibility for his pupil's welfare and formation as the Indian – a fact reflected by the modern English borrowing of the word *guru* from India. What is remarkable about the early Buddhist view of the relations between teacher and pupil is that just as the teacher has a duty to correct his pupil's faults the pupil has a reciprocal duty to criticize his teacher – not in general, to be sure, but if the teacher has taken up a wrong doctrinal position,[98] or is in danger of saying something unsuitable.[99] I know of no parallel injunction in other classical Indian traditions. Here again the particularistic ethic is replaced by a general, impersonal principle.

The formal organization of the Sangha

I have briefly depicted the limits within which monks were supposed to order their lives and shown how those limits could be bent. In the process I have said something of the Sangha's informal organization. Now we must turn to its formal organization, a topic of paramount importance for a proper understanding of its history – yet one which is still often misunderstood.

The Sangha has certain communal ceremonies. The word ceremony should not mislead. The Buddha opposed mere ritual activity. The Sangha's ceremonies are formalized, but purely functional. They are in fact called, baldly, 'Acts of the Sangha'. They are to this day carried out without ritual elaboration, and in their plainness contrast vividly with the public religious activities of the lay Buddhist population.

Two of these ceremonies are crucial: the higher ordination (*upasampadā*) and the communal rehearsal of the *pātimokkha*. The first two chapters of the *Khandhaka* portion of the *Vinaya Piṭaka* are devoted to these two ceremonies respectively.

As we have already indicated by talking of novices as well as monks and nuns, Buddhist ordination comes in two stages. We shall here give the details only for males. A boy can become a novice (*sāmaṇera*) when he is old enough to scare crows away,[100] which is interpreted to mean seven or eight. He must have his parents' consent.[101] His initial ordination, in English often called 'lower ordination', is in Pali called *pabbajjā*, an expressive word, for it means 'going out', that is from home to homelessness. This is *not* a communal ceremony; a single monk accepts the postulant, typically in the presence of no one but his immediate family; he is shaved and exchanges lay clothing for monastic; and he takes the Three Refuges and says a few more words after the monk.[102] The novitiate is a period of training; the novice is bound by his Ten Precepts[103] but not by the rules of the *pātimokkha* (except for those of decorum) and is not entitled to take part in the Sangha's ceremonies.

The higher ordination (*upasampadā*) cannot be taken till one is twenty (the age is however reckoned from conception, not birth).[104] It is a far more formal and elaborate affair. The postulant novice is presented by one monk, his 'teacher', to a formally constituted assemblage of monks presided over by another officiant, the 'preceptor', and is admitted as one of their number when he has shown himself duly qualified.

Originally the terms *pabbajjā* and *upasampadā* referred to the same thing: the Buddha gathered his first disciples, much in the manner of Jesus, by summoning them to follow him with the words 'Come, monk'. We need not here trace[105] how the two ordinations became separated and the higher one elaborated; we could not go much beyond the account of this evolution given in the *Khandhaka* itself.

The most important point for Buddhist history is that an ordination (and by this word from now on we shall mean the higher ordination) is not valid unless it is conferred by a quorum of monks – whose own ordination must of course be valid too. The monks should be learned and of at least ten years' standing.[106] The quorum was set at ten,[107] but five for 'border areas'[108] – *in partibus infidelium*, we might say. Five has been the quorum applied outside northern India.

Like all formal Acts of the Sangha, the ordination ceremony proceeds by the presiding monk putting the proposal to the assembly three times. Silence signifies consent, and unanimity is essential. When the proposal has thus been accepted the presiding officer states it a fourth and final time as a *fait accompli*.[109]

Before this proposal is put, the candidate is asked whether he is human, male, free from certain serious diseases, free from debt, not a slave or a soldier, whether he is of age and has his parents' consent.[110] He may also not be criminal, crippled or deformed.[111] He is also examined on his ability to recite a few canonical texts (though this is not prescribed in the *Vinaya Piṭaka*); the examination is almost a formality but does require preparation.

The monk, we have seen, is a self-reliant individual striving for his own salvation. By that criterion, his moral condition is his concern and no one else's. But he is also a member of a local monastic community, a *sangha* – even if he is a transient; and he is, willy-nilly, a member of the wider Sangha and thus represents Buddhism in the eyes of the laity. To that extent, his conduct is the concern of both his colleagues and interested laymen. How is the foolish, erratic or unscrupulous monk to be kept in line?

Ultimately the Sangha has only one sanction: expulsion. Even that they cannot fully enforce, in that they cannot remove a recalcitrant offender from the premises; but from their point of view a monk who has committed one of the four *pārājika* offences has thereby disbarred himself and is no longer in communion – he is *ipso facto* a layman again.

What of lesser penalties? Theravāda Buddhism knows no penances. If you have done, said or thought a wrong, doctrine says, nothing can simply cancel that out. But what you must do is be aware of what you have done and resolve to do better. There is no liturgy for repentance, only the rational exhortation to learn from one's mistakes. Even such psychological progress, however, can be institutionally aided if one is not merely to be aware of one's faults but declare them to another. Hence the monastic custom of compulsory confession.

For most of the offences in the code, confession is itself the main or only punishment. If one has acquired some unallowable possession, one forfeits it with the confession. There are also a few offences, the gravest after *pārājika*, for which the monk is suspended from full communion, the length of suspension depending on the length of time he has failed to confess the offence.

The *pātimokkha* code lists the offences (227 in the Theravādin tradition; but of these 75 are only the rules of decorum) in categories according to the penalty prescribed, from the gravest, the *pārājika*, to the least, the rules of decorum. This list is to be recited every fortnight at the *pātimokkha* ceremony, which Durkheim might have called the Sangha's solidarity ritual.

The ceremony is to take place every month on the days of the full moon and new moon.[112] These days, as well as the intermediate quarter days of the lunar month, are known as *uposatha* days, whence the Sinhalese word *poya*, which is also used by western Buddhists. The *pātimokkha* ceremony is thus also known as the *uposatha* ceremony. The senior monk present, reckoning seniority from higher ordination, recites the *pātimokkha* after a brief preamble.[113] At the end of each category of offence he asks three times whether all present are pure: he then announces that since they are silent they are pure. In an emergency, says the *Vinaya*,[114] he may also drastically abbreviate the recitation, so long as he asks about and announces the *sangha*'s purity. (As happened with food rules originally relaxed for a famine, I believe that this 'emergency' regulation has become generally current.)

Even abbreviated, the form of the ceremony shows that it was meant to be functional, to serve as the occasion for confession of one's faults. It is even possible that originally the demonstration was intended to edify the laity, for the text ascribes a part of the origination of the institution to a king's suggestion.[115] However, the character of the public recitation rapidly changed. The rule was laid down that laymen were not to be present;[116] this suggests to me that originally they were and it was felt to be embarrassing for them to hear the confessions. After the next development, however, excluding the laity lost its point, for the actual confessions came to precede the communal ceremony.[117] Monks confess one to another, in pairs, and assemble for the ceremony only when all, having confessed, are 'pure'.[118] The ceremony thus becomes purely expressive of that purity, and to that extent a mere ritual. This makes me think that here we do have a development which, though it is in the *Vinaya*, must post-date the Buddha's lifetime. It indicates an overwhelming desire not to lose face before one's colleagues.

Two or three monks can confess to each other and thus regain their purity (or confirm it, if they have nothing to confess). But the quorum for performing a *pātimokkha* ceremony is four.[119] Here we come to the truly communal dimension of the *pātimokkha* institution.

The Buddha attached the greatest importance to this ceremony; it answered the first principle he laid down for the prosperity of the Sangha when he modelled its constitution on that of 'tribal republics', acephalous polities (see above, p. 50): that it hold 'full and frequent assemblies'.[120] He laid down elaborate rules to ensure that it took place and that everyone attended. No one was excused unless he was too ill to be moved, and even so sick a man had to send a declaration of his purity by proxy; *in extremis* the rest of the Sangha was to come to hold the ceremony at his sickbed.[121] He clearly saw it as the focal point of *sangha* life. This in turn made it necessary to define a *sangha*. Since some monks lived scattered and isolated, and many were itinerant, the community had to be defined geographically: those within a certain area on the relevant day. Hence the importance in *vinaya* of the monastic boundary (*sīmā*). A correct *uposatha* cannot be held till a boundary has defined the community. (There is also a formal proceeding for laying such a boundary.[122]) The area encompassed is not to be larger than can be walked across to attend the ceremony and by the same token there should be no physical barriers such as uncrossable rivers within it.[123] Thus the real monastic community is defined geographically, like the Christian parish, but for quite a different purpose.

The displacement of confession to prior privacy did not disturb the *pātimokkha* ritual's *communal* function. It was the one thing which held the Sangha together. Each celebration, of course, was the announcement of the purity of a particular *sangha* and ensured their renewal of face-to-face relations - perhaps some had spent the intervening fortnight meditating in seclusion. But since monks moved between communities, these regular compulsory meetings bound the Sangha together as a whole. We must remember that there was nothing else to do so, both because of the difficulty of communications and because there was no hierarchy, no structure of command, after the Buddha's death.

Maintaining Buddhism in recognizable form must really have been a great problem for the first centuries. Central authority lay in the scriptures, 'the Buddha's word'; but even that depended on an oral tradition which could easily have become hopelessly fragmented. We know little about the mechanisms which bound all the far-flung *sanghas* together, though the texts give us glimpses. There were evidently occasions analogous to 'visits from head office', even though strictly there was no head office. A Pali commentary gives an example of those who project their own fears on to a lonely forest environment:

> There are monks who make their living in one of the 21 acquisitive ways, such as practising medicine, acting as messengers, or usury ... They hear that monks who know the 3 *Piṭakas* have set out on a mission to purify the Sāsana and will arrive today or tomorrow; they go into the forest and sit behind a bush and at the slightest sound of grass or leaf they are terrified, thinking 'Now we are lost', for they imagine those monks coming and catching them and making them put on white clothes [i.e. laicizing them][124].

Sect formation: Theravāda defined

But the Sangha did in fact split, into what historians have called 'sects'. How did this come about and what did it mean?

The Sangha's ideal is that all its Acts be carried out in unanimity. But this does not always work, and there is provision for voting in the case of disagreement. The crucial question then becomes the size of the minority. Since the quorum for holding a *pātimokkha* ceremony is four, a minority of less than four is of no account, because the dissidents cannot break away to form their own *sangha*. But four or more monks can do so. Therefore the *sangha* is only 'split' when there are at least four votes on each side.[125] Causing a split in the Sangha is one of the six heinous offences,[126] like parricide or shedding the blood of a Buddha; but it undoubtedly occurred. Presumably it was always the other side who were the splitters.

So splitting the Sangha is a technically precise matter. It occurs when a community, a *sangha*, has a disagreement which causes two groups of more than three monks to hold separate *uposatha* ceremonies. (It applies to other ceremonies too, but the *pātimokkha* recital is both the most frequent and the most important.) Monks who do not co-operate for the *pātimokkha* do not, *a fortiori*, co-operate for ordination ceremonies, and so different lineages arise within the Sangha.

Buddhist 'sects' are therefore bodies of monks (and nuns); they have nothing to do with the laity. Splitting is a matter of *vinaya*, of behaviour. If the split arises as the result of a disagreement, the disagreement itself is likely to be over a point of *vinaya* – of this recent Theravādin history furnishes us with many examples. But whatever the source of the disagreement, the result is measured in *vinaya* terms: holding separate *pātimokkha* ceremonies.

Monks cannot co-operate in a *pātimokkha* ceremony if they do not share exactly the same *pātimokkha* code. Differences in the code may have arisen not only from *sangha*-splitting, but also unintentionally, especially through the geographical isolation of different *sanghas*. In fact it seems likely, as Frauwallner has shown,[127] that most of the early sects originated from such regional variation, not through conscious disagreement. Once a monk becomes loyal to one version of the *pātimokkha* code he can only remain in full fellowship with others who share his view.

A sect is sooner or later perpetuated as a separate entity by holding its own ceremony of higher ordination. A body of monks who share an ordination tradition, a 'sect' if you like, is called a *nikāya*. As Bechert has written:

> In the first instance, a *nikāya* or sect can be described as a group or community of monks that mutually acknowledge the validity of their *upasampadā* or higher ordination and therefore can join together in the performance of … acts prescribed by Vinaya or Buddhist ecclesiastical law.[128]

It is important for western readers, used to a culture in which doctrine is the diacritic between religious bodies, and heresy the cause for expulsion, to appreciate that in India orthodoxy is less important than orthopraxy, doing the right thing, and that this has been true even of so intellectual a religion as Buddhism. Thus Mahāyāna, for example, is not a sect, but a current of opinion which cut across sects as properly defined. There is no such thing as a Mahāyāna *pātimokkha*. By the time that Mahāyāna doctrines arose, about the first century BCE, there were said to be eighteen sects in India. The number eighteen stayed constant in Buddhist historiography, and evidently became conventional.

This is of course not to say that when a body of monks separated from the rest it might not espouse some particular shade of doctrinal opinion. Human group loyalties often work in that way, and the set of eighteen 'sects' were associated with (often small) doctrinal differences. But the doctrinal opinion was unlikely to *cause* the split, which had in any case to be actualized by performing one's own *pātimokkha* ceremony.

Only now are we in a position accurately to define Theravāda. The term means 'doctrine of the elders', but this is not significant: all religious groups tend to claim that it is they who preserve the pristine doctrine. In doctrinal terms, Theravādins specified that they were *vibhajja-vādin*, which means 'analysts', and they delighted in classifying psychological states. A Theravādin monk, however, is one who adheres to the Pali version of the *pātimokkha* with its 227 rules, and is thus a member of the Theravādin ordination tradition – the two conditions are interwoven.

Originally there can have been only one Theravādin ordination tradition. Later, in ancient Ceylon, there were further splits, refusals to hold the *pātimokkha* together, and thus a further multiplication of ordination traditions. That story we reserve for chapter 6.

Before returning to the ancient Sangha, we should explain the term Hīnayāna. This word was coined by Mahāyāna polemicists, who called their own doctrinal position 'the great vehicle/course' (the word *yāna* is ambiguous) and that of their more conservative opponents 'the lesser vehicle/course' or, more politely, 'the disciples' vehicle/course' (*śrāvaka-yāna*) – the 'disciples' being those who personally heard the Buddha preach. It is unfortunate that the pejorative term gained currency in the west. Since Theravādins adhere to a pre-Mahāyāna view of Buddhism they are, from the Mahāyāna point of view, of the Hīnayāna; but the term has neither the same meaning nor the same reference as Theravāda, and is best avoided.

Maintaining conformity

We return now to the relation between the individual monk and his community. Was opinion indeed totally free? There is an offence in the *pātimokkha* code[129] which has been summarized as 'clinging to evil views'; does this not reveal a concept of heresy? The rule is long and complicated, and careful scrutiny shows that it does not. The offence is for a monk to put forward (not just think, but propound) a particular view: that what the Buddha taught to be obstructions are in fact not. The other monks are to ask him three times not to calumniate the Buddha, and the offence is if he persists after three such admonitions. The accompanying tradition is that the argument is about whether sexual activity is an impediment to the monastic life, obviously a basic point of discipline. So this is no exception to the principle that a monk has done no wrong unless he thinks so, and confesses it, himself. For, we repeat, it is a cardinal principle of Buddhism that the moral quality of an act lies in the intention behind it.

The *pātimokkha* thus appears a perfectly harmonious and consistent system of self-regulation. But alas, things are not quite so simple. For individual monks may act in bad faith; and it is also possible that corporate decisions may need to override the individual conscience. Thus it is that the *pātimokkha* is not the only system of monastic regulation in the *Vinaya*, though I feel sure it must have been the earliest. As I have mentioned above, there are other procedures for corporate acts of a *sangha*, procedures which were used for settling disputes and also occasionally for disciplining individuals. One such procedure is the appointment of a committee of senior monks.

> The committee is proposed to the disputatious sangha by the traditional announcement, and the appointment is ratified by unanimous silent consent. In so consenting, the disputing sangha also agree to abide by the decision of the committee.... The method ... clearly depends on the real authority structure of the Sangha, the gerontocracy.[130]

Respect for seniority and experience is another of the principles the Buddha enunciated for the welfare of lay polities and the Sangha alike.[131] Carrithers goes on to conclude:[132]

> In the absence of formal office and formal procedures of decision-making, the guidance of the Sangha is left to a small, learned group

of rugged individualists who must act harmoniously through reasoned face-to-face discussions.

Unanimity in decision was yet another of the principles which the Buddha laid down for the well-being of his Sangha.[131] This was not to be a merely formal matter. Many a time the Buddha told monks to live together in amity, looking at each other with eyes full of affection.[133] Buddhist loving kindness was no mere abstraction, no mere topic for meditation, but to be practised by the Sangha in their daily lives. During the rains retreats, when monks lived together for three months at a stretch, the Buddha forbade them to live in silence 'like dumb animals' – as, he said, other renouncers did.[134] And at the end of the retreat they hold a special *pātimokkha* ceremony at which each asks all his fellows to forgive him if he has offended them in any way during the retreat.[135] Monks in a good *sangha* were 'separate in body but one in thought.'[136]

Relations between ordained and laity

This brings us to relations with the laity. In the previous chapter we discussed Buddhist doctrine for the laity; here we must add a few words on clerical-lay relations. Buddhist monks are accustomed – and sensitive – to the accusation that they do not work actively for the welfare of their fellow creatures. Their answer is that their most important service is to show by example the way to end all suffering. 'The monk who dedicates himself to the Buddha's teaching lights the world like the moon coming out from behind the clouds,' says an ancient verse.[137] This was echoed to Carrithers by an elderly monk: 'We monks are like that street-lamp. . . . If we behave well, Sir, then the world can go along in our light.'[138] This would not excuse all callousness. Monks do what they can. 'Temporarily and provisionally it is possible and necessary to allay much suffering; but permanent and really effective alleviation is possible only for each individual in himself. . .'[139]

The Buddha from the outset conceived the Sangha as a missionary organization. Within a few weeks of his Enlightenment, when he had collected his first sixty disciples, the Buddha is said to have dispatched them with the famous exhortation which I have quoted in the Introduction (pp. 18–19). As mentioned above, monks and nuns were not allowed to turn down any invitation to preach. This may not seem so remarkable to us nowadays, but it seems to have been another innovation of the Buddha's. Brahminism was exclusive, so that the question of public preaching did not arise. The saints of other heterodox sects prided themselves on silence: according to a Jain tradition, the Jina, on attaining Enlightenment, no longer ate, slept or talked; but a divine sound emanated from his body and was interpreted by brahmin disciples, who on that basis composed the scriptures.[140]

The relations between the Sangha and their lay supporters were conceived as reciprocal generosity: the Sangha gave the Dhamma, the laity gave material support, rather disparagingly termed 'raw flesh'.[141] Naturally the laity were conceived as having much the better of the bargain. In fact, since giving to the Sangha brought them merit, they were favoured by both halves of the transaction. The Sangha could refuse to receive alms from someone by passing a formal act of 'overturning the alms bowl'[142] and this was evidently a feared sanction, no doubt because of the public opprobrium. This exception proves the rule that normally donations had to be accepted.

The scale of lay generosity must have been impressive. The texts often describe the Buddha as travelling with 250 or 500 monks; these are conventional round numbers but indicate a considerable entourage. When such a group accepted an invitation to a meal it must have required considerable organization and resources; and their alms round must have imposed quite a strain on the host area. No wonder that the Buddha's chief lay patrons are depicted as being extremely wealthy. Yet there are few if any stories of monks going short, except in famines. The historian may well conclude that the danger lay in the opposite direction: excessive lay generosity. The preceding pages have perhaps sufficed to show that lay pressure to accept gifts probably accounts for most of the Sangha's (recurrent) 'corruption'. The texts even suggest that kings were most dangerous in this respect. The Buddha's great patron Bimbisāra, King of Magadha, plays an interesting role. He was the first person, according to the canonical account, to invite the Sangha to a meal and to give them a monastery. Well and good. But he was also the person who gave them a whole village of five hundred people to be their servants. Of course we do not know whether these stories are literally true; but I suggest that even if they are not, they record the real problem of relations with state power and patronage. It was necessary to entertain such relations, if only because the Sangha needs state support to enforce its decisions – a problem even more crucial than excessive riches.

There are other indications that the Sangha early had to accommodate to the facts of political power. We have recorded that no soldier was admitted to the Sangha. The story behind this, according to the *Vinaya*,[143] is that once King Bimbisāra had trouble on his borders and sent crack troops to deal with it. But these soldiers decided that if they were to kill anyone they would sin and later suffer for it, so to escape their dilemma they became Buddhist monks. A minister advised the king that anyone who thus deprived him of his soldiers deserved to be executed. As the king was on good terms with the Buddha, he advised him that other kings might not take such a thing lying down. Reading between the lines, we can deduce that he warned the Buddha that for their own good the Sangha had better not ordain soldiers.

Probably a similar need to yield to the social order can explain the exclusion from ordination of thieves, debtors and slaves.[144] Since Buddhist monks were inviolate, ordination would have offered them an escape from their secular obligations. No doubt the slave-owners objected. The exclusion of slaves stands in striking contrast to the sermon in which the Buddha points out to a king that if one of his slaves were to leave and become an ascetic he would much improve his lot.[145] The king addressed is Bimbisāra's son; if that is historically accurate it makes it unlikely that the decision to exclude slaves really goes back to the Buddha himself; but the evidence is tenuous.

The issue of accommodation to political power is most explicitly addressed in a small anecdote, otherwise of little moment, of how King Bimbisāra once asked for the beginning of the rains retreat to be postponed. Agreeing, the Buddha said, 'I prescribe, monks, that you meet kings' wishes.'[146] This dictum from a specific context has been given far wider application.

This is not merely common prudence. The Sangha, and hence Buddhism, has a particular need of political patronage if it is to flourish. Monks can reach decisions to expel malefactors – or pronounce that they have automatically expelled themselves – but they lack the power to enforce those decisions. History has shown time and again that without state support – which need not mean *exclusive* state support – the Sangha declines for this very reason. Indeed, it falls prey to a vicious circle: when it cannot expel 'immoral' monks it acquires a reputation for being decadent, so that lay support further declines and it becomes increasingly impotent to set its house in order. In the next chapter we shall meet Asoka, the Buddhist model of how a king should behave to support the Sangha.

When we consider the decline and revival of the Sangha through history, corruption through political weakness seems to have been an even greater danger than corruption through economic power. The physical well-being of the Sangha – as of other segments of society – requires a measure of political security, but not direct access to power. What is required is that the secular arm lend the Sangha the strength to purify itself. Whether kings can go further and actually initiate such a purification is however dubious.

This problem of enforcement is not mentioned in the *Vinaya.* No doubt while the Buddha lived his authority carried all before it. But I can divine another reason for the silence: the problem was never solved in *vinaya* terms, and casuistry does not record unsolved problems. The only solution for the Sangha was to receive support from outside. That is why they have had 'to meet kings' wishes'.

CHAPTER FIVE

The accommodation between Buddhism and society in ancient India

A. BUDDHIST DEVOTION

In the first chapter we recalled that plans never turn out exactly as intended. The more people the plans involve, the more unintended consequences there are likely to be. In this sense a religion, like any other social movement, is bound to some extent to be a victim of its own success.

In the previous chapter we described a few developments which the Buddha can hardly have intended or even foreseen when he sent out the first sixty monks to spread the word: use of property by proxy, control of lay labour on a large scale, denying slaves admission to the Sangha, the refusal of those who had forfeited the right to remain in the Sangha to disrobe themselves – all these are plausible examples. For all but the last of these developments there is direct evidence in the Canon, where they are ascribed to the Buddha's lifetime, and of course to his intention – for piety could not admit that while he was alive such things could take place without his willing them. This chapter will deal mostly with developments which even the Buddhist tradition does not ascribe to the Buddha's lifetime, though in some cases it claims that he foresaw them. These attitudes and practices probably began among laity and are characteristic of lay Buddhist religiosity, but that is not to deny that they have also been part of the lives of the Sangha throughout recorded history.

It is sometimes said that the Buddha did not appeal to faith or that Buddhism is not a faith. Those who say such things are usually trying to draw a contrast with that strand in the Christian tradition (which of course is not the only strand) which says that one must believe Christian dogma however repellent it may be to reason: that such apparent conflict with reason is but a test of faith and all the more reason to believe: 'Credo quia absurdum' – 'I believe because it is absurd.' That is certainly quite un-Buddhist. But there is plenty in the Pali Canon about faith. The word most used is *pasāda*, which indicates emotion as much as belief, a calm and happy confidence that something is so. In the *Sutta-vibhanga*, the canonical commentary on the *pātimokkha* which constitutes about half the *Vinaya Piṭaka*, Wijayaratna has counted 409 occasions on which the Buddha criticizes conduct on the grounds that 'it is not going to instil faith (*pasāda*) in those who lack it or increase the faith of those who have it' (this is not a literal translation). Calm and happiness are themselves 'profitable', 'skilful' states of mind, little steps along the path to *nibbāna*.

The Buddha as an object of faith and devotion

A convert to Buddhism declared his faith in the Buddha, the Dhamma and the Sangha, and every Buddhist occasion begins in this way. But there is just one sentence which precedes even this 'taking refuge': a salutation to the Perfectly Enlightened Buddha. It is the Buddha himself who is the principal object of religious emotion; the Sangha arouse emotion primarily in so far as they are the Buddha's sons and daughters, his heirs, his representatives among us.

Whether or not he foresaw it, it is hard to think that the Buddha would have welcomed this 'personality cult'. In the text which describes his last days, the *Mahā Parinibbāna Sutta*, we get glimpses of his character which seem authentic. After the attack of dysentery which so weakens him that it leads to his death, the Buddha says that he has taught the Dhamma, so that now anyone who feels he can do it can take over the leadership of the Sangha;[1] he goes on to tell the monks to rely on themselves alone (quoted above, p. 89). Then, just before his death, he says that the Dhamma and Vinaya remain to instruct his disciples.[2] Yet the very same text reports beginnings of the personality cult, providing canonical justification for pilgrimage and the worship of relics. True, the Buddha's remarks were made to monks, and the devotional practices, it can be argued, are primarily for the laity. Yet the stark contradiction between 'having no refuge other than yourselves' and 'taking refuge' in the Three Jewels is striking. It seems hard to argue that Buddhist lay religiosity as we know it was just what he intended. However excellent a consequence of his teaching, I submit that it was not the Buddha's idea.

The Buddha himself was the prime object of faith and focus of devotion. The existence of gods, both here on earth and in the various heavens, was not usually questioned, let alone denied, but they were only kinds of superman, who could be propitiated for worldly favours but could not help one to progress on the path which is the only guaranteed escape route from suffering. (It is therefore considered inappropriate for members of the Sangha to worship them, though they too do not question their existence.) Theravādin doctrine has never wavered from the position that the Buddha is dead and no longer active in the world; in moments of great crisis some individuals do pray to him for help, but that is the spontaneous outburst of emotion and in their calmer moments they know that it can do no good except as a psychological relief to themselves. Buddhist saints, other Enlightened beings – they are commonly known as *arhats* – are similarly dead and of no influence on the world.

This seems to provide a very narrow ideological base for cult and mythology, and indeed that is a fair generalization about Theravādin culture. As we have explained in the Introduction and will exemplify later, Theravāda has co-existed with other systems of action and thought, derived both from Indian and local cultures, which the outsider can call 'religions', inasmuch as they are 'patterns of interaction with supernatural beings'. But at a very early stage, before it expanded outside India and largely indeed before it split into sects or developed doctrinal diversity, Buddhist culture did provide somewhat more material for creative artists to elaborate and pious Buddhists to adore than the personality and biography of Gotama Buddha. This material consisted of the Buddha's former births and a multiplicity of Buddhas.

The beginnings of both these developments are in the Canon, even in what are believed to be its oldest parts. An element of the Buddha's Enlightenment was that he remembered his former births – paradoxically infinite in number, as the world has no beginning. Stories of the Buddha's former births, called *jātakas*, became a major genre of Buddhist literature. Some originated among the Buddhists, others were adapted from Indian folk literature, especially animal fables. In all of them, whether he is man, animal or deity, the hero is identified with the future Buddha. The term for 'future Buddha' is *bodhisatta*, which in Sanskrit became *bodhisattva*.

The former Buddhas[3] are less interesting, for the biography of every Buddha follows much the same pattern; we can see that it is just modelled on that of Gotama. Why the doctrine arose is not clear. Possibly it was borrowed from the Jains. Another line of reasoning is that it provided the Buddha with some apparently external authentication, a prop for Buddhists in argument with non-believers whose own gurus claimed to have learnt doctrines handed down in a spiritual lineage. The Buddha had cognized the Dhamma by his own effort; but the Dhamma is eternal and so could be cognized by similar geniuses from age to age.

Like the Buddha Gotama's former births, the series of former Buddhas must stretch back to infinity. However, these two perspectives on the remote past were co-ordinated by creating a story that the future Gotama Buddha had formally embarked on his career as a *bodhisatta* by taking a vow at the feet of a former Buddha called Dīpaṃkara, who vouchsafed him the prediction that he would succeed. Dīpaṃkara was 24 Buddhas back and Gotama became, at least for Theravādins, the 25th (sometimes 28th) of those whose names are known to us; he renewed his vows at the feet of each. The stories of his former births were then standardized at 550 (a round number); during these births he behaved with a moral heroism which enabled him to accumulate the ten moral perfections (generosity, courage, fortitude, benevolence, etc.) which are the prerequisite for Buddhahood. The story of how the ascetic Sumedha, the future Gotama Buddha, fell at Dīpaṃkara's feet and made his great resolve is depicted in very many Theravādin temples and at least alluded to in innumerable works. Perhaps even more popular, and probably known to every Theravāda Buddhist child, is the last story in the *Jātaka* collection; in this the future Buddha, born as Prince Vessantara, attains the perfection of generosity by giving away not only all his material possessions but even his wife and children.[4] These stories are probably as important in Theravādin culture as the stories of Gotama Buddha in his final life.

The line of births culminating in Gotama Buddha is ended, but the line of Buddhas stretches into the infinite future. The next Buddha, Metteyya ('the Kindly One'), is already sitting in heaven waiting his time to be born on earth. Orthodoxy fixes the date of his arrival among us in the very remote future, and Buddhists who express the wish – as many do – to be reborn in the time of Metteyya are ready for the long haul. Metteyya should therefore have little effect on religion in practice. But he supplies material for messianic aspirations, a potential he has occasionally realized in Theravādin countries.

Pilgrimage

According to the *Mahā Parinibbāna Sutta*,[5] the Buddha declared before his death that an Enlightened person (or a world ruler) should be buried under a *stūpa*. A stupa (for which there are many synonyms) is a funeral mound, of which the main part by tradition is hemispherical and covered in masonry. Such memorials would serve to instil the tranquil joy of faith in all pilgrims, and so help them to obtain rebirth in heaven. This text serves as the charter for Buddhist pilgrimage. Indians seem always to have venerated certain spots – particular rivers, mountains, large trees – and the Buddhists felt the need for distinctively Buddhist sites to venerate. This does not mean that they had to stop venerating the others: faith in the Buddha did not require them to doubt that natural features were inhabited by more or less powerful deities. But for them the most important places to visit were those associated with the Buddha's life, especially the scenes of his birth (the Lumbinī grove near Kapilavatthu), Enlightenment (Bodh Gayā), first sermon (Sārnāth, near Benares) and death (probably near Pāvā in Bihar). The most important of these has always been Bodh Gayā; it drew pilgrims from all over the Buddhist world in ancient times and now again does so in the twentieth century, on a far larger scale than ever before.

The exact site of the Buddha's death seems early to have been forgotten. This diminished the already small number of places with sacred associations for Buddhists; and in any case, as Buddhism spread, few people in those days could hope to travel hundreds or even thousands of miles to Bihar. The number of pilgrimage centres was, however, early increased by the belief in former Buddhas; places associated with their – albeit mythical – biographies could be more widely distributed. But they were still all in India. When Buddhism spread overseas, new myths arose: every Theravādin country has a myth that Gotama Buddha paid it at least one flying visit, and the places where he touched down became pilgrimage centres.

Among the world's most famous journeys are some undertaken by individual Chinese monks in the first millennium CE to see the ground the Buddha trod. But pilgrimages are more commonly undertaken by Buddhist devotees, mostly laity, travelling in groups and devoting themselves to intensive religious activity over the entire period of the journey, so that the pilgrimage also has the latent function of cementing relations between the participants. However, the importance of the custom can be exaggerated. Pilgrimage is not an obligation, like the

Muslim *hajj* to Mecca. There is not even a Buddhist word for 'pilgrimage'; it is referred to as a 'worshipping journey' or some such. No one thinks the worse of a fellow-Buddhist for not having gone on a pilgrimage.

Relics

Far more important than pilgrimage is a development with which it is closely associated: the cult of relics. So far as I can discover, this was invented by Buddhists. This is the more striking, as their scriptures do not even claim that it was invented by the Buddha himself. But the same *Mahā Parinibbāna Sutta* says[6] that after the Buddha's cremation – though not at his behest – his relics were divided into eight parts and given to eight people, each of whom built a stupa over the relics and instituted a festival in their honour.

The general Indian belief is that a corpse is extremely impure, even after cremation. The Buddhist saint – and *par excellence* the Buddha – is, however, someone who has succeeded in going 'against the stream'; he has managed to reverse the normal process of nature. According to the *Mahā Parinibbāna Sutta*, the Buddha's own funeral symbolically reflected this reversal.[7] Corpses were normally disposed of outside the settlement, to the south (the direction of the god of death). The gods insisted that the Buddha's body be carried through the middle of the town near which he died and burnt to the east – the most auspicious direction. The preservation and worship of his physical remains follows the same symbolic pattern.

Stupas originated as tombs for the Buddha's relics – which of course multiplied as the demand for stupas grew. The text says that all Enlightened beings, *arhats*, are entitled to such tombs; and by extension the cremated remains of all monks in Theravādin countries are still buried under small stupa-shaped tombs; but to my knowledge it is only stupas which contain relics (however fictive) of a Buddha which are worshipped. In later times the relic entombed in a stupa was sometimes not a piece of bone or the like but a portion of scripture inscribed on gold; this reflected the Buddha's dictum (see p. 71 above) that 'he who sees the Dhamma sees me': the text was the Buddha's 'Dhamma-body'. Small portable relic caskets are also made in the shape of stupas.

By a later classification, relics are said to be of three kinds: corporeal; objects used (by the Buddha); reminders. Corporeal relics are always bone, teeth or hair. Objects used are such things as begging bowls, but also the tree under which the Buddha sat to attain Enlightenment (which is known as the Bo tree from *bodhi*, 'Enlightenment'), and in practice by extension other trees of that kind, the *ficus religiosa*. These two kinds of relics were venerated from very early days. The third kind may be a somewhat later addition. Its prototype is probably the stupa; originally it was held to be an object of worship only because of the relic it contained, but in due course it became a 'reminder', in particular of the Buddha's death.

In early Buddhist art – the earliest surviving dates from the second century BCE – the Buddha is not directly portrayed; his presence in the scene is indicated by some 'object used' such as a pair of sandals, which reinforces the general context. This significant absence presumably symbolizes the Buddha's reversal of nature and obliteration of what would cause him to be reborn. But very early in the first millennium CE statues of the Buddha began to be made and worshipped. The Theravādin tradition has been that such worship is justified by classifying the statue as a 'reminder relic'. In fact the statue is only treated as really sacred if it has a corporeal relic enshrined in it as well.

The doctrine of relics is thus fundamental to the practice of Buddhist worship, even if it looks rather like an *ex post facto* justification of devotional practice. It is also important to understand that in Buddhism – as in all Indian religions – such devotional practice is individual, not congregational. The layman makes his or her way to the shrine and offers flowers or incense before a Buddha image and recites Pali verses, as if in prayer, but it is all an exercise to purify one's mind. I have described this cult elsewhere.[8] All that need be said here is that it remains extremely simple, in contrast to Hindu ritual, and is for the most part carried on without professional intermediaries.

Mortuary rituals and 'transfer of merit'

The Theravāda Buddhist monk hardly ever acts as what we would call a priest. He officiates at no life crisis rituals except funerals – and even there he can claim to be present as preacher and consoler, not as officiant. We do not know whether the monk assumed this funerary role for Buddhists in ancient India, but it is quite logical for him to do so. Death is the perfect occasion for preaching on impermanence and the inevitability of suffering. Indian death rituals can only be said to begin with the funeral. In a series of complex rites, brahmins are fed in an attempt (among other things) to improve the lot of the dead man and cause him to be reborn in some agreeable situation. Buddhist monks substitute for brahmins in the rituals following the death of a Buddhist, and are formally fed a week after the death, three months after, and at annual commemorative rituals. On all these occasions the merit is ritually transferred to the dead person.

The 'transfer of merit' requires explanation. We saw above that Buddhism is a simple moral dualism: *kamma*, action — which the Buddha defined as intention – is either good or bad. And we said that 'the currency of good actions' was translated into 'the more fluid concept of mental purity'. But it was not always so translated; that was done by those who had acquired a sophisticated understanding of Buddhist doctrine. In particular it was done, one may presume, by the Sangha, those whose goal was *nibbāna*, to attain which would make their *kamma* irrelevant. But lay Buddhists, who were not so clearly differentiated from the rest of the population, were evidently setting their sights lower and aiming only to be reborn in heaven (or in a good station on earth); and their moral concepts were correspondingly more mechanistic. For them, merit was a kind of spiritual cash, a medium of exchange which could get you the things money cannot buy.

The doctrine of *kamma* places full responsibility for his fate on the shoulders of the individual. Yet evidence from Hindu as well as Buddhist sources shows that people cannot always accept the harshness of this doctrine, any more than Christians could accept the logic of predestination; they devise evasions at the price of logical consistency. A case in point is Hindu funerary ritual, in which there are several transactions in *kamma* and the mourners try to relieve the dead man of his sins. We have seen that this is also an arena for transferring *kamma* in Buddhism.

The precise details are complicated and the interested reader must consult secondary literature.[9] But Buddhist ideology, by having recourse to the fundamental doctrine that only intention counts in ethics, has performed a sleight of hand and invented a rationale for the process. If merit lies in good intention, a person who does a meritorious deed – be it feeding monks or going on a pilgrimage – can get a second lot of merit by thinking, generously, that he wishes other people could reap the benefits of his actions. Of course they cannot – that is the law of *kamma* – so he loses nothing, but he gets good marks, as it were, for wishing that they could. They too may wish that they could: they can empathize in his merit and *feel* as generous as if they had made the donation themselves; so they too collect good marks. The result is *as if* merit, spiritual currency, were transferred, with the difference that the original merit-maker does not lose his. Buddhists aptly compare the process to lighting one candle from another.

The transfer of merit (as it is rather inaccurately known in English) plays a large part in Theravādin practice. For example, when one feeds monks they say a Pali formula which invites one to offer the merit – strictly speaking, to offer the chance to empathize in the merit – to the gods. In return for this favour they will accord their protection. It is no good objecting that the gods could have empathized whether the offer was formally made or not; the answer can come pat that otherwise the matter might have escaped their attention. Since gods give help in this world, the custom of transferring merit to them links Buddhism to the local communal religion.

This dedication to the gods of the merit of offering a meal occurs in the Canon, though as far as I know only once – again in the *Mahā Parinibbāna Sutta*.[10] But the rather simplistic treatment of merit as spiritual currency often crops up when the context concerns laymen; even in the *Vinaya* a lay donor is told that he has 'generated' merit and so achieved heaven.[11] The treatment of ethical action as a currency fits Buddhism's commercial background. But there is a discrepancy: real economics is a zero sum game, so that within the system gains are equal to losses, whereas in Buddhist spiritual economics you gain by giving away. I must add that Buddhists do not consider the possibility of transferring sin/demerit, as sometimes occurs in Hinduism; the best one can do to avoid the fruition of a bad action is to do so much good that the result of the bad keeps getting pushed to the back of the queue.

In Sri Lanka any public or collective expression of Buddhist piety is simply called a 'meritorious act'. It usually takes place around monks. The most common 'meritorious act' is indeed the feeding of monks, an event so common and central to Sinhalese Buddhism that it has appropriated the ordinary word for 'donation'. I mention the Sinhala because I am acquainted with its vocabulary, but one can assume that these developments occurred among Buddhists of the first generations in ancient India. At a 'meritorious act' merit is both made and transferred. One can participate even if one is too poor to give, and it is possible to argue that religious activity is thus a process of sharing and so strengthening communal ties. But one cannot press this argument too far, for my experience is that, whatever doctrine may say, people still feel surer of their merit if they have actively given than if they have been passive onlookers; they are not confident that the coin of 'empathy' carries the same purchasing power.

This may sound like common sense; I do not, however, think it is trivial. Buddhist spiritual economics is no zero sum game, but on the other hand the feeling is that spiritual capital gains interest. The rich have the resources to make donations; that means that they can afford to be generous with their merit – that is, use it for making more; and they get the protection of the gods into the bargain. Once one is on the right road one can thus set up a virtuous circle. The corollary is also true: the wicked man sinks on the scale of being and is reborn as a bug or even in hell, where he has almost no chance to make merit. This may be a depressing picture to the sentimentalist. But it is a picture of a universe of moral order, in which power and other pleasant things directly correlate with virtue.

I must not leave an impression of merit-making as a dry metaphysical mercantilism. Carrithers catches the spirit of lay Buddhism:

> Merit, *puñña*, is not only a sort of intangible religious good, but is also a psychological good, in that giving to (well-behaved) monks inspires laymen to generosity, happiness, peace, and so forth. Hence the atmosphere at a hermitage during an alms-giving ceremony . . . is strikingly quiet and pious, and, for those laymen susceptible to piety, an occasion of happiness or even reflection. The virtuous monk . . . 'inspires faith'. This is faith, however, in the psychological efficacy of the Dhamma, rather than in some entity.[12]

B. SECULAR POWER: ASOKA

The most important Buddhist layman in history has been the Emperor Asoka, who ruled most of India for the middle third of the third century BCE. On the capital of one of the pillars Asoka erected is beautifully carved a wheel with many spokes. This representation of the wheel of Dhamma which the Buddha set in motion is the symbol chosen to adorn the flag of the modern state of India. The lions on the same capital are on the state seal. Thus India recalls its 'righteous ruler'. Asoka is a towering figure for many other reasons too, but we confine ourselves to his role in Buddhist history. Before Asoka Buddhism had spread through the northern half of India; but it was his patronage which made it a world religion.

We know very few hard facts about the history of Buddhism in the century or two between the Buddha's death and Asoka's accession – if we knew more, we would be less vague about the chronology. The most important events were the Councils, or rather Communal Recitations. Soon after the Buddha's death five hundred senior monks – as the tradition has it – assembled in Rājagaha and rehearsed his teachings together; this is plausibly claimed to be how the Canon originated. A second such rehearsal of the scriptures, probably with additions, took place after the settlement of a major dispute over discipline in the town of Vesālī; the tradition says that this took place a hundred years after the Buddha's death, but the presence at it of several monks who had been ordained in the Buddha's lifetime suggests that that must be an exaggeration. These are the only two Councils accepted by all Buddhist traditions, because after the second the Sangha began to split. It is only the Theravādins who consider that the third Council was one held in Pāṭaliputta, Asoka's imperial capital, in the middle of his reign; evidently it concerned only them. It is reasonable to assume that the parts of the Canon which are unique to the Pali version (in particular the *Abhidhamma Piṭaka*, the 'basket' concerned mainly with classifying psychological and ethical elements) were definitively added at this Council and that what was recited was much like the Pali Canon that has come down to us. We return to this Third Council below.

Asoka was the grandson and second successor of Candragupta, who founded the Mauryan dynasty and empire about 324 BCE. We have very little evidence about the precise extent of what Candragupta conquered and even less about the activities of his son Bindusāra, but Candragupta's empire may already have covered northern India from coast to coast and probably comprised about two-thirds of the sub-continent. Bindusāra and Asoka extended it further to the south. The capital was the city of Pāṭaliputta, which had been founded as the new capital of Magadha fairly soon after the Buddha's death; modern Patna is on the same site. The Mauryan empire was a political unit of a new order of magnitude in India, the first, for example, in which there were speakers of Indo-Aryan languages (derivatives of Sanskrit) so far apart that their dialects must have been mutually incomprehensible.

Asoka's precise dates are controversial. Eggermont, the scholar who has devoted most attention to the problem, proposes 268–239 BCE.[13]

For our purposes there are two Asokas: the Asoka known to modern historians through his inscriptions, and the Asoka of Buddhist tradition. We shall say something about each in turn and then try to reconcile the two.

Asoka's inscriptions

Asoka left a large number of inscriptions on rocks and pillars. He dictated his edicts to scribes in Pāṭaliputta and had them carved in conspicuous places throughout his vast kingdom. They record a personality and a concept of rule unique not merely in Indian but perhaps in world history. The idea of putting up such inscriptions probably came to Asoka from the Achaemenid empire in Iran; but whereas Darius had boasted of winning battles and killing people, and considered his enemies products of the forces of evil, Asoka recorded his revulsion from violence and his wish to spare and care for even animals. He had begun in the usual warlike way, but after a successful campaign in Kalinga (modern Orissa) he had a change of heart. He publicly declared[14] his remorse for the sufferings he had caused in the war and said that henceforth he would conquer only by righteousness (*dhamma*). This remarkable conversion from what every proper Indian king considered his *dharma* to a universalistic *dhamma* of compassion and ethical propriety presumably coincided with the conversion to Buddhism which Asoka announced in what may well be the earliest of his edicts. In that edict[15] he says that he first became an *upāsaka* but did not make much progress for a year; then, however, he 'went to' the Sangha, and made a lot of progress. We cannot be sure just what he meant by 'going to' the Sangha – the Buddhist tradition that it meant going and living with monks may be an exaggeration – but in any case it clearly involved getting to know more about Buddhism; as explained above, only through the Sangha could the laity have access to the scriptures.

Almost all of Asoka's inscriptions are about *dhamma*. By this he did not mean specifically Buddhism, but righteousness as he understood it. And it is clear that his understanding was greatly influenced by Buddhism. The best traditions of both Buddhism and Indian kingship coincided in Asoka's declared support for all religions. This support went far beyond passive toleration: he dedicated caves to non-Buddhist ascetics,[16] repeatedly said that brahmins and renouncers all deserved respect, and told people never to denigrate other sects but to inform themselves about them.[17]

Asoka abolished the death penalty.[18] He declared many animal species protected species[19] and said that whereas previously many animals were killed for the royal kitchens, now they were down to two peacocks and a deer per day, 'and the deer not regularly – and in future even these three animals will not be killed.'[20] (Here as so often the rather clumsy style seems to have the spontaneity of unrevised dictation.) He had wells dug and shade trees planted along the roads for the use of men and beasts, and medicinal plants grown for both as well.[21]

The influence of Buddhism appears in both substance and style. The Buddha took current terminology and twisted it to his purpose: who is the true brahmin; what should one really mean by *kamma*, etc. Asoka does this repeatedly with his *dhamma*. Other kings have victories; he has *dhamma* victories.[22] Other kings go on hunting expeditions; he gets much more pleasure out of *dhamma* expeditions, on which he makes gifts to brahmins and renouncers and senior citizens,[23] tours the country and finds instruction in the *dhamma*. Other kings have officials; he has *dhamma* officials to promulgate virtue and to look after such disadvantaged groups as old people, orphans and prisoners.[24] In an edict addressed to these officials[25] he tells them to follow 'the middle path' – almost certainly echoing the Buddhist term – by avoiding such vices as jealousy, cruelty and laziness. In another edict[26] he says that people go in for all sorts of ceremonies on family occasions such as marriages, and women especially perform all kinds of paltry and useless rites for good luck, but the only rewarding ceremony is to practise *dhamma*, which means treating your slaves and servants properly, respecting your elders, acting with restraint towards all living beings, and making gifts to brahmins and renouncers.

Readers will notice how closely this edict echoes the *Advice to Sigāla* and other sermons on lay ethics which we have quoted.[27] Given that Asoka is most unlikely to have had a text available, the resemblance could hardly have been closer. Like Sigāla, Asoka's subjects are to substitute ethical action for traditional ritual, and what they are to do is just what the Buddha recommended. Our comment on the *Kūṭadanta Sutta* (p. 83) above), that the ideal king portrayed by the Buddha is the ideal layman writ large, fits Asoka perfectly. To follow all the details one should read these wonderful human documents for oneself.[28] I shall just cite two more points at which Asoka commends what we have identified as distinctively Buddhist values. He says, 'It is good to have few expenses and few possessions.'[29] And he not only urges diligence on others, but leads by example: he attends to business at any time, whether he is eating, in the women's quarters, in his bedroom, in his litter, in the garden, or even – if our understanding is correct – on the toilet. 'For I am never satisfied with my efforts and with settling business, because I think I must work for the welfare of the whole world.'[30]

Near the end of his last and longest inscription,[31] after summarizing his efforts to propagate *dhamma*, Asoka says, 'People's progress in *dhamma* is achieved in two ways, by *dhamma* rules and by conviction. Rules count for little; most is by conviction.' A perfect Buddhist sentiment, which I find touching in the context.

Some scholars have questioned Asoka's Buddhism on the grounds that he never mentions *nibbāna* or other key concepts of Buddhist soteriology. Our description of Buddhist lay religiosity, both in the Canon and after, proves that this objection is foolish. There are also certain inscriptions, apart from the announcement of his conversion, which have a purely Buddhist content in the narrowest sense. In an inscription found at the site[32] he announces that he has visited Lumbinī, the Buddha's birthplace, and remitted the village's taxes. In another[33] he says that he has doubled the size of the stupa of a (named) former Buddha and come himself to worship at it. So Asoka went on Buddhist pilgrimages. There are also two remarkable inscriptions addressed to the Sangha. In one[34] he recommends that they study certain specific texts; most but not all have been identified. In another, which has been found at three sites[35] (though badly damaged at two), he says that any monk or nun who splits the Sangha is to be made to wear white clothes (i.e. revert to lay status) and made to leave the monastery; the laity are to come each *uposatha* to check that this is done. We have seen that this issue, the unanimity of the Sangha, is a central one in the *vinaya*, and that, in lending his authority – indeed, his practical help – to the expulsion of dissidents, Asoka is acting as the perfect Buddhist king who enables the Sangha to keep itself pure.

We have left to the last the passage in an inscription[36] which mentions Asoka's missions. In it he says that he has won a *dhamma* victory by sending messengers to five kings and several other kingdoms. The kings, all of whom ruled in the Hellenistic world, the Near East, have been identified; from their dates we can deduce that the inscription was dictated in 256 or 255 BCE, and this gave modern scholarship the key to dating not merely Asoka but the whole of ancient Indian history. Unfortunately most of the other countries mentioned have not been securely identified. An overlapping list of countries, equally problematic, is mentioned in another inscription[37] in a similar context. We shall return below to the vexed problem whether these missions correspond to the missions recorded in the Buddhist chronicles.

Asoka in Buddhist tradition

The missions had a great influence on world history. But in other respects the Asoka who influenced later Buddhists, serving as the model for Buddhist rulers, was the Asoka portrayed in the Buddhist chronicles. A large body of stories grew up around him. We shall, however, restrict ourselves to the Theravādin chronicles, and in particular to the account of the *Mahāvaṃsa*[38] (see p. 140 below).

Most features of the Asoka of legend are perhaps simple-minded inflations of the truth. Thus he is said to have built 84,000 monasteries and as many stupas; it seems that in later times almost every old stupa was attributed to him. He is also said to have been preternaturally wicked before his conversion, killing 99 half-brothers.

The story of Asoka's conversion is that one day he chanced to see a Buddhist novice walking down the street and was so impressed by his tranquil deportment that he conceived *pasāda* and invited him in. (There is a romantic tale that, unbeknown to the king, he was his nephew; but that is not the point of the episode.) 'The king said, "Sit down, dear sir, on a suitable seat." Seeing no other monk present, he went up to the throne.'[39] This establishes that the most junior monk has precedence over the highest layman, the king. Again significantly, the novice preaches to the king about diligence (*appamāda*); he is thereupon converted and starts to feed monks on a vast scale. In due course Asoka's younger brother, his son Mahinda and his daughter Sanghamittā enter the Sangha.

The lavish state patronage has an unintended consequence: it tempts non-Buddhists to join the Sangha, or rather, to dress up as monks. The true monks cannot co-operate with them, so no *uposatha* ceremony is held for seven years. The king's first attempt to rectify this leads to disaster when his too-zealous minister has some real monks beheaded for this non-co-operation. He then invites the venerable elder Tissa Moggaliputta, who first assures him that without evil intention there is no bad *kamma*. The king and the elder then proceed to the big monastery the king has founded in Pāṭaliputta, and the king cross-examines its inhabitants to weed out the non-Buddhists. (Notice that this says nothing about doctrine within Buddhism or Buddhist sect formation: the men who merit expulsion were never Buddhists at all.) Finally Asoka says to the elder, 'Since the *sangha* is purified, let it perform the *uposatha* ceremony,'[40] and they do so in concord. Tissa then organizes the Third Council; they compile the scriptures (by reciting them) and he composes the *Kathāvatthu*, the last book in the Pali *Abhidhamma Piṭaka*. In effect he thus as it were seals off the *Tipiṭaka*, the Pali version of the Canon, with the possible exception of the large 'Collection of Minor Texts'

(*Khuddaka Nikāya*) of the *Sutta Piṭaka*, the contents of which remained somewhat fluid for many centuries. The *Kathāvatthu* establishes or reaffirms Theravādin orthodoxy on a host of points, mostly minor, on which they differed from some or other Buddhist schools.

The story of the Third Council is peculiar to the Theravāda tradition; evidently it concerned only them. The story of Asoka's intervention to purify the Sangha is found in other Buddhist traditions too, though with variant details. It is not corroborated by inscriptional evidence, as the inscription cited above does not say that Asoka has actually expelled monks himself; on the other hand, it is almost certain that many of Asoka's inscriptions have been lost – new ones are still being discovered – and the argument from silence is weak. The surviving inscription certainly proves that Asoka took an interest in the unanimity and purity of the Sangha. Scholars have treated the Theravādin account with scepticism because of various implausible features in it. Certainly it confuses the fortunes of one sect, or perhaps even just one monastery, with those of Buddhism throughout India: it is impossible to believe that no *uposatha* ceremony was held in all India for seven years, and in any case Asoka's expulsion of pseudo-monks from one monastery would only have rectified matters in that particular *sangha*, not in the Sangha as a whole. It also seems odd that it should be Asoka, a layman, who tests monks on their doctrine. Yet this is hardly out of character for a king whom we know to have put up an inscription telling the Sangha which texts to study. It is the occupational hazard of rulers to think they know best.

Whether the story is essentially accurate or inflates a minor incident in which Asoka did not personally participate, it serves in the Theravādin literature to complement the *Vinaya*, supplying the missing piece to the puzzle of the Sangha's regulation. Buddhist kings ever after Asoka saw it as their duty to act as Defender of the Faith – to use the Christian phrase – by expelling malefactors to purify the Sangha. For a Buddhist, to defend the faith is to defend the Sangha.

Asoka has been the model for rulers all over the Buddhist world. Within the next thousand years at least five kings of Ceylon prohibited the killing of animals.[41] In Burma, Asoka's example has constantly been invoked by kings;[42] and President U Nu, modelling himself on Asoka, had innumerable small stupas put up.[43] The great Khmer ruler Jayavarman VII (1181–after 1215) saw himself as a 'living Buddha' and in his inscriptions expressed Asokan sentiments on the material and spiritual welfare of his subjects and announced that he had had hospitals built.[44] In eleventh-century Thailand, King Rāmā Khamhaeng ordered that for urgent business he should be disturbed even on the toilet.[45] In fifth-century China, the Buddhist emperor Lian-u-thi went and lived in a monastery with monks.[46] Of course no one before the nineteenth century had access to the inscriptions, or even knew they existed; they based themselves on Buddhist literary sources. In modern times Asoka's precedent has been no less invoked but more distorted. The great Sinhalese Buddhist reformer Anagārika Dharmapāla (see below, p. 188), whose assumed name Dharmapāla means 'Defender of the Faith', called Asoka's 'the greatest democratic empire',[47] while the Sinhalese polemicist D.C. Vijayavardhana, who regarded the Buddha as somehow anticipating Karl Marx, described Asoka as 'the Lenin of Buddhism'.[48]

The missions: interpreting the evidence

Curiously enough, the Theravādin chronicles do not credit Asoka directly with what we naturally think of as his most important achievement, the dispatch of missions which established Buddhism over a far wider area, within the Indian sub-continent and beyond. According to those texts, it was the elder Tissa Moggaliputta who sent out nine missions to 'border areas'. This was in c. 250 BCE. Each mission was headed by an elder whom the texts name and consisted of five monks, the quorum required for conferring higher ordination in remote parts.[49] The mission to Ceylon will concern us in the next chapter. Here we need only say that it was headed by the elder Mahinda, whom Theravādin tradition considers to have been Asoka's son; his daughter Sanghamittā followed in due course to establish the Order of Nuns in Ceylon.

There is archaeological evidence to corroborate a piece of the chronicles' story. Five named monks are said to have gone to various parts of the Himalayan region.[50] In Bhilsa (= ancient Vidisā) in central India, relic caskets of the right period, the early second century BCE, have been found inscribed with the names of three of these monks and stating that they are of the Himalayan school.[51]

Nevertheless, the great Buddhologist Étienne Lamotte not only argues that these missions cannot be those to which Asoka refers in his inscriptions; he is even sceptical whether there was a concerted missionary enterprise at all.[52] He points out that Asoka's '*dhamma* messengers' or ambassadors of righteousness can hardly have been Buddhist monks, because the emperor protected all faiths and used *dhamma* to mean something much more generally acceptable than

Buddhist doctrine. He argues that the lists of destinations in the Buddhist sources on the one hand and the inscriptions on the other are discrepant, though they overlap; that some of them were already familiar with Buddhism by that date; and that the dates too are discrepant.

Erich Frauwallner, on the other hand, accepts the Buddhist account in most particulars.[53] But he identifies it with Asoka's embassies and thus holds the emperor directly responsible. He further argues that the missions set out from Vidisā in central India, where the missionaries' remains were found. He identifies the geographical names in the Theravādin sources with some of those in the inscriptions, and glosses over the difficulty of the date.

On the whole I side with Frauwallner. The geographical identifications are too uncertain to help us. While Lamotte is right to point out that some of the areas visited, notably Kashmir, had Buddhists already, that does not disprove that missions could be sent there. The chroniclers, as so often happens, had no interest in recording a gradual and undramatic process, and allowed history to crystallize into clear-cut episodes which could be endowed with edifying overtones; but this over-simplification does not prove that clear-cut events never occurred. We know from the inscriptions that they did. There is a discrepancy of about five years in the dates; as the dates of Asoka's embassies are certain, within a year or two, I suggest that we must not flinch from concluding that on this point the Buddhist sources are slightly out. Maybe Frauwallner is also right about where the missions left from, for the Ceylonese sources say[54] that Mahinda stayed a month at Vedisa (= Vidisā) before going to Ceylon.

Asoka's ambassadors of righteousness would certainly not have been men travelling alone. Such a mission could well have included monks – perhaps even representatives of more than one religion. So Lamotte's objection about the nature of *dhamma* can also be parried.

The monks who composed the chronicles would not have been pleased to record that Buddhism travelled as a sideshow. Nor indeed would it have been relevant to their main purpose as chroniclers, which was to show how valid ordination traditions came to be established. I agree with Frauwallner that the missions to remote parts were probably responsible for the creation of several of the early sects, which arose because of geographical isolation. What is really most implausible, in my view, is that it should have been Tissa Moggaliputta who sent out all the missions. The strong evidence of the *Kathāvatthu* demonstrates that he was a polemicist for the particular doctrinal interpretations of the Pali school, whereas we know that Kashmir, for example, had other sects and schools (i.e. *vinaya* and doctrinal traditions), not the Theravāda or *vibhajja-vāda*. Evidently Tissa Moggaliputta was the chief Theravādin intellectual of his day, and the Theravādin chronicles therefore grossly exaggerated his role in general Buddhist history. Just as he cannot have presided over the purification of the entire Sangha throughout India, he cannot have been the prime mover in dispatching missions throughout the known world. Indeed, there is one account which does not connect him with Mahinda's mission.[55] Asoka may well have sought his advice and secured his co-operation, but these missions – as we shall see – were from court to court, a product of state patronage.

CHAPTER SIX

The Buddhist tradition in Sri Lanka

For more than half of its history Theravāda Buddhism has existed mainly in India and Ceylon. Its history in India is, however, disappointingly obscure; it is hard to disentangle it from the history of Buddhism in general, and even that is fragmentary and has to be gleaned from disparate evidence, notably from the texts which survive only in Chinese and Tibetan translations. Buddhism in India did not write its own history.

Like Ceylon, Burma has a tradition that it is the Theravādin country *par excellence*, and being a Theravāda Buddhist is as central a part of the Burmese as of the Sinhalese national identity. Like Ceylon, Burma has a national chronicle (the *Sāsana-vaṃsa*) which claims that the Buddha himself visited the country and foretold its future as a stronghold of his Sāsana; the chronicle then presents the history of Burma as that of a Buddhist kingdom (though it is far briefer than its Ceylonese counterpart). However, while archaeological and literary evidence proves that the Ceylonese historical account of Buddhism in the island, from Mahinda's mission on, is substantially true, there is reason to be sceptical about the early history of Theravāda in Burma. The Sinhalese chronicle refers to a mission sent by Tissa Moggaliputta to Suvaṇṇa-bhūmi, 'The Land of Gold'. This name has been applied to various parts of southeast Asia, and Theravādin tradition could be correct in identifying the monks' destination as lower Burma, though some modern scholars think it more likely to have been central Thailand.[1] However, the earliest archaeological evidence for an Indian writing system in Burma is not older than the second century (CE, and for Pali, the hallmark of Theravāda, not older than the fourth century.[2] Though there is plenty of evidence for Buddhism in Burma in the succeeding centuries, it is largely in Sanskrit. There is evidence dated c.600 CE for Pali, and hence for Theravāda, in the kingdom of Dvāravatī in central Thailand, and this civilization may have extended into lower Burma.[3] To upper Burma, however, Theravādin ascendancy came only in 1057, when King Anuruddha (Burmese: Anawrahta) captured Thaton, capital of the Mon kingdom in lower Burma, and took back to his own capital of Pagan both Theravādin monks and manuscripts of the Pali Canon.

The Sinhalese Buddhist identity

The monastic chroniclers of the fortunes of Buddhism in Ceylon have ensured that with those fortunes have been identified the fortunes of the Sinhalese people, indeed, the Sinhalese nation. There have been Hindu invasions (most destructive in the fifth, ninth, tenth, eleventh and thirteenth centuries), culminating in the establishment of the Hindu kingdom of Jaffna in the north of the island from the thirteenth to the fifteenth centuries. There are Muslim settlements, notably on the east coast. And there was massive interference from Christian colonial powers who ruled coastal areas from 1505 on and the whole island from 1815 to 1948. But despite all these alien intrusions, Theravāda Buddhism has dominated the religious and cultural life of the country throughout its recorded history, which can be said to begin with the arrival of Mahinda in c.250 BCE (though the chronicle begins earlier). In particular, for most of the period virtually all Sinhalese have been Theravāda Buddhists; the only numerically significant exception is the Roman Catholic community on the west coast, many of them fishermen, converted by the Portuguese in the sixteenth century.

Ceylon is an island just over 25,000 square miles in size. Its inhabitants at the dawn of history were apparently homogeneous – for Väddas, once thought to be a distinct aboriginal population, have been shown to be marginal Sinhalese. Though there were other foreign incursions, the destructive invasions of ancient times all came from the nearest part of the Indian mainland, which at its closest is only just over 20 miles away. The mainlanders from that area spoke Tamil and were mostly Śaiva Hindus. The Sinhalese national identity was thus built on the two contrasts of language and religion: Sinhala/Tamil and Buddhist/Hindu. On this foundation were elaborated stereotypes, of which the most important element is the contrast 'pacific Sinhalese v. aggressive Tamil'.

For the first millennium of the Common Era, in so far as Theravāda Buddhism existed at all outside Ceylon, it left little trace. The Sinhalese are well aware of their part in keeping this great religious tradition alive. It is held that as he lay on his deathbed the Buddha, who had visited Ceylon three times, knew that Vijaya, the ancestor of the Sinhalese race, had just reached the island of Lankā (=Ceylon) from India. He said to Sakka, the king of gods, who was in attendance, 'My teaching will be established in Lankā, so give him and his followers and Lankā full protection.'[4] Thereupon Sakka entrusted the protection of Ceylon to the god Viṣṇu. Viṣṇu is still believed to have this responsibility.

Periodization of Sinhalese Buddhist history

Pre-modern Ceylonese history is conventionally divided into periods by the location of the Sinhalese capital. It was continuously at Anuradhapura till the late eighth century, when invasions from southern India became a regular problem. Polonnaruva, further east, was better sited to cope with them. The capital oscillated between these two cities for over a century and the last king to rule from Anuradhapura died in 896.[5] After the Tamil invasions of the late tenth and early eleventh centuries the political unity of the Sinhalese kingdom became precarious. It was reunified and ruled from Polonnaruva by Vijaya Bāhu I (1070–1110), Parakkama Bāhu I (1153–86) and the latter's successors till the Tamil invasion of 1215, and again for a period later in the thirteenth century. The northern part of the island was then lost by the Sinhalese. The capital shifted several times till in the sixteenth century, after the Portuguese had taken the west coast, it settled in Kandy. It remained there till the British conquest in 1815, when the island was reunified and ruled from Colombo.

While the Sinhalese have always been Buddhists, the fortunes of Buddhism as institutionalized in the Sangha have fluctuated under the pressures of foreign invasion and internal decay, the former sometimes hastening the latter. Many cultural traditions were lost in the troubled eleventh and early twelfth centuries. The decisive event which halted this decline was the 'purification' of the Sangha and council held by Parakkama Bāhu I and the elder Mahā Kassapa in 1164/5. In the sixteenth century the Sangha so declined that the indigenous ordination tradition was lost; and a valid ordination tradition was not successfully re-established in Ceylon till the Thai mission of 1753. It is this date, not 1815, which is a watershed in Buddhist history. The largest body of monks in Sri Lanka today, the Siyam Nikāya, traces its ordination tradition back, as the name shows, to that Thai visit to Kandy. It should, however, be added that the Thai tradition derived in turn, via Burma, from Polonnaruva, so that the modern Sangha are not only the cultural heirs of the ancient but have maintained the pupillary succession.

Given this remarkable continuity, and given that the Anuradhapura period lasted for more than half the time between the introduction of Buddhism into Ceylon and the present day, it seems reasonable to concentrate on that period in attempting a succinct account of traditional Sinhalese Buddhism. Most, though not all, of the characteristic features of that Buddhism began to develop quite early in the period. On the other hand, our sources mainly inform us of the doings of monks and kings. To supplement these public events and dramatic developments with a view of Buddhism in the wider society we have to use modern, even contemporary observations of Buddhism as it lives in traditional villages.

Sources

The sources for the history of the Anuradhapura period are scriptures, chronicles and inscriptions. Of the scriptures more will be said below. Though inscriptional evidence begins in the second century BCE, it does not become an important source of historical information till the Polonnaruva period.[6] Most important are the chronicles, especially the *Mahāvaṃsa*, 'The Great Chronicle'. The first part of this was composed in Pali verse early in the sixth century by a monk called Mahānāma 'to arouse *pasāda* in good people'. It was modelled on a briefer fourth-century chronicle, likewise in Pali verse, the *Dīpavaṃsa*, 'The Island Chronicle'; the latter may have been composed by nuns, for it takes much interest in their affairs. The other sources of the *Mahāvaṃsa* have been lost. They included the 'merit books' in which it was customary, at least for the rich and powerful, to keep a record of their pious donations and good works.[7]

The first part of the *Mahāvaṃsa* ends abruptly in the middle of chapter 37. Its second part, up to chapter 79 inclusive, was written by a monk in the thirteenth century, and further instalments were added till the eighteenth century. (A later addition has not acquired the same recognition.) The continuations are sometimes known collectively as the *Cūlavaṃsa*, 'The Lesser Chronicle'.

The chronological coverage of the *Mahāvaṃsa* is extremely uneven. Naturally, several chapters are devoted to the mission of Mahinda, beginning with its antecedents in Asoka's conversion and what the chronicle calls the Third Council. But then more than a quarter of the first part is devoted to a single reign, that of King Duṭṭhagāmaṇi (Sinhala: Duṭugämuṇu) (101–77 BCE)*. Similarly, King Parakkama Bāhu I occupies a quite disproportionate share of the second part.

Sinhalese Buddhist nationalism

The *Mahāvaṃsa* is the charter of Sinhalese Buddhist nationalism. Its account of the Polonnaruva period devotes several chapters to wars against the Tamils, mentioning Buddhism only incidentally. This reads like the secular history which we modern readers unthinkingly expect, so we are apt not to notice how odd it is in a book which ends every chapter reiterating that it is composed for the edification of the pious. But the identification of religion and nation goes back to the account of Duṭṭhagāmaṇi. (To what extent to the king himself and to what extent to his chronicler we cannot tell.) Duṭṭhagāmaṇi defeated the Tamil king who at his accession was ruling in Anuradhapura. He proclaimed that he was fighting not for a kingdom but for Buddhism, and put a Buddhist relic in the spear which served as his standard.[8] Monks left the Sangha to fight in his army.[9] Most startling of all is the advice the king was allegedly given by some Enlightened monks. Perhaps recalling Asoka's remorse, the king, after his victory, asked them what consolation he could have for causing a great slaughter. They replied:

> That deed presents no obstacle on your path to heaven. You caused the deaths of just one and a half people, O king. One had taken the Refuges, the other the Five Precepts as well. The rest were wicked men of wrong views who died like (or: are considered as) beasts. You will in many ways illuminate the Buddha's Teaching, so stop worrying.[10]

The *Mahāvaṃsa* has exerted a powerful influence. We learn from it[11] that when Parakkama Bāhu I purified the Sangha he was playing Asoka to Mahā

* Like Rahula, I am keeping to the chronology established by Geiger (1912). According to Mendis (1947), Duṭṭhagāmaṇi's rule should be dated 161–137BCE and all Sinhala dates from then on till the end of the fourth century be moved back 60 years. The problem is that somewhere between Devānampiya Tissa and the late eleventh century the *Mahāvaṃsa* put in 60 regnal years too many. Geiger thinks it is in the fifth century, at the very beginning of the *Cūlavaṃsa*; Mendis argues that it is between Devānaṃpiya Tissa and Duṭṭhagāmaṇi. I find Mendis' arguments plausible but not conclusive.

Kassapa's Tissa Moggaliputta, both presumably guided by *Mahāvaṃsa* chapter 5. But Duṭṭhagāmaṇi came to provide yet another royal model, albeit a very different one from Asoka. So when Parakkama Bāhu II (1236–71) set out to fight the Tamils, according to the chronicle, he first recalled all the non-Buddhist Tamils who had usurped the throne – presumably basing his recollections on the *Mahāvaṃsa* itself.[12]

When I interviewed Sinhalese monks,[13] most (but not all) of them were reluctant entirely to accept the view propounded to Duṭṭhagāmaṇi, for they realized its incongruence with Buddhist ethics. The stereotypes are, however, too strong to be easily demolished, and least of all by historical fact. The same *Mahāvaṃsa* records that after some victories over the Tamils Parakkama Bāhu II brought from Tamil-nadu many virtuous and learned monks to help him restore the local Sangha.[14] Theravāda Buddhism seems indeed to have flourished in south India from the earliest times till as late as the seventeenth century.[15] Even in Ceylon there were evidently Tamil monks and Tamil patrons of Buddhism.[16] But these facts are now little known. It is notable that the Buddhist missionary efforts of modern times have been directed at countries overseas, from Indonesia to the United States, but rarely at the local Tamil population.

The *Mahāvaṃsa* provides a model of and a model for the Sinhalese Buddhist identity, and the resultant stereotypes are one element in the Sinhalese Buddhist world view. Though 'communal religion' finds its main expression, when it is in small, face-to-face communities, in (ritual) action, in larger social units it finds expression in some more or less developed system of ideas. A central element in the brahmin ideology of *dharma* is who they are. The more egalitarian Sinhalese have long held a view of their communal identity which is closer to modern nationalism. Their comparative egalitarianism has been fostered by Buddhism, and their self-definition in contrast to Tamils by events in their early history, reinforced by the way in which those events were recorded.

Cosmology

For the rest, the traditional Sinhalese Buddhist view of the world is a local variant of the cosmology outlined in chapter 3. The system organizes material which has arrived from India at various times; many details will be found in my book *Precept and Practice*[17] and references there cited. The phenomenal world operates under the aegis of 'our holy king Buddha', though strictly he is no longer part of it (the same ambiguity about being at the top of and being outside as we noted for *nibbāna* (p. 95), having delegated his authority. The Dhamma is put into effect by a cosmic hierarchy who operate through a series of such delegations, 'warrants' like the one the Buddha issued to Sakka and Sakka in turn issued to Viṣṇu. The king is not equated with a particular god, as he has been in Hindu states – that would be alien to Buddhist rationality – but he occupies a position on earth analogous to that of Sakka above, and like Sakka derives his legitimacy from his humble recognition of the suzerainty of Buddhism as embodied in the Sangha and such sacralia as relics; we shall give instances below. In particular, the legitimate king must be in possession of the Buddha's tooth relic. It is still the custom for newly installed governments in Sri Lanka to visit Kandy to pay their respects at the Temple of the Tooth.

The analogue between the cosmos and a unified state occupying the entire island of Ceylon is also perceptible in the religious geography. There are traditionally sixteen sites of Buddhist pilgrimage on the island, all of them hallowed by the Buddha's visits as recounted in the first chapter of the *Mahāvaṃsa*. Eight of them are at the ancient centre, Anuradhapura, while the others are so distributed as to take the pilgrim to the extreme north, south, east and west, and so do a circuit of the island. A traditional pilgrimage also recalls the hierarchic organization of cosmos and state. Pilgrims set out from their village only after getting the formal permission of their village god; they then go to pay their respects at the headquarters of the regional god; and so advance up the hierarchy of the Buddha's representatives to the moral centre. The same structure can be found within the complex of religious buildings at a village temple: the local godling, the regional god and the Buddha are housed next to each other but in such a way that the spatial arrangements reflect the hierarchy. In modern times it can be observed that the analogy between the power structures of the pantheon and the state is often quite explicit.

A Buddhist society

Until the nineteenth century, Sinhalese society was almost wholly rural and agricultural. Apart from a small landowning aristocracy, it consisted of a rice-growing peasantry, various craftsmen (metal-workers, potters, etc.), a few service personnel (washermen, load-carriers, etc.) – and the Sangha. In caste terms, the laity consisted of a dominant, land-owning caste and several smaller service castes. This enumeration omits coastal fishing communities and the castes created by colonialism, such as cinnamon-pickers. What is striking is that there was no indigenous merchant class. Foreign trade seems always to have been entirely in the hands of foreigners (i.e. non-Sinhalese), internal trade mainly so. This means that whereas Buddhism began with the rise of an urban merchant class, Theravāda has survived in virtually antithetical conditions, as the religion of a peasant society who persistently differentiated themselves from non-Buddhist traders. (This is true not only of Sri Lanka but also of the Theravāda countries of continental south-east Asia.) We shall see in the latter part of this chapter how this affected the Sangha.

Though from many points of view Sinhalese society appears a regional variant of the south Indian pattern, Buddhist values have modified even so Indian a feature as caste. The Indian caste system, we saw, is articulated in the language of purity and impurity, and Hindu life is accordingly hedged about with taboos. The fact that the bearers of Sinhalese cultural values are not brahmins, the class at the apex of the caste hierarchy, but monks, who in theory represent the value of castelessness, so lightens the emphasis on purity that the Sinhalese lead lives of an utterly different quality in this respect from their Hindu neighbours (even those within the island). There is no real untouchability in Ceylon – whereas nearly a quarter of all Hindus are untouchables. Ideas of pollution connected with death, parturition, etc. exist but are far milder than among Hindus. As we saw in the case of relics (p. 123), pollution cannot affect Buddhist sacralia. No one is ever barred from visiting a Buddhist shrine or monk or from Buddhist observance on account of impurity.[18] While Hindu women are regarded as so impure during menstruation that they may not touch anyone or enter the kitchen, let alone approach the gods, whether a woman is menstruating is of no relevance to her Buddhist activities. It is relevant if she wants to take part in an activity concerning the gods. But the spillover effect from Buddhism into daily life is very great, so that she is not forbidden the kitchen or made to shun human company. It may be part of this same spillover effect that the general status of women is so much higher in Sinhalese than in Hindu society.

Speaking very broadly, one could say that Sinhalese folk religion is closely related to that on the adjacent mainland, but that the place held in India by brahmins is taken here by the Sangha, a change with far-reaching effects. Sinhalese magic and exorcism seem largely to derive from the region which is now Kerala, while the higher gods are mostly pan-Hindu with a strong south Indian coloration.[19] But the Buddhist values of compassion and non-violence have dictated that no god can receive a blood-sacrifice: any supernatural being who demands an animal victim is *ipso facto* a devil, inherently cruel and therefore below man in the scale of being. Indian brahminism likewise defines recipients of blood sacrifices as demonic, but its hierarchic view of the world leaves plenty of room for them to take place, as it were 'among the lower orders', whereas in Sinhalese society they are extremely rare, being banished altogether from public ritual and confined to the occasional killing of a chicken in some dreadful nocturnal rite of exorcism.

Similarly, both brahminism and Buddhism oppose possession and commend self-control, while the communal religion of the Sinhalese, as of the Indian, village centres, and has probably always centred, on a cult of local deities whose priests become possessed and so act as mediums to help villagers solve their practical problems. In traditional Ceylon these priests acknowledge Buddhist values by never becoming possessed on a *poya* day; in my experience they also have rather low prestige and tend to put up somewhat half-hearted performances, as if feeling that trances are not quite dignified. Again we see that while brahminism and Buddhism share a value, brahminism relativizes and particularizes, highlighting the value by allowing or even prescribing its absence among non-brahmins, whereas Buddhism universalizes: monk and layman have complementary responsibilities but acknowledge the same ideals.

On the other hand, brahminism is in the first place a ritual, Buddhism an ideological system. This leads to a stark contrast between the roles they play in their respective societies. Theravāda Buddhism has generated from within itself amazingly little of the ritual which societies seem to need for their functioning. We have seen (p. 124) that death is the only life crisis in which anything specifically Buddhist is involved. The traditional Sinhalese wedding is a variant of non-brahminical south Indian marriage. Similarly, the Sinhalese New Year festival, on 13 April, is secular and much the same as that of many Hindus. There are, however, some distinctively Buddhist calendrical festivals, all of them held on full moon days; the most important, the full moon of the lunar month Wesak (May–June), commemorates the Buddha's birth, Enlightenment and death.

In one area of life brahmins seem to have been indispensable: the court. There was no Buddhist form of coronation (though at least one coronation has been held in a monastery).[20] Kings in Ceylon and throughout continental southeast Asia depended on brahmins for their royal rituals – presumably they brought them from India. The monastic authors of the chronicles, not surprisingly, hardly mention the court brahmins, but they are glimpsed occasionally.[21]

Worship of Buddha images

The manner in which Buddha images are worshipped in Ceylon[22] owes a great deal to south Indian Hindu temple worship, which in turn is modelled on court ceremonial. Especially in the Temple of the Buddha's Tooth in Kandy,[23] and to a lesser extent as one moves away from that essentially royal, paradigmatic institution, the Buddha image is treated like the King's person. The last dynasty to rule in Kandy, till 1815, was also from South India; it is reasonable to suppose that what can still be observed in Kandy reflects the ritual of their court.

Nowadays Buddha images are mass produced; but it is unlikely that before modern times they were ever treated as casual objects. The origin of the Buddha image is contentious;[24] but from the fourth century CE onwards our sources often refer to shrines containing them. A Buddha image is technically a relic of the third class, a 'reminder relic' (see p. 124). The central image in a temple is normally upgraded by placing a physical relic, a fragment of bone, inside it when it is consecrated; that this is a true relic of the Buddha is a *fable convenue*. The ceremony of consecration involves painting in the image's eyes,[25] another Hindu borrowing. Though a consecrated image is treated with great deference, and cannot be moved, anyone can have access to it, and it is rare to encounter, for example, an objection to photographing it: outside the consecration ceremony, the Hindu idea that consecration has endowed it with life is absent. Traditionally, Buddha images were probably found only at sacred, public spots; it is possible that aristocrats had private shrine rooms, but I doubt even that. The modern multiplication of images is due first to Christian influence and then to the technical possibilities of mass reproduction.

Role of the village monk

The essence and *raison d'être* of a Buddhist temple, however, remains that it is the residence of a monk. A temple begins when a monk settles, though at this stage it may still be called only a 'residence' (*āvāsa*). It becomes a temple (*vihāra*) as other objects of worship are added: a consecrated Buddha image, installed in a building; a stupa; and a Bo tree. (Often it is the presence of a Bo tree which has made the monk choose that site.) Not all these three things need be there, but it is unusual to lack more than one of them unless the temple is still new.

Most Sinhalese villages have a local temple with a resident incumbent, and sometimes also some other monks or novices, the incumbent's fellow monks or pupils. But he does not function like the English village vicar. Villagers who need a monk to conduct mortuary rites must by custom invite him (and other monks only through him), and he must accept; but these are the only rites for which such a presumptive link is recognized, even though the villagers feed him and his fellows, and generally use the local temple for most of their 'merit-making'. In other words, they are responsible for him, not he for them; he is not a pastor, a shepherd to his people. His twin functions – we postpone the question of how a 'renouncer' came to have any 'function' at all – have traditionally been to teach and to preach.

In modern times the monk's role of teacher has been taken over by the school system (and we shall see in the last chapter that this poses a major problem for the Sangha today). But traditionally the Sangha have functioned in Ceylon, very like the brahmins in Indian society, as the cultural and literary specialists, the preservers of intellectual tradition. They were the educators, in the days when there was less distinction than nowadays between formal education and general acculturation. Monks taught reading and writing (mainly but not only to boys), and at the same time taught moral values and literature: virtually all literature was Buddhist and inculcated Buddhist ethics.

The preacher is half teacher, half ritualist. Sermons are a less frequent and routine occurrence at village temples than in Christian churches; they are also more or less the only occasion on which Buddhist laity form into what Christians would recognize as a congregation. Such preaching will normally be in Sinhala. But the formalized chanting of Pali scriptures is also a form of preaching, and one specific form of such recitation constitutes the only significant regular involvement of the Sangha in communal religion.[26] This recitation is called *paritta* in Pali and *pirit* in Sinhala; the words mean 'protection'. Any competent person may chant *pirit*, but it is usual to invite monks to do it – and of course to feed them before and/or afterwards, thus increasing the merit. At a formal ceremony at least two monks normally chant together; often many more are involved and they chant in relays. It may take from about half an hour to seven days and nights, depending on the form of ceremony chosen. The texts are from a set repertory (the *pirit* book) which monks are supposed to know by heart. Only the length, not the occasion, of the ceremony determines (with a few exceptions) which texts are recited. The occasion can be anything from a state ceremony like the opening of Parliament to a service in a private house to commemorate the dead – and make merit for them. Most people regard *pirit* simply as a means to bring luck and avert misfortune; it thus appears to them as an impeccably orthodox Buddhist ritual for this-worldly benefits. Sophisticated Buddhists will point out that some of the texts address potentially malevolent spirits and preach Buddhist compassion to them; for the sponsors and human audience, they will say, the ceremony only works in so far as they too are affected by the message of the texts, and in so far as their participation manifests their virtuous intentions. What to the sophisticated has a spiritual application can be interpreted by simple people as a form of white magic.

From a comparative point of view it is remarkable that Theravāda affords so few examples of such ambiguous practices. After every public Buddhist act the Sinhalese offer the merit to the gods; in return for this spiritual good, the gods are supposed to look after the affairs of this world for them. Not only do the gods have 'nothing to do with religion'; they deal with this world so that Buddhism is left free to concern itself with ultimate things.

The achievements of Mahinda's mission

From the Theravādin point of view, then, the contents of this chapter so far have dealt only marginally with Buddhism. The history of the Sāsana in Ceylon must be the history of the Sangha. So we return to its beginning, the arrival of Mahinda.

The three surviving accounts of the mission, all in Pali, probably depend on a common lost source. The oldest and briefest is that in the *Dīpavaṃsa*; another in the *Mahāvaṃsa.* Dated between the two chronicles is the historical introduction to his great commentary on the *Vinaya*, the *Samanta-pāsādikā*, by Buddhaghosa (on whom see below, p. 154). All three versions were composed by members of the Sangha, primarily with a monastic audience in mind, so naturally they are much concerned with *vinaya.* This is especially true of Buddhaghosa, who is aiming to establish the authenticity of the *vinaya* tradition in which he stands.

Besides the four other monks he would need for performing a higher ordination in remote parts (see p. 107), Mahinda brought with him to Ceylon a novice and a layman. Not surprisingly, the story abounds in miraculous detail. The party arrives by air,[27] and Mahinda so arranges matters that his first encounter in Ceylon is with the king, Devānaṃpiya Tissa, who is out hunting with forty thousand retainers.[28] Mahinda preaches the king a sermon from the Pali Canon on the life of a Buddhist monk. The king and his entourage are converted; they take the Three Refuges. The layman who has come with Mahinda is then given both the lower and the higher ordination; this apparently serves an exemplary purpose. After converting hosts of divine beings, Mahinda proceeds to the capital, Anuradhapura. On seeing the seats prepared for the monks, soothsayers predict, 'They will be the masters on the island.'[29] Mahinda preaches to and converts women of the royal household, said to number 501. He then gives a public sermon and converts a thousand townsfolk. The sermons are specifically said[30] to be in the local language and the names of the canonical texts he preached are given; whether or not these details are accurate, it means that the chronicler thought that Mahinda translated texts from Pali into the local language. Further sermons are recorded, the converts make spiritual progress, and the king makes the Sangha his first gift, a park to serve as their monastery. This is what is to become the Mahā Vihāra, 'The Great Monastery'. There is no reason to doubt that this was the first monastery founded in Anuradhapura. The tradition which has survived is that of the Mahā Vihāra. The *Mahāvaṃsa* was composed by a monk in that tradition and Buddhaghosa worked there. Our view of the history of Buddhism in Ceylon is therefore that of the Mahā Vihāra, which naturally presents itself as the guardian of orthodoxy. It does seem to have been the most conservative centre.

As the king donates the land for the Mahā Vihāra the earth quakes, which according to the *Mahāvaṃsa*[31] – but not the other two accounts – Mahinda explains as a sign that the Sāsana is now established on the island. Moreover, all the religious foundations are justified by saying that the sites have been sanctified and the acts prefigured during the visits not only of Gotama but of the three previous Buddhas.

A crucial act is the establishment of the first *sīmā*, the monastic boundary of the Mahā Vihāra. The king himself drives a plough to mark out the line the monks have determined. Formal acts of the Sangha, such as the *uposatha* ceremony, can now be properly performed. Not quite consistently, the *Mahāvaṃsa*[32] defines this too as constituting the establishment of the Sāsana.

Mahinda and his colleagues duly pass a rainy season in Ceylon, and then Mahinda says to the king,

'It is a long time since we saw our teacher, the Buddha. We have

> been living without a protector; there is nothing here for us to worship.' 'Reverend sir, did you not tell me he was dead?' 'Seeing his relics is seeing the Buddha.'[33]

(Compare this with the Buddha's statement, 'He who sees the Dhamma sees me.') The king thereupon sends off the novice who came from India with Mahinda to get relics. With Asoka's help, he gets from Sakka, king of the gods, the Buddha's right collar bone, and over this is erected with due pomp Ceylon's first stupa. In due course Asoka's daughter, the nun Sanghamittā, comes too, so that the Order of Nuns can be established. She brings with her a branch of the Bo tree under which the Buddha obtained Enlightenment; this cutting takes root in Anuradhapura, where the tree is worshipped to this day, and from that tree it is propagated to monasteries all over the island.

In Ceylonese tradition, Buddhism (the Sāsana) has three constituents: learning, practice and realization. Each depends on the previous one. The decline of the Sāsana in our day is marked by the fact that realization, Enlightenment, is already rare if not obsolete, and practice, i.e. virtue, especially monastic virtue, is also fading. Five thousand years after the Buddha's death, according to tradition, his Sāsana will die out. At this point learning too will disappear. The texts of the Pali Canon will be lost, starting at the end. The last to go will be that which stands first in the Canon, the *Vinaya Piṭaka*, and the first part of that, and therefore the last to go, will be the *Sutta-vibhanga*, which contains the *pātimokkha*. When that is gone, all is lost: Buddhism has disappeared from the face of the earth.

In the same spirit, Buddhaghosa's account of the establishment of Buddhism in Ceylon culminates in the establishment of a local tradition of *vinaya* learning. Mahinda declares, after monasteries have been founded and relics imported, that though the Sāsana is now established, it will have taken root only when someone born in Ceylon of Ceylonese parents is ordained in Ceylon, learns the *Vinaya* in Ceylon, and recites it in Ceylon.[34] A son of King Devānaṃpiya Tissa, who has become a monk, then ceremonially recites the *Vinaya Piṭaka*, and as soon as he has uttered the first words of the *Sutta-vibhanga* the world convulses in exultation.[35]

Establishing Buddhism in a new country

In his admirable account of these events the Ven. Dr Rahula writes:[36] 'The idea of the "establishment" of Buddhism in a given geographical unit is quite foreign to the teaching of the Buddha ... Buddhism is purely a personal religion.' It is true that Buddhism is primarily a personal religion, what I have called a soteriology. But the chronicles are recording the establishment of the Sangha, and that does require formal attachment to the terrain by putting down a *sīmā* before it can perform valid acts like the *pātimokkha* recitation. When the soteriology, the Dhamma, is institutionalized as the Sāsana, it has to find local habitations. For in the Theravādin tradition the Sāsana exists through the Sangha. To survive, the Sangha immediately and constantly requires material support, and in the long run requires the means to perpetuate itself by ordaining recruits.

These aims can be most easily achieved by acquiring royal patronage. That Mahinda began his mission by converting the king may, like the rest of the story, be a gross simplification; and the numbers of his early converts must be absurdly exaggerated: no king goes hunting with forty thousand attendants, who in this case would have constituted a sizeable slice of the population. But it is true that the most realistic course for a missionary in those days would have been to make straight for the largest town and preferably for the palace. Only there would he have found the opportunity to preach to a large crowd; and without wealthy and powerful patrons he could not possibly have established a monastery. Though Ceylon was probably prosperous and well developed by the standards of those days, communications must still have been rudimentary, and Anuradhapura was probably the only considerable town and the king the only person with a great command over resources. Similar considerations would have applied in any country in ancient times, so the tendency of Buddhist historians to describe the spread of Buddhism as a series of missions to courts cannot be dismissed as naive fabrications.

Why did Buddhism spread so successfully? The major factor has no doubt been the power and beauty of its thought. It offered both a coherent, universalistic ethic and a way to salvation from suffering. When it reached the peasant societies of south and southeast Asia (not only in its Theravāda form), it encountered no rival ideology but filled an intellectual and religious gap, for those societies had no soteriology and no literate culture of their own. Many centuries later, it was challenged in some of those societies by new soteriologies, first Hindu devotionalism and then Islam. In its struggles with them (in arenas such as Indonesia and central Asia) whether the king continued to support the Sangha must have been crucial in determining the outcome.

The Sangha's duty to preserve the scriptures

The Sangha preserves the scriptures, and Buddhism is perhaps peculiar among world religions in the extent to which it depends on the preservation of its scriptures. Unbiased scrutiny of mass religiosity the world over should convince anyone that the doctrinal content of their religion which most people can articulate is minimal. Islam's rapid spread must have been facilitated by the fact that it could be subscribed to in a single sentence: 'There is no God but Allah and Mohammed is his Prophet.' Most Hindu soteriologies have hardly any doctrinal content which is known outside a small learned élite, just an injunction to love God; for the rest, one carries on with the duties prescribed by the traditional communal religion. For Christianity, Keith Thomas has collected impressive and amusing evidence of popular religious ignorance in England, his examples ranging from the Middle Ages to the nineteenth century.[37]

For Islam, simplicity is strength. Buddhist strength lies elsewhere, in its ethos and in the cogency of its ideas. The ethos is best conveyed by living exemplars. The ideas are not terribly complicated in their essentials, but they certainly cannot be reduced to one or two sentences. Moreover, the proposition that no one has any abiding essence or soul is counter-intuitive. To this extent Buddhism is ineluctably an intellectual religion and requires a professional intelligentsia who can preserve and expound its doctrines.

The Buddhist scriptures were the cultural treasure and patrimony of Sinhalese society. But preservation of an oral tradition can be somewhat precarious. Late in the first century BCE, civil wars and Tamil invasions led to a terrible famine. The *Mahāvaṃsa* records:

> Formerly clever monks preserved the text of the Canon and its commentaries orally, but then, when they saw the disastrous state of living beings, they came together and had it written down in books, that the doctrine might long survive.[38]

(In how many copies it was written we are not told.) This is the earliest record we have of Buddhist scriptures being committed to writing anywhere.

At that time a conference of monks debated the question whether learning or practice was the basis of the Sāsana. The majority decided, according to a Pali commentary: 'Even if there be a hundred or a thousand monks practising insight meditation, if there is no learning none will realize the Noble Path.'[39] Everywhere those who share in and benefit from an institution feel a responsibility to preserve it for future generations. In favourable circumstances, the interests of the present and the future need not conflict, but at a crisis one has to decide between investment and current consumption. Thus we have reason to feel grateful for that decision. Maybe the sense of crisis was engendered not merely by the recent troubles but also by the tradition that the Buddha had predicted, when he was persuaded to found the Order of Nuns, that his Sāsana would last only 500 years. This means that by the Theravādin chronology of the time its end must have been expected late in the first century BCE. Maybe only when this calamity was averted was the tradition amended to its modern form: that the Sāsana will last 5,000 years.

The decision that the primary institutional goal of the Sangha must be to preserve the scriptures was formalized in the creation of two roles, duties or 'yokes' for monks: the 'book yoke' and the 'insight yoke'. Ever since then, monks have formally specialized either in learning and preaching, or in meditating. The choice of one's role is an individual matter, but in ancient times there was apparently pressure to take the academic role.[40] Nowadays the division between book and meditation roles tends to coincide with another, between 'village dwelling' and 'forest dwelling', which will be explained below.

The use of Pali: Buddhaghosa

A social history must discuss the availability of information. To whom were texts accessible, to whom were they intelligible? Even in Mahinda's day, Pali could not have been intelligible to an untutored Sinhalese. Both languages derive from Sanskrit, but Sinhala had already undergone far greater change. The first missionaries must therefore have learnt the local language, which strictly speaking we would call Sinhala Prakrit, for their preaching.

According to Buddhaghosa, Mahinda brought with him the commentaries on the Pali Canon and translated them into Sinhala.[41] This must be at least an over-simplification, for two reasons. Firstly, though the commentaries that have reached us are only about as long as the Canon, the Canon is very repetitious, so that they have a far higher information content. Memorizing a commentary involves also memorizing the text commented on. Individuals have been known to memorize the whole Canon, but even that is a formidable feat, and monks were normally organized to specialize in particular groups of texts.[42] So we deduce that Mahinda and his little party can hardly have brought the whole body of Canon and commentaries: the texts must have arrived more gradually, in the heads of several people.

Secondly, although scholarship has still done little to establish how much of the commentaries was composed in India and how much in Ceylon, Adikaram has shown that they were added to till about the middle of the first century CE,[43] which would mean that the last additions were made about half a century after they were written down.

The commentaries that have reached us are all in Pali, and most of them were composed in the early fifth century in Anuradhapura by Buddhaghosa, who according to tradition was born a brahmin in India. Buddhaghosa is Theravāda's great scholastic; his position is even more dominant than that of St Thomas Aquinas in the Roman Catholic tradition. His first work was the *Visuddhi-magga* ('The Path to Purity'), a compendium of Theravādin doctrine which has been regarded as authoritative ever since. It is arranged in three sections, according to the old hierarchical triad: morality, concentration, wisdom. Though full of quotations from the Canon and other literature, it is an original work, not a mere compilation. The prose style is much more elaborate than that of most Pali texts and probably shows the influence of a Sanskrit (and therefore brahmin) education. The contents strictly concern the life of a monk. Though enlivened by some anecdotes by way of examples, they are fairly austere and afford few glimpses of devotional sentiment or popular practice. It is above all a handbook for meditators.

The rest of Buddhaghosa's work is commentarial, and in it he is editing older material. On this basis he composed commentaries on the *Vinaya*[44] and on the most important sermons and doctrinal texts. Most of this older material was in the local Sinhala and some probably was already in Pali.

After Buddhaghosa, work on Buddhist doctrine tended to be in Pali. Other monks wrote what proved to be definitive Pali commentaries on the canonical texts he had not covered, and in due course also sub-commentaries in the same language.

The general shift from the vernacular to Pali had clear reasons and important consequences. Being a living language, Sinhala constantly changes. By the time of Buddhaghosa, the Sinhala texts written down in the first century BCE must have become hard to understand. Since the Canon was in Pali, that language was in any case the foundation of monastic education. More convenient than to study another dead language was to preserve the commentaries in the same language as the Canon. Around 400 CE a Sinhalese monk translated the Pali Canon into Sinhala,[45] apparently for the first time, but this work has disappeared without trace, no doubt because it became unintelligible in its turn. Some of the older commentaries survived Buddhaghosa for a few centuries, but in the end they too were all lost. Inscriptions apart, the oldest Sinhala texts that survive – and all the early literature has a strictly Buddhist content – date from the Polonnaruva period.

The positive effect of Buddhaghosa's reversion to a classical language was to internationalize the Theravādin tradition. From then on, Theravādin monks and nuns could communicate and interact across linguistic boundaries, like Latin-speaking priests in pre-modern western Europe. Despite local differences in their pronunciation of Pali, the Theravādin Sangha from that day to this has shared a common language, and this has enabled Sanghas which are nationally in decline to renew themselves from abroad. If Buddhaghosa was indeed an Indian brahmin, this would not only explain his preference for writing in a learned language but also make it likely that the use of Sanskrit throughout India made him aware of the cultural advantages of having such a *lingua franca.*

The drawback, of course, is that a dead language is unintelligible to ordinary uneducated people. The shift to Pali did not perhaps change things all that much: we have suggested that Buddhist scriptures were never widely available, so that the need for professional clergy to purvey their contents was there from the beginning. Nevertheless, the transformation of monks, seeking their own salvation, into priests, making salvation available to others, was thus furthered by the sheer process of linguistic change.

Translation and popularization

Buddhists have been among the world's great translators. In the early days in India, the Buddhist monks who memorized the texts spoke related dialects, so that 'translation' was a matter of little more than phonetic change, the sort of thing that occurs spontaneously as people talk in varying contexts. The same could even be said of putting the texts into Sanskrit, which was a matter of 'talking posh'. But when Buddhism reached more remote parts, where the vernacular was not just a related dialect, the local monks had to master the texts in what was to them a foreign language. So long as the scriptures were preserved only orally, systematic translation of such a large body of material was simply not feasible. The Chinese have managed to translate versions of the entire Canon – much of it, indeed, several times – and so have the Tibetans, but it is worth reflecting how rarely, till very recently, a nation has mustered the organized academic resources necessary for such a project. If the anonymous monk referred to above managed to translate the whole Canon into Sinhala in c.400 CE, his feat stands alone, for, despite a recent government project for a team of translators to do so again, they are still far from completing their work.

The idea behind the modern government project is of course to democratize access to the scriptures: it seems unsatisfactory that those Sinhalese who know no Pali should have to turn to English translations. But this is a modern aspiration. We can be sure that the translations made in ancient times were for the benefit of fellow members of the Sangha. What was translated or paraphrased into Sinhala for the laity in pre-modern times was almost exclusively the *Jātaka* and similar story literature, the bulk of it not strictly canonical but commentarial. Should one wish to reassemble the texts which were familiar to the typical Buddhist layman, the Canon, excepting a few short poems, would be fairly useless.

As is true for mediaeval Europe, a fair impression of popular scriptural knowledge might be gained by surveying what was painted on the walls of temples.[46] Most of it concerned the lives of the Buddha. The subjects were normally chosen by the local incumbent. There was a tradition that the unworldly should not have aesthetic interests: one monk is reputed to have been so wrapped in meditation that for twenty years he lived in a cave without noticing that there were paintings on the ceiling.[47] But such abstraction was not expected of the village-dwelling monk, and we even know of a novice in the eighteenth century who painted temple murals himself.[48]

Village dweller and forest dweller

The only cultural specialities which required literacy, apart from transmitting Buddhism, were astrology and medicine. So it is not surprising that despite the Buddha's warning against involvement with such matters[49] monks often practised astrology and medicine – though of course they were not supposed to do so for pay.

Such non-religious activities have characterized the village-dwelling monk. Village temples are often so situated, e.g. on high ground at the edge of the village, as to render visible the ambivalence of the monk's position (see p.95): is he outside society or at the top? In Indian terms, does he reflect the tradition of the renouncer or of the brahmin? The contrast survives, but moderated – in true Buddhist spirit. Unlike the Indian renouncer, even the most forest-dwelling, eremitic Theravāda monk is no wanderer; while unlike the brahmin, the village-dwelling cultural specialist has achieved, not inherited, his role – even if we shall see below that access to that position has sometimes been socially restricted.

'Forest dwelling' is one of the classical ascetic options (*dhutanga*) for individual monks; it can be undertaken either temporarily or for life. However, such ascetic life-styles have tended to become institutionalized in pupillary lineages; and once this happens there is an inexorable drift back to the monastic norm. This is not only because the ascetic practice is undertaken out of a personal commitment which is hard to routinize. As shown above, the ascetic virtuoso is constantly being nudged back to normal comforts by the 'relentless piety' of the laity who shower him with donations. An example of this is furnished by another nominally ascetic group, the *paṃsu-kūlika*. At various times in the Anuradhapura period, monks who undertook the recognized ascetic option of dressing only in rags (*paṃsu-kūlika*) organized into separate monasteries. They came into prominence round 700 CE, and within a few years the king 'is reported to have given even the fine garments worn by himself to the *paṃsu-kūlika* monks for robes'.[50] In the eleventh century *paṃsu-kūlika* monks joined in a mass exodus of monks from Polonnaruva in protest against royal confiscation of monastic property.[51]

'Forest dwellers' are referred to from about the sixth century.[52] By the time of Parakkama Bāhu I the division of monks into 'village dwellers' and 'forest dwellers' seems to have been thoroughly institutionalized. We do not know whether the pupil of a 'forest dweller' was invariably regarded as one too, but the division into the two types of 'dwellers' survived Parakkama Bāhu's re-organization of the Sangha.[53] It was revived when the Sangha was reconstituted in 1753. But that was just a formality: monastic lineages which were then designated 'forest dwelling' are just as village dwelling nowadays as the rest. That merely illustrates the drift. But what is important is that individuals with a vocation for the eremitical life continue to go off to live in 'forests', i.e. in simple hermitages away from densely inhabited areas. However, one must not jump to the naive conclusion that all forest dwellers are rigorously ascetic meditators, let alone that village dwellers are more learned but also more self-indulgent. Formal roles and ideal types do not always coincide.

The structure of the Sangha in Ceylon

As explained above, monks and nuns throughout the Buddhist world are split into lineages, ordination traditions, which do not co-operate in formal acts of the Sangha, and therefore live apart and tend not to co-operate in informal contexts either. In Sanskrit and Pali such separate bodies of monks are called *nikāya*. All Theravādin monks share the same *pātimokkha* code, but they may differ over its interpretation or over *vinaya* matters not covered by the code. They may also split for geographical or other reasons. If Theravāda is to be called a 'sect', a *nikāya* formed within Theravāda should be called a 'sub-sect'; but a better translation might be 'fraternity'. Literally it is a vague term like 'group', but it refers to a body of monks fissile and combinable but ultimately determined by a willingness to hold ordination ceremonies together.

The first recorded split in Theravāda occurred at about the time when the Canon was written down, late in the first century BCE. After his war against the Tamil invaders, King Vaṭṭagāmaṇi gave a monastery in Anuradhapura called Abhayagiri to a monk who had helped him. The *Vinaya* knows no precedent for such a gift to an individual. The monks of the Mahā Vihāra charged the monk with an (ostensibly unrelated) offence and expelled him, whereupon a group of his disciples moved to Abhayagiri and severed relations with the Mahā Vihāra.[54]

The second split came in the fourth century CE. King Mahāsena came under the influence of a monk from south India; according to the tradition of the Mahā Vihāra monks, he wanted to convert them to Mahāyāna. They left the capital in disgust. The king had their buildings demolished and the materials used for new buildings at Abhayagiri; the Mahā Vihāra site was sown with beans.[55] Though these changes were soon reversed and the south Indian monk assassinated, the king built a new monastery called Jetavana in the grounds of the Mahā Vihāra and gave it to another monk whom he favoured. History repeated itself: the monk was accused of an offence and expelled. Like Abhayagiri, Jetavana survived as a separate *nikāya*. The Abhayagiri tended to be much more open than the Mahā Vihāra to new, i.e. Mahāyāna, influences from India, while the Jetavana vacillated. But we must remember that points of doctrine are not relevant to the differentiation into *nikāyas* unless and until they encroach upon the *vinaya*; after that one can of course accuse the splitters (always the other side) of unorthodoxy too.

From the fourth century till Parakkama Bāhu's 'purification' in the twelfth century there were three Nikāyas in Ceylon – or so historians tend to tell us. But it might be more accurate to say that there were three Nikāyas in the capital. We do not know whether every monastery in the island formally came under one of the three, but if we include the forest hermitages it seems unlikely. In modern times, every monk in Ceylon has to receive his higher ordination with the co-operation or at least the agreement of the headquarters of his *nikāya* – in most cases he has to go there for the ceremony – but we have no evidence that this was so before Parakkama Bāhu's reform. There are said to be three Nikāyas in Sri Lanka today: the Siyam, the Amarapura and the Rāmañña; and yet this is a kind of fiction, the pattern being set by the glories of the ancient past. The modern Nikāyas are much subdivided, some by disagreement over a point of *vinaya* and some geographically; and some forest hermitages recognize allegiance to none of the three – in fact in 1968 they got government recognition to form their own Nikāya, which means essentially the right to confer their own higher ordinations. Nevertheless, in both ancient and modern Ceylon (though not from the twelfth to the nineteenth centuries) the Sangha has conventionally been said to consist of 'the three Nikāyas'. It is rare for a monk to change *nikāya*; if he does, he has to be reordained.

Formal state control of the Sangha

Parakkama Bāhu I set up a single authority structure for the national Sangha, and had all ordination ceremonies performed at one time of year in the capital,[56] presumably so that he could supervise them. Though the chronicle says that he reunited the Sangha,[57] this expression glosses over the fact that what he did was to abolish the Abhayagiri and Jetavana Nikāyas. He laicized many monks from the Mahā Vihāra Nikāya, all the monks in the other two – and then allowed the better ones among the latter to become novices in the now 'unified' Sangha, into which they would have in due course to be reordained.[58] Acting on the advice of Mahā Kassapa, a forest dweller, he then promulgated a *katikāvata*, which is a royal edict about monastic discipline. Several kings in Ceylon issued such edicts, which have the force of *vinaya* regulations; Parakkama Bāhu's was the most important. It provided for the Sangha to be headed by a monk who came to be known as the Sangharāja, 'King of the Sangha', and ruled by him with two deputies; these officers were appointed by the king on the Sangha's advice. Mahā Kassapa became the first Sangharāja.

Such a political organization for the Sangha was something quite new. It has been imitated at times in the Theravādin countries of continental southeast Asia. However, the system of unified control breaks down if the secular government allows new *nikāyas* to form. Parakkama Bāhu's organization survived in theory into the fifteenth century,[59] but when the

Sinhalese state fell on hard times it can have had little reality. When the Sangha was formally reconstituted in 1753, the great monk Välivița Saraṇaṃkara was appointed Sangharāja, but the office died with him in 1778. In the early nineteenth century the British government allowed separate *nikāyas* to form which did not obey any central, state-appointed authority. Furthermore, once the British had taken over the whole island there was no Buddhist king left to appoint such a person.

Nevertheless, vestiges of Parakkama Bāhu's system survive to this day. We have seen that the Siyam Nikāya was formed with two moieties, 'village dwellers' and 'forest dwellers'. Each moiety has a head, a deputy head, and an executive committee or cabinet. Nowadays, the head and deputy head are elected by the executive committee. These clerical authorities control such matters as ordination into their Nikāya; and to ensure that control they require all ordinations to take place during one month annually at their headquarters in Kandy, the capital in the time of the last Sangharāja. The other, newer Nikāyas have partially imitated these arrangements.

Parakkama Bāhu's centralization represents a stronger formal control of the Sangha by the state than existed during the Anuradhapura period. However, this organization did not supersede any of the Sangha's older authority structures: it just added to them. Moreover, evidence from Thailand, where the Sangharāja system, elaborated into a whole hierarchy of office, is in full operation today,[60] suggests that progress in this monastic career structure still does not command the kind of respect traditionally accorded to a monk for his personal qualities.[61]

Sangha and state in Anuradhapura

The kings of ancient Ceylon considered themselves to stand in the tradition established by Asoka and to be responsible for the well-being of the Sangha. The relations between church and state were more like those between brahmin and *kṣatriya* in Hindu India, where what we might call the complementarity between the sacred and the secular was well understood, than the relations between Pope and Emperor in early mediaeval Europe. Rather than rivalry, there was in general a community of interest; 'the kingship by which the state was represented was the firmest support of the Buddhist church and the latter that of the kingship.'[62] Even if there was in fact more friction with the king and more impiety than the monastic chroniclers cared to record, it is clear that kings normally treated the Sangha with immense deference, and we shall mention below some striking instances of kings' personal devotion. Once in the seventh century, the monks of the Mahā Vihāra formally refused to accept alms from a king, the closest Buddhist equivalent to excommunication, and we hear of no attempt by the king to retaliate. But since such a decision by one *nikāya* would not have bound the others, perhaps he could afford to ignore the insult.

Many kings tried to follow in Asoka's footsteps by working for the public good. For example, King Buddhadāsa (late fourth century) put up resthouses on the highway and homes for cripples and the blind,[63] and allegedly had a hospital, staffed by a doctor, in every village.[64] He also practised medicine himself, even on a cobra.[65] He is said to have lived the life of a *bodhisatta*,[66] and certain later kings are said to have aspired to Buddhahood,[67] which means that they regarded themselves as *bodhisattas*. Finally in a tenth-century inscription a king proclaims that only *bodhisattas* can become kings of Ceylon.[68] Whether sincere or purely rhetorical, this is tantamount to stating that the king dedicates himself unreservedly to the welfare of others. Incidentally, the penetration of this *bodhisatta* ideology into Ceylon seems extraordinarily slow: such future Buddhas multiplied in Mahāyāna Buddhism and became extremely important in India by about the first century CE.

Asoka's crucial act as defender of the Sāsana, we recall, was his 'purification' of the Sangha. It had two aspects: getting rid of those who had only joined the Sangha for an easy life, and reuniting the Sangha in its formal acts. In other words, the 'corruption' had two aspects: luxurious living, and consequent disharmony.

The Sangha as landlords

In so far as the established Sangha had a recurrent problem with wealth, it is arguable that the kings themselves contributed to it, not merely by the scale of their munificence but also by its character. We have seen (p. 102) that the *Vinaya Piṭaka* mentions a case in which a king gave a village of five hundred monastery attendants for the service of an elder, but this curious story there stands alone. It is mentioned almost in passing: the point of the passage in which it occurs is quite different. With this dubious exception (which was a gift of labour rather than land), the holding of large-scale or immovable property by individual monks seems to have started in Ceylon. In Theravādin countries today the law recognizes the difference between property held by the Sangha corporately and that held by individual monks; one may give to either, though custom regards an offering to the whole Sangha as more meritorious.

The reign of King Vaṭṭagāmaṇi in the late first century BCE seems to have been a period of rapid change. The king is the first person recorded to have given the Sangha usufruct of real estate.[69] The gift was made to Mahā Tissa, the same monk to whom, a little later, the king gave Abhayagiri monastery as his *personal* property,[70] thus indirectly causing the Sangha to split. We recall that this was also the time when the scriptures were first written down and their preservation declared to be the Sangha's first duty. Like the climacteric in the Sangha's history under Parakkama Bāhu I, this period of rapid change followed immediately upon invasion and civil war, a secular crisis which had nearly obliterated the Sangha. In both cases the reaction of the king, understandably, seems to have been to try to restore the Sangha by involving himself and his successors more closely with its welfare. In the long run these measures had some unintended consequences.

Land grants to monks and monasteries became very frequent after Vaṭṭagāmaṇi, so that monastic land-holding became a major feature of the economy. Grants were of various kinds: 'the grant of a village could involve the right to taxes, to labour from its inhabitants, to proprietary right over its land, or a combination of these.'[71] In traditional India, control over land normally implied some control over its population, so that giving land often meant giving the labour of its inhabitants. In India brahmins, and later temples, were commonly given land by the king for their upkeep; the land was tax-free and the labour of its inhabitants normally went with it. Not only were such gifts irrevocable by the giver: they were supposed to be honoured by his successors in perpetuity.

Buddhaghosa's commentary on the *Vinaya* shows that at least by the fifth century – but probably a good deal earlier – a whole gamut of legal fictions were enabling the Sangha to deal with property. Another of his commentaries says that the Sangha could not accept slaves under that name, but if they were called monastery servants (*ārāmika*) or legalizers (*kappiya-kāraka*) (see p. 102) it was all right.[72] Even this nicety of nomenclature came to be ignored, for at one point the *Vinaya* commentary says in so many words that kings gave slaves to monasteries, and that they could not be ordained unless they had first been freed.[73] Inscriptions record that people gave money for the specific purpose of maintaining monastic slaves – and offered the resulting merit to all living beings.

> If granting endowments to maintain slaves at monasteries was considered meritorious, freeing them from slavery was considered even more meritorious. Thus the device of offering slaves to monasteries provided a two-fold way for the acquisition of merits.[74]

We shall see that kings would offer and redeem themselves as a dramatic act of humility. But this practice was not confined to royalty: inscriptions show that it became popular between the fifth and eighth centuries.[75] In such cases the slavery was a kind of fiction; but as late as the fourteenth century a monk could write 'that in order to liberate oneself from evil tendencies one should liberate slaves'.[76]

The system of 'monastery villages' has not yet quite disappeared from Sri Lanka. A monastery may own the territory of a village, or part thereof, and the right to the labour of its inhabitants, who must till the monastery's fields and provide other services according to their caste, such as bringing and washing cloth and making music at religious occasions. (Recently the terms of service have been mitigated and the labour can be commuted for cash.) Though we have detailed information on the provision of these feudal services only since the sixteenth century, presumably a very similar system of tied labour employed many of the villagers of ancient Ceylon as 'monastery attendants'.

Monastic landlordism caused ideological problems to the Sangha – and no doubt practical problems to the laity. In theory, monks and nuns cannot get rid of anything given to them. Originally it was not envisaged that they could acquire things surplus to their needs. The Sangha are 'the supreme field in which to sow merit', the object of charity. The *Mahāvaṃsa* records[77] that when Mahā Tissa found King Vaṭṭagāmaṇi in need of food he gave him his alms, but only after he had touched the food himself; thus the king was technically not receiving a gift from a monk but just eating his leftovers. By this standard it should be impossible for the Sangha corporately to dispose of its property; and in the tenth century we find King Mahinda IV prohibiting the sale or mortgage of monastic land.[78] This edict would not have been promulgated had there been no such practice; and in fact 'as early as the second century AD monasteries could, at least theoretically, dispose of their lands'[79] in that they had full proprietary rights. Monasteries also behaved like normal business corporations in buying land, in selling its produce, in deriving income from commerce,[80] and in particular in receiving interest on deposits made in money or in kind with the merchants' guilds.[81]

All such financial transactions could be 'laundered' through lay administrators. The *vinaya* rule, according to Buddhaghosa's commentary, was that the Sangha could accept property only to meet the cost of 'allowable articles' or of maintaining the monastic buildings.[82] So, for example, water from the Sangha's irrigation system was not 'sold' but only used to ensure the flow of 'allowable articles'. The passage containing this sophistry is worth quoting:

> If people, bent on helping the *saṅgha*, construct an irrigation reservoir on the land belonging to the *saṅgha*, and thenceforth provide 'allowed articles' from the proceeds of the crops raised with the water from the reservoir, it is permissible to accept them. And when it is requested, 'Appoint a *kappiyakāraka* for us,' it is in order to appoint one. And if these people, being oppressed by the tax demands of the king, were to give up the land and go away, and if others who occupy their land do not give anything to the monks, it is permissible to stop the supply of water; but this should be done in the ploughing season and not in the crop season. And if the people were to say, 'Reverend sirs, even in the past people raised crops with water from this reservoir,' then they should be told, 'They helped the *saṅgha* in such and such manner, and provided the *saṅgha* with such and such articles.' And if they say, 'We too, shall do so,' it is permissible to accept what they offer.[83]

If over the centuries kings and other pious landowners were making land grants to the Sangha, while the Sangha was not supposed to divest itself of property and probably rarely did so, the Sangha must gradually have acquired a considerable share of the country's material resources, and of its manpower too. Fa Hsien, the Chinese pilgrim who visited Ceylon early in the fifth century, says that about 60,000 monks were fed from their common stores, so that they did not have to beg their food. His compatriot Hiuen Tsiang, 250 years later, recorded on hearsay that Ceylon had 20,000 monks.[84] We have no figures for nuns. Unfortunately I know of no estimate of the population of Ceylon in ancient times. Malaria seems to have arrived in the second quarter of the present millennium and decimated the population,[85] so that modern population figures (see pp. 173 and 202) offer no clue to the ancient ones. If however we look at modern Burma, that so high a proportion of the population and other resources should be devoted to Buddhism is not incredible: Spiro reports estimates that in 1960 monks constituted about 10 per cent of the male population.[86] Even if with Bechert[87] we divide this by about nine, it is still impressive.

Such a curtailment of the king's ability to mobilize men and resources must have been a grave disadvantage in time of war. This modern reflection runs counter to the belief that Buddhist piety was the best guarantee of national safety. That belief must have been powerful, for not till the twelfth century did a king (Vikrama Bāhu I, 1111–32) confiscate monastic property on a large scale.[88] It is noteworthy that despite concerted protest by all three Nikāyas neither he nor any of his successors down to and including Parakkama Bāhu I seems to have restored what had been taken.[89] The custom of granting land and labour to monasteries did not die out, but thereafter assumed a more modest scale.

Although legal fictions were devised to justify the Sangha's *communal* involvement with property, the economic transactions of individual monks seem inevitably to conflict with their professed ideal. Firstly we must make clear that in ancient times, as in modern, the administrators of monastic revenue were not always laymen. According to Mahinda IV's tenth-century inscriptions, one of which states that the rules it lays down are drafted on the basis of earlier ones,[90] 'monks were in charge of the revenue received from the villages and lands'.[91] It is even more surprising to find that 'the monks themselves were "paid" for their work. For example, different grades of "payments" were fixed for monks who taught *Vinaya*, *Sutta* and *Abhidhamma* and those who looked after the monastery.'[92] To such systematic 'payments' I know of no modern parallel. Recently some monks have taken up paid employment as school-teachers, amid fierce controversy; they tend to defend their position by saying that they pass their salaries on to the Sangha. Even if they do not, they are not being paid for performing the duties of the monastic role.

Since monks came to own monasteries, it was natural for their property rights to become heritable (though this probably never meant that they could alienate property to laity[93]).

> The law of succession and incumbency of Buddhist temporalities in the early period is not known. Most probably the chief monk of a monastery was appointed by the Sangha.... The first evidence of incumbency through pupillary succession can be detected in [a tenth-century inscription].[94]

Though we lack firm evidence for what actually happened earlier, Buddhaghosa's *Vinaya* commentary certainly envisages not merely that a monk own a building as his personal property but that he leave it to his disciples.[95] Moreover, this passage is cited as the opinion of an old Sinhala commentary, which strongly suggests that inheriting monastic property from one's teacher may go back to at least the first century CE.

Inheriting personal monastic property profoundly affects the character of the Sangha. In recent centuries, monks in Ceylon have been entitled to inherit incumbencies from their teachers or from kinsmen. The latter case, by which rights to monasteries are simply vested in families, existed during the Kandyan period (i.e. up to 1815) but is now obsolete. The modern system is that it is normal for the incumbency of a monastery to pass from the abbot to his senior pupil, who is defined as the first pupil to whom he gave the lower ordination and who is still in robes. The two systems can be made to approximate to each other if the incumbent ordains a close kinsman as his first pupil, and my impression is that this was till recently quite common in traditional villages but is now becoming rare.

Decline . . .

Though these developments have moved far from the original ideal, they are not perhaps too hard to explain. Monks in Ceylon were never wanderers; they were settled throughout the countryside. The 'village dwellers', who were always the vast majority, inevitably became members of the village community. Normally a village temple contains only one or two adult monks. The monk thus spends most of his life in contact not with other monks but with his fellow villagers. Small wonder then if he gradually absorbs their values and assumes their customs.

If one looks at Indian civilization as a whole, one sees that brahmins follow the same pattern. Their ideal is a moderately ascetic way of life, 'contentment with little'; yet they are the prescribed object for the generosity of the Hindu king, and most Hindu high-caste rituals involve feeding them. For the most part they live in villages, far from any central authority which might enforce discipline. (Indeed, for the most part no such authority exists on any formal level.) So they are almost universally stigmatized as greedy and corrupt. They are, in fact, altogether too much like everyone else.

The Sangha's life as landowners in peasant communities led to yet a further deviation from the pristine ideal: organization by caste. We know next to nothing about this before 1753, but the logic of the situation suggests that what we can observe since then continues a much older state of affairs.[96] Though at least two low-caste monks were ordained in Kandy by the Thai mission in 1753, within a few years the Kandy headquarters were refusing to ordain anyone who was not of the dominant, landholding caste which makes up about half the Sinhalese population.[97] While acknowledging that this contravenes the spirit of Buddhism, they maintain this restriction till today. Indeed, they have been imitated by some branches of the other Nikāyas, while yet others restrict entry to other particular castes; those which admit pupils of any caste are in a small minority.

When monks are landlords, it is not surprising that they should drift into being of the same caste as other landlords. It is part of the same phenomenon as the succession by blood relationship. Before 1753 there were no true monks left in Ceylon but only men called *gaṇinnānsē*. These had taken the lower ordination but wore white (i.e. dressed as householders) and were not necessarily celibate; they lived in monasteries and kept the property in the family. We are not sure just how long this sad state of affairs had been in existence, but probably since the reign of the Śaiva king Rājasiṃha I (1580–91), for he had persecuted Buddhism and his successor had brought monks from Burma to restart the ordination tradition. Another such mission came from Burma in 1697. It seems, however, that these two missions were invited not in order to initiate a genuine religious revival, but to legitimize the claims of incumbents to their temple lands. In fact it was often a branch of the family of the local lord, the chief landholder of the village, which inhabited the temple – a situation familiar to historians of mediaeval western Europe.

Conditions before 1753 thus seem to have replicated those before 1164, when 'in the villages belonging to the Sangha the good morals of monks consisted only in their supporting their wives and children'.[98]

... and revival

How can the Sangha recover from such catastrophic decline? Three factors have proved crucial: royal patronage; the international character of the Theravādin tradition; and Buddhism's scriptural foundation.

Having (in my view) contributed to the disunity and corruption of the Sangha, the kings, who surely did not see their actions in that light, were often ready to emulate Asoka by purifying it. Several are recorded to have held such purifications,[99] sometimes following them by a communal recitation of the scriptures, on the model of the Third Council. In theory they could intervene only at the invitation of the Sangha, executing its decisions, but apparently it was sometimes the kings or their ministers who took the decisions.[100] We recall that the story of Asoka's intervention has the same ambiguity.

We can assume that most of these purifications consisted of expelling *pārājika* offenders (see p. 104) from a particular *sangha*. Only one of them followed the myth (rather than the probable reality) of Asoka so far as to reunite the whole Sangha: Parakkama Bāhu's act of 1164/5. The sorry state of the Sangha at that time is not surprising, considering that the country had just suffered nearly two centuries of Tamil invasions and internecine civil wars. It is in this period that the Order of Nuns died out in Sri Lanka. At one point, during a comparative lull, the king, Vijaya Bāhu I (ruled in Polonnaruva 1070–1110), had even found that there were not five monks available to hold an ordination ceremony and had therefore imported some from Burma for the purpose.[101]

It was the export of the Theravādin ordination tradition that allowed the Ceylonese Sangha to re-import it when need arose. Vijaya Bāhu I was the first king to do so. Unfortunately we do not know exactly when Theravādin monks or nuns first went from Ceylon to Burma, but probably it was during that troubled period,[102] within the reign of the Burmese king Anuruddha (c.1044–c.1077).[103] A Burmese monk who had stayed about ten years in Ceylon under Parakkama Bāhu I, studying the scriptures, returned to Burma in about 1181 with the usual four associates and set up a separate *nikāya*, the 'Sinhalese Sangha', which became the main monastic tradition there.[104] It is apparently through this 'Sinhalese Sangha' that Theravāda reached Thailand in the thirteenth century, though later the Thai also drew on direct contact with the Sangha in Ceylon. It was those contacts in turn which made possible the Thai mission to Kandy in 1753.

The nuns have been less fortunate, even though in ancient times their international contacts too were extensive. 'Three groups of nuns and a group of monks went from Sri Lanka to China in the fifth century. Such movements persisted until at least the eighth century.'[105] It is thus possible that some – or even all – of the Buddhist nuns who survive in the Far East derive their ordination tradition from Sri Lanka. Ceylonese nuns also established an ordination tradition in Burma, where it lasted longer than in Ceylon: there is inscriptional evidence for a Burmese nunnery in 1279.[106]

Royal purifications and the transfer and restitution of the ordination tradition represent the formal side of the Sangha's revival. But the revival of Buddhism is always founded on the revival of scriptural knowledge. Carrithers has devoted a fine book[107] to such a revival, the forest hermitage movement which has gathered momentum in Sri Lanka over the last hundred years. He demonstrates[108] that even the intimate practice of meditation has probably been revived from written sources, not handed down from teacher to pupil in uninterrupted succession. *A fortiori*, more overt practice can be and has been revived by reference to books. The scriptures, once written down, have been able to bridge the gaps in living tradition created by historical vicissitudes.

In Sinhalese public opinion there seem always to have been two conflicting views about the state of the Sāsana. The view that it is in decline goes back, we saw, to the Buddha himself. There is a popular tradition in Sri Lanka that the last Enlightened person in the country died in the first century BCE.[109] On the other hand, the Pali commentaries and chronicles both state and imply that ancient Ceylon was full of Enlightened monks. There are even anecdotes about how people tested or contested claims to sainthood. Curious laymen devised little ruses to see whether an alleged saint took fright easily or salivated at the sight of food. A major component of the popular image of the saint was that he controlled his body and always preserved decorum.[110] Rahula sums up his fascinating chapter on this topic by saying that saints 'were evidently not expected to be entirely free from … minor blemishes, such as pride and love of display', but 'should have a reputation for deep piety and scrupulousness in observing the precepts' and miraculous powers were a bonus.[111] I doubt whether expectations are very different today.

The character of Sinhalese Buddhist religiosity

To conclude this outline, I give a few brief indications of the place Buddhism has held in the hearts of the Sinhalese. Some kings in the Anuradhapura period went so far as to offer the kingdom as alms, either to the Sangha or to a relic (in practice not an important difference). Others offered themselves and/or their families to the Sangha as slaves and then redeemed themselves, thus combining a symbolic gesture of total humility with extreme munificence.[112] (There are Hindu parallels: one mediaeval rite was for the king to weigh himself against gold or silver, which he then distributed to brahmins.[113]) The king in the first century CE who 'offered himself, his queen, his two sons, his state-elephant and his state-horse to the Sangha,'[114] despite the monks' remonstrances, and then redeemed the offering with vast munificence to both monks and nuns, was probably trying to emulate the generosity of the Buddha, who in his penultimate birth on earth, as Prince Vessantara, was banished for giving away the state-elephant, then gave his horses and carriage, and finally gave his wife and two children – but got everything back in the end, when his father the king had redeemed the children against their weight in gold.[115]

Many other instances of great royal piety are recorded. King Duṭṭhagāmaṇi is said never to have eaten without offering food to the Sangha.[116] A later king always ate from the Sangha's public refectory, presumably after the monks, like a servant of theirs.[117] One king in the first century CE had such respect for a certain learned monk that when the monk had a boil on his finger he took the finger in his mouth (a recognized remedy for that affliction) and then when the boil burst was too deferential to spit out the pus but swallowed it.[118]

Since our records of ancient India sadly lack such detailed stories from real life, and moreover are rarely so well dated, it is worth remarking on the quality of piety such incidents reveal. In Hinduism, the kind of extravagant devotion (Sanskrit: *bhakti*) which is manifested in self-surrender (*prapatti*) and servitude (*dāsya*) to the object of adoration is usually considered to begin towards the middle of the first millennium CE. We have shown how Buddhists from the earliest times declared their conversion by 'taking refuge' in the Three Jewels. This expression is a hallmark of Hindu theistic devotion, but it seems to occur in Hinduism for the first time in the *Bhagavad Gītā* and other parts of the Hindu epic, the *Mahābhārata*, which are not normally dated before the third century BCE at the earliest. The Pali commentaries specify a form of 'taking refuge' in which one dedicates one's labour to the Three Jewels in voluntary servitude.[119] Such religious servitude is also reflected in proper names like that of Buddhadāsa ('Buddha's slave'), the late fourth-century king of Ceylon.

Royal gestures of humility are often merely rhetorical, and may tell us little about personal feelings. But swallowing pus does not have the ring of a mere publicity stunt. Modern writers conventionally portray – or caricature – Theravāda Buddhism as a religion of bloodless reason in contrast to the emotional warmth of theistic Hinduism. But these stereotypes probably depend in part on the nature of our sources. The subject deserves more research; but my guess is that the apparent dearth of emotion in early Indian religion is due to its being censored out by the intelligentsia, both brahmin and heterodox, just as they censored out the widespread practice of possession. The Sangha, guardians of Buddhist orthodoxy, have allowed emotion to play little part in their soteriology, but these fragments of evidence suggest that emotional worship and religious self-surrender came early to Theravāda Buddhism.

For the mass of the Sinhalese people, however, the single most important feature of Buddhism is undoubtedly the ideal it presents of civilized conduct.[120] Robert Knox, the shipwrecked English sailor who lived as a captive among the Sinhalese from 1659 to 1679, during a black period for the Sāsana, wrote of them: 'They do much extol and commend Chastity, Temperance and Truth in words and actions; and confess that it is out of weakness and infirmity, that they cannot practice the same . . .'[121] When at least the precept survives, practice can always follow.

So much for kings and commoners. As for the Sangha, the range of life-styles from pomp and pelf to the humblest frugality has been a social reality. But few monks live at the extremes, either joining in the life of the world to the exclusion of any personal piety or shunning mankind and striving for salvation without a care for others. It is the duality of purpose, to care for oneself *and* others, which has provided the dynamic for the Sangha's historical development.

CHAPTER SEVEN

Protestant Buddhism

The nineteenth century was a watershed in the history of Buddhism in Ceylon. In 1796 the British succeeded the Dutch as rulers of the maritime provinces, the 'Low Country', a term which referred to the now comparatively populous and developed west and south of the island, with its capital at the port of Colombo. In 1815 they acquired control of Kandy, the city in the central highlands which had been the capital of the Sinhalese kingdom since the sixteenth century; they thus acquired political control over the whole island, a control they were not to relinquish till 1948. While a few of the kings over the previous centuries had favoured Śaivism at the expense of Buddhism, 1815 was the first time in its recorded history that the whole island had been brought under foreign domination and Buddhism had accordingly lost its symbolic place at the head of the nation's affairs. On the other hand, it was also the first time since about the end of the twelfth century that the island was brought under single rule. There were small local uprisings against the British in the Kandyan provinces in 1818 and 1848, and disturbances (Buddhist-Muslim riots which the government aggravated by seriously over-reacting) in 1915; but otherwise the country was not only unified but completely peaceful till Independence.

The Sangha was used to a history of decline and reform. After a long period of decline under the earlier kings of Kandy, when not only the higher ordination but all contact with the ancient monuments and centres of civilization in the northern plains was lost, a revival was initiated in the mid-eighteenth century by the monk Saraṇaṃkara and his patron King Kīrti Śrī Rājasiṃha (ruled 17 who was a great benefactor to Buddhism, probably for political re rather than from personal piety.[1] The re-introduction of the hig ordination from Thailand in 1753 marked a notable revival in Buddhist learning and in the power and wealth of the Sangha. When the dynasty fell and the kingdom came to the end of its two-thousand-year history, it must have seemed that the revival was destined to be brief. Gradually, indeed, the Sangha did begin to suffer the effects of the lack of state support and control which we have discussed above – and which this period enables us to trace and document in detail for the first time. Unity was lost and laxity went unchecked. But this time not all was decadence. The government interfered very little with traditional Sinhalese culture and social arrangements, and the country was prosperous. In 1824 the population of the entire island was only about 850,000;[2] by 1891 it had risen to over 3 million, of whom 2 million were Sinhalese.[3] It doubled again before Independence. In 1891 there were nearly ten thousand members of the Sangha, and there were internal reform movements of the traditional kind looking for purification in the simple life. Hardly an institution in its death throes. Around 1960 there were about 17,000 monks and novices in a Sinhalese population of about 7 million.[4]

If one takes the long view of history, one can argue that such fluctuations in the fortunes of the Sāsana were perhaps neither greater nor different in kind from some previous vicissitudes. It is for a different reason that I consider the nineteenth century a watershed. It is because during that century Buddhism began to change its character. Not in the countryside or the Kandyan provinces, not as yet in a way to affect more than a very small segment of the Buddhist population. But by the end of the century quite a new kind of Buddhism had taken definite shape and begun to spread from the middle classes in Colombo. In 1892 the Anglican Bishop of Colombo published a rather well-informed book about Buddhism, in which he wrote:

> There are two Buddhisms now in Ceylon: the residuum of the old Buddhism of the past centuries, as it lingers in out-of-the-way places, and as it has shaped the habits and ways of those who are not under European influence; and a new revival, much more self-conscious and artificial, which aims indeed only at reviving what Buddhism always professed to be, but which has been influenced, in its estimate of that profession, very largely by Europeans.[5]

This new kind of Buddhism has been brilliantly analysed by modern scholars. Professor Bechert has called it 'Buddhist modernism', Professor Obeyesekere 'Protestant Buddhism'. Like Dr Malalgoda, on whose fine work I draw heavily in the following account of its origins, I shall use the latter name because it has so many illuminating implications. For this movement in Theravāda Buddhism – which began in Sri Lanka but has by no means been confined to it – both originated as a protest (against Christianity) and itself reflects Protestantism. Its salient characteristic is the importance it assigns to the laity – and the correspondingly lesser importance it assigns to the Sangha. Indeed, we can begin our account of it by pointing out that the very view of Buddhist history on which this book has been based, that which identifies the fortunes of Buddhism with those of the Sangha, would be questioned by Protestant Buddhists. For they regard all adherents of a religion as equally responsible for its welfare. It is precisely because this view appears as a natural one to modern western readers, with their centuries of Protestant experience, that its novelty needs to be emphasized.

To the creation of Protestant Buddhism two kinds of influence have contributed. The primary credit must go to Protestant missionaries, and to a handful of other westerners influenced by them, anti-missionary missionaries: the Theosophists. But their seed would not have fallen on fertile ground – to use the kind of image they loved – had the peace and prosperity of the nineteenth century not brought about socio-economic changes. A new Sinhalese middle class of bureaucrats, businessmen and professionals (lawyers, doctors, school-teachers, intellectuals) arose, centred on Colombo; the kind of religious individualism which had appealed to businessmen in northwest Europe from the Reformation on appealed to them too. As had happened when the Buddha first preached, the urban middle class seized the religious leadership; Buddhism for the second time began a Protestant reformation. This time, as in the European case, it was based on another effect of British rule: the use of printing, and hence the increase of reading (in this case, notably of reading English).

The disestablishment of the Sangha

The two stories, that of the Sangha's disestablishment and of its loss of influence to the laity, are connected. The traditional identification of the Sangha with the Sinhalese 'establishment' is encapsulated in the refusal by the Sangha's headquarters, in the late eighteenth century, to ordain anyone not of the top caste.[6] All forms of power and prestige were the prerogative of the dominant caste. But in the maritime provinces, long under European rule, the dominant caste no longer dominated. The 'fisher' caste, there second in rank and size, was rising in entrepreneurial activity; the castes third and fourth in rank and perhaps in size (it is no accident that these tend to be correlated) rose with them. All these three castes are sparsely represented in the Kandyan region. In 1799 a monk from the *salāgama* caste, who had mainly been cinnamon-pickers and soldiers, set off with five novices and three laymen for Burma. His enterprise was financed by a layman of his caste. 'Upon their arrival in Amarapura, the then capital of Burma, the Ceylonese party was received by the reigning monarch Bodawpaya (1782–1819) himself';[7] and the Burmese Sangharāja presided over their ordination in 1800. They returned to Ceylon in 1803. In 1807 three further and separate missions, one from each of the three castes mentioned, set off for Burma, and all in due course returned successfully with higher ordinations.[8] Together, these groups constituted the Amarapura Nikāya. By degrees, they obtained official recognition from the British government. Registration with the government became the act critical for a *nikāya* to establishing legal authority.

As Malalgoda says, the creation of the Amarapura fraternity was unprecedented. It did not depend on the patronage of the Sinhalese king but on the relatively small-scale initiatives of private citizens; 'on the other hand, in adopting as its raison d'être the protest against a royal decree (relating to caste exclusivism) it successfully questioned for the first time the right of secular authorities to regulate the affairs of the order.'[9] It was monks of this Nikāya who were to lead the protesting reaction to Christianity.

In 1815, when the British were invited by Kandyan nobles in revolt against their king to assume control, they promised in their treaty with the chiefs that 'The Religion of Boodhoo professed by the Chiefs and Inhabitants of these Provinces is declared inviolable, and its rites, Ministers and Places of Worship are to be maintained and protected.'[10] The treaty was drawn up by John D'Oyly, an Englishman who had lived for some years in the area and knew Sinhala well; an English friend described him as 'little different from a Cingalese hermit', and some even suspected him of being a crypto-Buddhist. This article of the treaty embarassed the British government, and was strongly attacked by evangelicals such as William Wilberforce.[11]

In the Kandyan kingdom the king was not only ultimately responsible for the supervision of monastic temporal possessions and the enforcement of ecclesiastical juridical decisions; he also appointed the heads of many monasteries.[12] Even the recent Hindu dynasty had fulfilled these functions, realizing no doubt that this was a sign of their legitimacy – something also perceived by D'Oyly and the contemporary governors. But the missionaries campaigned against the connection between the British Crown and 'heathenism', so that after D'Oyly's death in 1824 the government gradually dissociated itself from Buddhism.[13] This withdrawal accelerated in 1839 when the Methodist missionary Spence Hardy published his pamphlet *The British Government and the Idolatry of Ceylon.* Immediately the British Governor refused to sign the 'Acts of Appointment' of monastic incumbents, making it an issue of conscience. These Acts of Appointment had replaced the Kandyan ceremonies of installation as legal recognition of ecclesiastical office. As the government withdrew, monks could enforce their rights only through the civil courts, and for that they needed valid acts of appointment. Till 1840 the British courts upheld traditional monastic jurisdiction. But when officials became reluctant to sign Acts of Appointment, all fell into chaos; for instance, one of the two chief monasteries in Kandy was without a head in 1845–9 and 1851–3. In 1853 the government decided, though still against missionary opposition, to issue 'Certificates' of appointment; but these certificates merely stated as fact that an incumbent had been duly elected by the other monks. Unlike the Acts, the Certificates stated no approval; crucially, they did not command the office-holder's subordinates to obey him.[14] Though the Supreme Court decided in 1871 that the British Crown had inherited from the Sinhalese the right to exclude monks from their temples for wrong-doing,[15] the ecclesiastical hierarchy had lost government support to enforce its authority, and could neither control misuse of their temporalities, nor, even more important, enforce expulsions from the Order on account of immorality, without recourse to civil courts, a 'costly and uncertain'[16] affair. In so far as the British Christian government did harm to traditional Buddhism, this process of disestablishment was its single most important cause. It was an unintended, though to the British not an unwelcome, consequence of the government's action (or inaction). In 1847 the British government gave up its custodianship of the Buddha's tooth relic in Kandy,[17] the traditional palladium of Sinhalese royalty; instead, they allowed a large Anglican church to be built next to the Temple of the Tooth. It is perhaps fair to add that the Anglican church was disestablished in Ceylon in 1880.[18]

The British missions

The main missionary organizations were established in Ceylon between 1805 and 1818; the most important were those of the Wesleyans (Methodists) and of the Church of England.[19] Despite their association with the ruling power, their lack of success is remarkable. The number of Christians in that period is hard to gauge, because births could only be registered after baptism in a Christian church, and such registration was vitally important for legal claims to legitimacy and inheritance. The missionaries were worried by the problem of nominal Christians, but at the same time could rarely resist the temptation to maximize their conversion figures.[20] Even so, the Christian population in 1891 was only just over 300,000, about 9½ per cent of the total,[21] and of these the large majority were Roman Catholics, descendants of those who had been converted under the Portuguese. The main Christian influence on Buddhists was by reaction.

The missionaries propagated Christianity in three main ways: by education, preaching, and pamphleteering. Every mission station had a primary school, and the Church of England ran a collegiate institution to train school-teachers and ordinands. The government also controlled some parish schools, which survived from the Dutch period, and administered them through the School Commission, a body heavily weighted with Christian clergy. This body was replaced in 1869 by the completely secular Department of Public Instruction. Till then, it totally controlled government schools and made financial grants to others which qualified. Although the traditional Sinhalese system of education, temple schools run by local monks, persisted all over the island, those schools never qualified for grants, even after the secularization of government control, because the monks failed to meet official standards in such matters as regular attendance and approved curricula. All the officially approved schools were Christian; and all Christian schools taught in English, and were thus the necessary approach to government service and worldly advancement.[22] The first hour of the day was dedicated to religious instruction; in 1841 parents were given the right to object, but we know of several schools where this right was never used.[23] Not only did they not wish to displease the teachers; the non-exclusivist traditions of Buddhism were still operating, so that probably most of them really did not mind. Most pupils continued to be Buddhists at home and attend Buddhist festivals. Presumably more males than females were converted. Being used to the idea that different religious systems catered to different spheres of life, presumably Buddhists could adapt to the idea that Protestant Christianity (which in Ceylon includes Anglicanism) was now the religion of state ceremonial and public life. This is not to deny that someone who attends church and studies the Bible, for whatever reason, may be influenced by the content of what he hears and reads.

The missionaries were crippled by their inflexibility. They worked hard to learn Sinhala, but then insisted that the Bible be translated into 'plain speech', using only one word for 'you', the second person pronoun. The result would be absurd in almost any language but English, and to make matters worse, trying to keep close to the Biblical 'thou', they chose the pronoun *tō*. This was not in ignorance. The chief translator admitted: 'To apply *tō* to a man of respectable class is an actionable offence: and, I believe, damages have actually been awarded for it ...' When the translation was introduced in church in Colombo the Sinhalese walked out in protest against the insult to God, and petitioned the bishop against it.[24]

The same rigidity characterized the missionaries' dealings with Buddhists, and hampered them in their preaching. From the first they courted encounters with the Buddhists, and were merely infuriated by the refusal of monks to take up the challenge. In 1823 it was written of a Methodist missionary:

> influenced by a desire to become intimately acquainted with the superstitions of the natives, that he might be the better prepared to expose their absurdity and sinfulness, Mr. Clough took every opportunity of being present at their religious services, and endeavoured on such occasions to engage the priests in conversations on religious topics, in the hearing of their followers.[25]

During a great religious festival outside Colombo, the local C of E missionaries systematically destroyed their hitherto amicable relationship with the local Buddhist monks by turning up every night for the whole week of the festival and distributing a specially printed pamphlet on 'the sin and folly of image-worship' with particular reference to the on-going ceremony.[26]

However, the missionary preferred to venture alone *in partibus infidelium*. In 1849 the headmaster of the Government Central School in Kandy resigned to be a full-time missionary, 'following the example of the Apostles, yea of the Saviour himself' by travelling on foot and enduring privations.[27] Since preaching is of course also a Buddhist practice, the itinerant missionaries might have made some impression had they made concessions to local custom; but this was quite contrary to their spirit and intention. Not only did they continue 'plain speech' and address their audience indiscriminately with a derogatory pronoun; they ignored all questions of decorum and Sinhalese notions of suitable time, place and manner for preaching. The result was that the Baptist missionary Ebenezer Daniel wrote in 1840, 'We often meet with little but contempt, opprobrium and laughter,' and recorded that villagers often asked him, 'Will you give us arrack if we listen to you?'[28] The question is significant. In 1848 the Government Agent of the Central Province (Kandy) pointed out that in 30 years of rule the government had opened four schools in his province and licensed the erection of 133 arrack taverns. After 1850, some missionaries did engage in temperance work (now that the need had arisen), but Malalgoda notes that they never voiced as much opposition to the government's connection with the liquor trade as they had previously voiced to its connection with Buddhism.[29]

The great technical innovation of the missionaries, and one which was to have a profound influence, was their use of the printing press. The first Sinhala press had been established by the Dutch government of Ceylon in 1736; it was used mainly to print Christian propaganda. The second was imported for the same purpose by the Wesleyans in 1815. The Anglicans and the Baptists then each set up their own.[30] From the start, what was printed was more polemical than merely expository. With typically military metaphor, Gogerly, the manager of the Wesleyan Press, wrote in 1831, 'At present it is by means of the press our main attacks must be made upon this wretched system.... We must direct our efforts to pull down this stronghold of Satan.'[31] Those responsible estimated that between 1849 and 1861 1½ million tracts (in both Sinhala and English) circulated among the Ceylonese population[32] of about 3 million, of whom many could not read.

For the first 50 years of this onslaught the Buddhist response was eirenic. About 1835, to Christian horror, a Buddhist priest wrote a tract saying that Christ had been incarnated on earth after an existence in heaven (just like a Buddha), was virtuous and benevolent, and taught the truth in so far as he understood it.[33] Unlike many brahmins in

India, Buddhist monks did not shun contact with Europeans, and two learned monks had even assisted with the first translation of the Bible into Sinhala (not the one using *tō*). Some monks allowed missionaries to use their preaching halls, and were puzzled when their reciprocal requests were refused.[34] Writers in the 1850s remark on the lack of hostility to Christianity and on the monks' co-operative attitude in lending manuscripts from their libraries and explaining their contents. But this lack of opposition merely irritated the missionaries. The most famous one, the Methodist Spence Hardy, when on his preaching rounds, usually spent the night at the village temple, where the monks treated him kindly. This he could only attribute to their 'indolence, apathy and indifference in all matters concerning religion'.[35] Of monks' faces he wrote that 'there is often an appearance about them of great vacancy, amounting almost to imbecility'[36], and he believed that many were illiterate. He wrote in 1850, 'It is almost impossible to move them, even to wrath.'[35] But on returning to Ceylon after an absence of 15 years, Hardy was delighted to note that the pernicious vice of tolerance was on the wane, that monks would no longer co-operate with missionaries, would no longer explain or lend their books, but had bought presses and were printing tracts.

> I have formed bright anticipations as to the future. There can be no doubt as to the result of the contest now carried on; for although it may be prolonged and severe, it must end in the total discomfiture of those who have risen against the Lord and his Christ, and in the renunciation of the atheist creed that now mars the happiness, and stays the enlightenment, of so many of the dwellers in Lanka.[37]

The Buddha would go the way of 'Jupiter and Mars, Woden and Thor'.[38] That was in 1863.

If for a long time Buddhists made no attempt to refute the missionaries' arguments this was mainly because nothing was put forward that seemed worth refuting. But in 1832 the Methodist Daniel Gogerly started learning Pali, then learnt Sinhala, and in 1849 published *Kristiyāni Prajñapti* (*The Evidences and Doctrines of the Christian Religion*). Part 2 of this work, on the evidences for Christianity, such as miracles, was based on Paley's famous work of 1794; part 1, more original, compared Buddhist and Christian doctrine. This work was reissued several times, and Gogerly's Sinhalese protégé, David de Silva, published many tracts based upon it. The appeal now was rather to reason than to emotion, and Gogerly's work contained many quotations from the Pali scriptures.[39]

Early Buddhist reactions

Theravāda Buddhists had not yet printed their scriptures, and indeed it was a long time before some monks could be persuaded of the utility of doing so. The first Buddhist press was in Colombo. Significantly, it had originally been imported by the Church Missionaries (Anglican) in 1823; they sold it off to an employee in 1855. The second was set up independently in 1862 by a Buddhist monk in Galle, the largest town in south Ceylon; he kept it going with the help of his friend King Mongkut of Siam, who himself during his monkhood had been the first Siamese to establish a printing press.[40]

Who wrote for these presses? Two monks spear-headed the Buddhist response. The Galle publications were mainly by Hikkaḍuve Sumangala (1826–1911), a monk of much learning and generally traditional opinions. It is typical that he had been baptised in infancy; this merely indicates that he came from a good-class family.[41] In Colombo, the leading Buddhist was Mohoṭṭivatte (*alias* Migeṭṭuvatte) Guṇānanda (1823–90), who in 1858 became the sole incumbent of a suburban monastery. In 1862 he founded a society, the Sinhala name of which, literally translated, was The Religious Society for Giving Increase to the Teaching of the Omniscient One, but in English was called The Society for the Propagation of Buddhism, in imitation of the Society for the Propagation of the Gospel. These discrepant translations epitomize a contrast between Buddhism and neo-Buddhism. This society acquired the press which had belonged to the Church Missionaries, and their first publication was a reply to *Kristiyāni Prajñapti*, begun as a monthly periodical in June 1862. Next month Gogerly started a rival periodical and in the same year Sumangala started his. For three years there was a succession of such periodicals on both sides. Gogerly died in 1862, and was succeeded as head of the Wesleyan mission by Hardy, who set about learning Pali. But after a while no one would teach him, 'even for high reward'. Times had changed. Hardy returned to England in 1865, this time for good, and Christian leadership in controversy devolved on David de Silva.[42]

At almost the same time as the Buddhists took to printing tracts, they at last began to accept the Christian challenge to public debate. In

1864 the Anglican Seminary challenged the monks of the local temple, and were surprised – and presumably gratified – when they accepted. They were even more surprised in February 1865, when the debate took place, for nearly fifty monks, including Sumangala and Guṇānanda, turned up, and so did about two thousand Buddhist laymen. Because of disagreement on procedure, this debate finally took the form of an exchange of questions and answers in writing; and a similar event later in the year took the same form; but this was followed by a series of live public debates.[43] In almost all the major encounters Guṇānanda took the leading part on the Buddhist side. Indeed, he plausibly claimed in 1887 that over 25 years he had given over 4,000 public lectures and sermons.[44] The most important debate in which he took part was held at Pānadura, south of Colombo, in 1873, with David de Silva as his principal opponent. It took two days. On the first day the audience was estimated at 5,000, on the second day at over 10,000. This debate was a turning point. The audience was of course predominantly Buddhist and fiercely partisan; their shouts of victory echoed far and wide.[45] The missionaries realized now that they had misjudged the situation, and issued no further challenges. But to consider the debate a victory of Guṇānanda, one did not have to be present. The entire debate was published in the newspapers, both Sinhala and English, and the English version then appeared in book form. It was this book which reached Colonel Henry Steele Olcott, co-founder of the Theosophical Society, with far-reaching consequences.[46]

It is in these beginnings that the mirror-image nature of the Buddhist reaction to Protestant attacks is particularly evident. Traditionally Buddhist monks preach seated, and often holding a fan in front of their faces, in order to render the sermon as impersonal as possible. We know that Guṇānanda, at least in public debate, adopted the Christian style of preaching; he spoke standing, gesticulated, and generally acted the orator.[45] To some extent his matter too was copied from the Christians; as they questioned the historicity of his scriptures, he impugned the historicity of theirs, and so forth. An example: though the issue may seem to us rather peripheral, a favourite subject of Christian attack was Buddhist cosmology, with its numerous heavens and hells, as it was 'in antagonism to the most obvious teachings of science'. But for Guṇānanda this was child's play: he counter-challenged his evangelical opponents to locate their own heaven and hell in the cosmos, and when David de Silva said that no explorer had yet discovered Mount Meru, the traditional Indian *axis mundi*, Guṇānanda countered by asking where lay the Garden of Eden.[47] He and other Buddhist controversialists relied at first solely on their own ideas and Biblical reading, but soon discovered useful material in western authors. The great English secularist Bradlaugh was first translated into Sinhala in 1872, the year before the Pānadura debate. Christian scholarship also came in useful. In 1863 Spence Hardy introduced his book *The Sacred Books of the Buddhists Compared with History and Modern Science*: 'the method that Bishop Colenso employs, unsuccessfully, in his attack upon the Pentateuch of Moses, we may employ, successfully, in exposing the 'unhistorical' character of the Pitaka of Buddha.'[48] One can imagine how this approach boomeranged.

For all his adoption of Christian techniques, and even his use of western materials with which to attack Christianity, Guṇānanda's view of his *own* religion was still a traditional one; he was a Buddhist monk who had learnt Buddhism from his preceptor in the traditional way. Religious controversy by public debate was not untraditional in Buddhism – in fact there had been a good deal of it within Ceylonese Buddhism earlier in the nineteenth century – and in his method of argument Guṇānanda was still decisively influenced by the old school. In 1878 he republished a classical Pali text, *The Questions of King Milinda*, in which a monk unravels knotty points in Buddhist doctrine, and remarked in the preface that it was 'unsurpassable as a means for learning the Buddhist doctrine ... or for the suppression of erroneous opinions.'[49] Indeed, within a decade he was to attempt to suppress the erroneous opinions of Protestant Buddhists. Already, in the Pānadura debate he explicitly dissociated Buddhism from Newtonian cosmology. By contrast we shall see below that when Buddhist laymen came to take the lead in religious controversy they claimed that Buddhism was not merely rational but had anticipated the discoveries of modern astro-physics[50] and other sciences.[51]

The rise of the Buddhist laity

The salient characteristic of Protestant Buddhism is the enhanced importance of the laity. In 1904 Sumangala was among several prominent monks who addressed a Memorial of the Sangha of Ceylon to King Edward VII; in it they wrote 'By the laws of Buddha the laity form no part of religion. The Sangha are the only living representatives of Buddhism on earth.'[52] This slightly exaggerated statement was provoked by remarkable developments within Buddhism in the previous 30 years, some of them unintended consequences of Sumangala's own actions. It was in the field of education that the Buddhist laity first came to the fore. Monks could and did answer the misionary challenges in preaching and printing, but for the running of schools they lacked the organizational structures and probably the administrative experience. During the first fifty years of British rule the small village temple school seems to have flourished in the Low Country, but declined in the Kandyan provinces. However, these schools, with their archaic curricula and lack of English, could not compete with the Christian schools. In 1869, the year in which the Department of Public Instruction was founded, a Buddhist monk organized the opening of the first non-monastic Buddhist school in Ceylon, with a headmaster who was a convert from Christianity and had been educated at a mission school.

There is very little evidence about the extent of literacy among the Sinhalese laity before the nineteenth century. In 1821 male literacy was estimated as being 'almost as general as in England'.[53] That has been estimated for the period at just over 60 per cent.[54] It seems reasonable to suppose that even in its periods of decline the village Sangha had imparted literacy to a fair number of high-caste males. But as there was hardly any Sinhalese printing before the nineteenth century, and manuscripts were virtually confined to monasteries, even the literate can have had nothing to read: earlier lay Buddhists lived in an essentially oral culture. Schools and printing presses combined in the late nineteenth century to produce a lay reading public for the first time in Sinhalese history. For the middle classes, however, this literacy was primarily in English. This gave them access to modern knowledge and allowed them to communicate with the wider world; at the same time, it often alienated them from the traditional culture.

The danger of such alienation was apparent to active Buddhists, and they began to harness the educational revolution to their own requirements. A landmark in the history of Buddhist doctrine was the foundation of Vidyodaya Piriveṇa, a Buddhist ecclesiastical college, in 1873.[55] Already in 1864 two prominent Buddhist laymen from Colombo had written a letter to the press suggesting the establishment of a college of Buddhist studies, with £10,000 capital. The idea was novel and it took nine years to raise enough money to start Vidyodaya.[56] In this decade the institutions started by monks, notably the two presses and the non-monastic Buddhist schools just mentioned, ran into financial difficulties and collapsed. Sumangala became the principal of Vidyodaya. In this capacity he was assisted by a lay management committee which included several leading entrepreneurs, including a

Colombo furniture dealer called Hewavitharanage Don Carolis, and his father-in-law Don Andris Perera.[57] Two years later, in 1875, two monks founded Vidyālaṃkāra, a similar Buddhist college.[58] Both these colleges admitted both clergy and laity. These two institutions, both in Colombo suburbs, continued for nearly a century as the leading educational institutions for Buddhist monks; they were given full University status in 1959. They have both been cradles of Protestant Buddhism, and crucial for feeding that movement back into the mainstream of Buddhism via the clergy whom they educate.

The impact of the Theosophists

Enter the Theosophists. The Theosophical Society was founded by Madame Blavatsky and Colonel Olcott in 1875 in New York; its headquarters moved to Adyar, near Madras, in 1879. In that year Bishop Copleston, the Anglican Bishop of Colombo, wrote to the Society for the Propagation of the Gospel:

> The secretary of an obscure Society – which, however, for all the Sinhalese know, may be a distinguished one – has been writing, it appears, to several Buddhist priests here, hailing them as brothers in the march of intellect, and congratulating one or two of them on the part they took so nobly against Christianity in a certain ill-judged but insignificant public controversy which took place years ago in a village called Panadura. These letters the priests have printed in a little pamphlet, along with some selections from an English book, which describes some spiritualistic performances of Buddhist priests in Thibet.[59]

The secretary was Olcott, and the English book was *Isis Unveiled*, which Madame Blavatsky had presented to Guṇānanda. In the same year the same bishop wrote: 'Buddhism as a whole is not conquered, or near it.... There is little doubt that Buddhism is far more vigorous in Ceylon than it was 150 years ago.'[60] He was more observant than Spence Hardy, and perhaps more prescient.

A few months later, in May 1890, Blavatsky and Olcott arrived in Ceylon. They took the Three Refuges and the Five Precepts, thus formally embracing Buddhism. For the Buddhists this was a victory indeed. Olcott was a colonel and a judge; he was also an experienced organizer and fund-raiser. Moreover, as an outsider he was in a unique position to unite the different factions among Sinhalese Buddhists. Two weeks after his arrival in Ceylon he lectured at Vidyodaya on 'Theosophy and Buddhism'. His aim was to set up a branch of the Theosophical Society in Ceylon; the Sinhalese of course were more concerned with their confrontation with Christianity. In the event Olcott set up two branches, the purely Theosophical one, which never flourished and soon died, and the Buddhist Theosophical Society (BTS), which was Theosophical only in name. Buddhist Theosophy was in fact Protestant Buddhism.[61]

In 1881 Olcott published – of course in English – his *Buddhist Catechism*, which was his attempt to formulate the basic tenets to which he felt all Buddhists in the world should be able to subscribe. This document, which has gone through many editions, not all of them bearing Olcott's name, deserves to rank as a Theosophical rather than a Buddhist creed, but this is not widely realized, notably in Britain, where the connections between Theosophy and organized Buddhism have been intimate. The *Buddhist Catechism* represents the beginning of the modern world Buddhist movement. Olcott likewise devised the Buddhist flag which has been adopted by the World Fellowship of Buddhists[62] and is in widespread use today; it is composed of the five colours of the Buddha's halo. The very idea of having a Buddhist flag springs from Olcott's American background. I think that the institution of singing carols at Wesak, the traditional anniversary of the Buddha's birth, Enlightenment and death, is Olcott's answer to Christmas carols; the English ones have fallen into desuetude, but Protestant Buddhists still sing Sinhala songs at Wesak. The same analogy with Christmas underlies the flourishing modern trade in Wesak cards.

Olcott was delighted by his reception in Ceylon, and continued to visit it nearly every year until his death in 1907. The Buddhists trusted him so well that in 1884 they made him their representative to the Colonial Office with full discretion, and empowered him 'to accept and register as Buddhists persons of any nation who may make to him application to administer to them the Three Refuges and Five Precepts and to organize societies for the promotion of Buddhism'. This was written by seven monks headed by Sumangala, who till his death was chairman of the clerical division of the BTS. His traditional Buddhist ideas made him a personal rather than an ideological friend of Olcott. In 1903 Olcott wrote of the clerical division, 'I have not been able, during an intimate intercourse of twenty-two years, to arouse their zeal', and for his part Sumangala resigned from the BTS in 1905, in protest at what seemed to him Theosophy's greater identification with

Hinduism, though he withdrew his resignation on Olcott's personal assurance and appeal. Relations between Olcott and Guṇānanda were worse: in 1887, shortly before his death, Guṇānanda wrote in Sinhala a kind of Buddhist catechism in answer to Olcott's, and in its preface he emphasized the need to reassert the true doctrines of Buddhism. In the same year he invited Olcott to lecture at his temple, and after Olcott's address delivered a passionate attack on Olcott and the BTS in Sinhala.[63]

Guṇānanda's attack on the BTS was probably motivated, like Sumangala's later resignation, by the spectacle of Buddhist leadership passing into lay hands; for it was the lay division of the BTS, with its local sub-divisions, which was really active and effective. This part of the BTS ran the schools which Olcott helped to found, and which were perhaps the most enduring part of his achievement in Ceylon. In 1881 he went on fund-raising tours especially to raise money for Buddhist education, and by 1889 there werre 63 BTS schools and another 40 Buddhist schools (mostly with lay managers) registered with the government. BTS schools were modelled on the missionary schools, down to the cricket; education was in English, and Buddhism took the place Christianity held in the missions. Monks were not prominent as either teachers or managers of BTS schools.[64] Some of these schools became very important, and their sponsorship only changed in 1961, when the government nationalized almost all independent schools.

From now on Buddhist lay organizations proliferated, and continued to be modelled on Christian organizations. The Young Men's Buddhist Association was founded in 1898 by a Buddhist convert from Roman Catholicism; one of its aims is: 'to advance the moral, cultural, physical and social welfare of Buddhists'. In practice the YMBA has paid little attention to the Y, but developed into the most important lay Buddhist organization in Ceylon, its leadership being known nowadays as the All Ceylon Buddhist Congress.[65] It was the YMBA which set up a national network of Buddhist Sunday Schools and commissioned, printed and distributed the texts for them, till these functions were taken over in the 1960s by the government. The BTS founded two newspapers, the Sinhala one in 1880 and the English one in 1888. In 1889 Buddhist laymen began to be involved in the administration of the Sangha's temporalities.[66] The management of Sangha property has remained a controversial topic, and the reports of the largely lay commissions which have been set up to investigate it are important documents of Protestant Buddhism.[67]

Anagārika Dharmapāla

We must return to the family of Hewavitharanage Don Carolis. His father-in-law, Don Andris Perera, was president of the Colombo branch of the lay BTS from 1883 to 1890.[68] His son, born in 1864, became the most important figure in the modern history of Buddhism. His given name was Don David Hewavitarne, but he is usually known as Anagārika Dharmapāla, a name and style which he assumed in 1881.[69] Shortly before his death in 1933 he became a monk and took a new name, but that too is little remembered. The name Dharmapāla means 'Protector of the Dhamma' – Defender of the Faith. The title *Anagārika* was an innovation. The word is Pali (and Sanskrit) and means 'homeless'; traditionally it was one of the epithets of Buddhist monks, but never a title. Dharmapāla used the term to designate a new status, to which we return below.

Dharmapāla was to become a national hero of Sri Lanka. For a time in the 1960s there was even a national holiday in his name, though later, because of the proliferation of holidays, it was subsumed in National Heroes' Day, which is January 1st. All over the Sinhalese parts of Sri Lanka urban streets are named after him. His biographer has even proposed him as a *bodhisatta*, and he apparently considered himself to be one.

His father was a social parvenu in Colombo, so that Dharmapāla was born into a rising but perhaps somewhat frustrated middle-class family. He was educated at a Roman Catholic primary and an Anglican secondary school in Colombo, there being no Buddhist schools there then. His recollections of his schooldays are strongly coloured by his hatred of Christianity, and we must allow for exaggerations, but it does appear that he despised his Anglican schoolmasters for eating meat and drinking alcohol, and above all for shooting birds. 'The gentle religion of Buddhism' he associated with his Buddhist mother; like most pupils at mission schools, he practised Buddhism at home. Nevertheless he was obviously good at his scripture lessons; he learnt chunks of the Bible by heart, and his later writings and speeches are full of Biblical quotations and Biblical language. His biographer tells us:

> One Sunday he was quietly reading a pamphlet on the Four Noble Truths, when [the boarding master of the school] came up to him and, true to missionary tradition, demanded the offending work from him and had it flung out of the room. . . . The climax of his criticism was reached when he drew a picture of a monkey

> and wrote underneath it 'Jesus Christ', for which piece of juvenile impudence he was threatened with expulsion from the school.

However he finally left the school not because of religious odium, but because he found the food inedible. (Food of course is a symbolic idiom.)

David Hewavitarne, as he still was, heard the Panadura debate, and came into personal contact with Mohoṭṭivatte Guṇānanda in 1878. He met Olcott in 1880 on his arrival in Ceylon, sometimes acted as his interpreter, and worked for the lay BTS in several capacities until he quarrelled with the Theosophical Society and parted company with it in 1898.[70] In 1884 he visited the world headquarters of the Theosophical Society at Adyar, near Madras, with the Society's leader, Madame Blavatsky. He adored her and considered her a Buddhist, whereas she seems to have acted as something of a mother figure to him till her death in 1891. Later in life he was patronized in a similar way by an elderly American widow. While working for the Theosophists, Dharmapāla travelled widely. In 1889 he accompanied Olcott to Japan and established the first direct contact between the Buddhists of Japan and Ceylon.

In 1891 he visited Bodh Gayā, the spot where the Buddha attained his Great Enlightenment, Mahā Bodhi. The focus of Buddhist pilgrimage was then almost derelict, and the site owned by a Hindu priest, the incumbent of a modern Śaivite temple nearby. In his poem *Buddha at Kamakura* Rudyard Kipling wrote in 1892:

> Yet Brahmans rule Benares still,
> Buddh-Gaya's ruins pit the hill,
> And beef-fed zealots threaten ill
> To Buddha and Kamakura.

It became Dharmapāla's principal ambition to change all that. He took up the struggle against beef-fed Briton and superstitious brahmin. In 1891 he founded in Ceylon the Maha Bodhi Society, with Hikkaḍuve Sumangala as President and himself as Organizing Secretary. The primary aim of the Society, which was only realized long after Dharmapāla's death, was to win back for Buddhists ownership of the Bodh Gayā site: the case was pursued through law courts. Another aim was to found at Bodh Gayā an international Buddhist high school; though this has never been done, it betokens the close involvement of early Protestant Buddhism with schooling. Within a year Dharmapāla moved the headquarters of the Maha Bodhi Society to Calcutta, where they have been ever since. One reason for the move was that Dharmapāla's militant Buddhist nationalism was getting him into difficulties in Colombo. But the move also served his general purpose: to unite and activate the Buddhists of the world. The Maha Bodhi Society has in a general way been quite successful and can be said to represent the reality rather than the rhetoric of a world Buddhist movement in modern times.

In 1893 Dharmapāla, still under Theosophical patronage, represented Buddhism at the World Parliament of Religions in Chicago. He made less impact there than Swāmi Vivekānanda, who represented Hinduism and made himself a figure on the world stage. Vivekānanda and Dharmapāla occupy comparable positions in their respective religious and national traditions; they share many attitudes and aspirations, and even their English rhetoric is similar. It is striking that although Dharmapāla, who was finally exiled from Ceylon in 1915, was to spend much of the rest of his life in India, Buddhists and Hindus have never paid any attention to the similarity, nor did the two leaders make common cause. (They seem to have fallen out in 1897.) From the Indian side this is understandable because politically, and even culturally, Dharmapāla represented only a tiny minority of a very small nation. But the Buddhists' total lack of interest in Hindu nationalism and reform[71] requires more explanation. The tradition of the *Mahāvaṃsa* which defined Sinhalese Buddhist identity in contradistinction to Tamil Hinduism provides part of the answer. However, as we have briefly indicated, for most of their history the Sinhalese Buddhists, though intermittently in conflict with the Tamils, remained open to Indian cultural influences. Kandy was even ruled by an Indian dynasty for the last centuries of its independence. But colonial rule weakened the links between Ceylon and the mainland, especially after the British took control of the whole island. India and Ceylon came under different ministries in London. In Ceylonese schools Britain, not India, was the foreign civilization presented for emulation, and to this day Sinhalese schoolchildren learn next to nothing about India; even Gandhi is little known.

His indifference to India was thus typical of Dharmapāla's background and of the people he influenced. His Sinhalese Buddhist nationalism was perhaps the one feature of Dharmapāla's ideology and activity which one could consider perfectly traditional; but even this found novel expression. In 1906 he founded a nationalist newspaper,

Siṃhala Bauddhayā ('The Sinhalese Buddhist'). In his writings he idealized the pre-colonial past. Both style and content of his nativist rhetoric owe much to a Christian education. 'The sweet gentle Aryan children of an ancient historic race are sacrificed at the altar of the whisky-drinking, beef-eating belly-god of heathenism. How long, Oh! How long will unrighteousness last in Ceylon.'[72] In *A Message to the Young Men of Ceylon*, first published in 1912,[73] he wrote,

> But the Sinhalese today being ignorant of the deeds of their noble ancestors, have lost all hope of development. Our ancestors like the ancient Greeks were free from pride, envy, crime and luxury. There were no capitalists and landowners, but every one had his own garden, hena field, and the village forest, and the village pasture ground gave them the right to graze their cows and cut firewood. Buddhism gave them the religion of the Middle Path, and the Sinhalese did not care for wealth but cared more for virtue and courage.[74]

He wrote in Sinhala as well as in English, but his Sinhala was in a sense a mere translation from the English, what linguists call a 'calque'; he did not write in a traditional Sinhalese manner, or address himself to a traditional Sinhalese audience, but to an educated bourgeoisie, most of them probably bilingual.

Dharmapāla gave the layman a new place in Buddhism which went much further than organizational leadership. Traditionally lay Buddhists did not meditate; those who wished to meditate gave up the lay life. Moreover, there seems to have been very little meditation in Ceylon in the late nineteenth century. In 1890 Dharmapāla found in an old Buddhist temple a text on meditation, which he studied and ultimately caused to be published.[75] He practised meditation on the basis of this study, and thus became, so far as is known, the first Buddhist to learn meditation from a book without recourse to a master. Moreover he initiated the fashion for lay meditation, which has become so popular among the bourgeoisie of Colombo and Rangoon that few if any of them realize the untraditional nature of their activities.[76]

Lay religious activism

We come now to the heart of the Protestant Buddhist ethos. It is encapsulated in the title Anagārika. With it Dharmapāla invented a status half way between monk and layman as these roles were traditionally understood. Instead of the monk's yellow robe he wore a white robe, and he did not shave his head, but he formally undertook a life of chastity and ascetic abstention. He took the Eight Precepts (see above p. 76). Traditionally Buddhist laymen may take these vows on Buddhist holy days (*poya* days) for spells of 24 hours; and a few old people take them permanently; but Dharmapāla took them for life while still a young man. He thus made a dramatic public commitment to devoting his life to Buddhism, but without renouncing worldly – notably political – activity. By devoting his life to Buddhism Dharmapāla meant not merely, in fact not primarily, seeking his own salvation, but promoting the Sāsana, and indeed the general welfare of Buddhists as he saw it. Dharmapāla accepted the Christian criticism of monks as selfish, even to the extent of publishing a reference to 'monks who ... exist only to fill their spittoons.' Spence Hardy could have done no better.

The historical Anagārika became a popular symbol, but the new status failed to catch on; the reason for both things is that within a short time many monks became socio-politically active, while many laymen became this-worldly ascetics. This convergence superseded the need for a label – everyone, so to speak, is an Anagārika now. The influence of Christianity is even more clearly visible in the present situation than in the case of the *anagārika* status, which, though it arose out of the confrontation with Protestantism, was not founded on a Christian analogue. Now, on the other hand, we have Buddhist monks who are prison chaplains, even army chaplains, who are missionaries abroad, and who work as salaried teachers in lay schools, and court involvement in politics and social welfare activities. Their role is very like that of a Christian clergyman. And the Protestant Buddhist layman sees his role much as the Protestant layman sees his: he is not content with a merely supportive role, dependent on the clergy, but is independently active, even in doctrinal debate. Such Buddhists are not the majority of Sinhalese Buddhists, who until recently were still peasants, but a large minority, typically urban or suburban and socially mobile.

In general terms it is clear that this Protestant revolution in Buddhism was connected, like the original rise of Buddhism itself, with urbanization and the rise of a bourgeoisie. On this occasion the priestly class whose religious monopoly the newly prosperous laity wished to break were not brahmins but Buddhist monks. The Protestant Buddhist emphasis on control of formal education was significant. In seventeenth-century England, Peter Laslett has written, the clergy lost 'their function as the official intelligentsia'.[77] We can conjecture that the phrase would be applicable to the brahmins of Bihar in the fifth century BCE. It was doubly appropriate to the monks who witnessed the rise of a middle class in a British colony in the late Victorian era. The first generations to be exposed in school to the vast array of modern secular knowledge held those unaware of the modern world in some contempt. This explains how Dharmapāla, a Buddhist nationalist campaigning against British rule, could at the same time write:

> Europe is progressive. Her religion is kept in the background [... and used] for one day in the week, and for six days her people are following the dictates of modern science. Sanitation, aesthetic arts, electricity, etc., are what made the Europeans and American people great. Asia is full of opium eaters, ganja smokers, degenerating sensualists, superstitious and religious fanatics. Gods and priests keep the people in ignorance.[78]

Dharmapāla worked hard – and successfully – to inculcate into the middle classes of Colombo (it can at first hardly have amounted to more than that) some of the values of this-worldly asceticism (as Weber characterized Calvinism). Like all Protestant reformers, he preached such virtues as honesty, diligence and thrift. We have seen that these were the values that the Buddha preached to the laity. The *Advice to Sigāla*, the Buddha's most famous sermon on lay ethics, which we have discussed above, was sometimes known in Sinhala as the 'Disciplinary Code for the Laity'. Dharmapāla published a Sinhala pamphlet under precisely this title, *Gihi Vinaya*, in 1898. It has run through some 20 editions and sold about 50,000 copies. It can be said to apply Protestant values to the details of daily life, very much on the model of any late Victorian manual of etiquette. The aim throughout is to elevate rustic manners. The pamphlet contains 200 rules on such subjects as conduct recommended for women, children and servants, table manners, and how to use the lavatory. In its more ethical aspects, as in relations between the master of the house and his dependants, the booklet stands in the tradition of the *Advice to Sigāla*. But when Dharmapāla prescribes use of the fork, an object hardly known in Sri Lanka below the upper-middle class, the specifically western model is evident. This was true in less trivial matters as well. Thus Dharmapāla and the other early Protestant Buddhist lay leaders preached a sexual puritanism to such effect that not only has monogamy become the norm of the Sinhalese bourgeoisie; it is believed, quite incorrectly, to be the traditional norm. The bourgeoisie have adopted western Victorian morality, and the contemporary West is considered lax and corrupt in falling from that standard. By a similar misunderstanding Dharmapāla considered caste to be un-Buddhist.

This last misunderstanding is of great importance for what has perhaps been the most insistent theme of this book. Religious individualism – which we have tended to dub 'Protestantism' – does to some extent imply religious egalitarianism. Certainly for the Christian Protestants it carried that implication. It carried it for the early Buddhists too, in that they believed all human beings to share the capacity for spiritual progress. But that did not lead them (as it did the more extreme Christian Protestants) to deny all social status: they accepted a fundamental divide between those who had left the world and those who remained in it, and the social distinctions prevalent among the latter. They thus accepted also, as I have shown, a distinction between a soteriology and a communal religion appropriate to those who remained in society.

Dharmapāla accepted the western Protestant view of religion as one and the same for everybody. It would never have occurred even to his anti-Christian friends the Theosophists, with their own Protestant backgrounds, to question this assumption. So Dharmapāla saw Buddhist soteriological doctrine and activity as equally applicable to everyone. Laymen should meditate. 'Gods and priests', the stuff of communal religion, could have no place in the lives of good Buddhists. The communal religion which in fact the Sinhalese were practising must therefore be due to pernicious Hindu influence.

Other characteristics of Protestant Buddhism

As early as 1847 a Sinhalese Christian wrote in an essay 'On the Corruption of Buddhism . . .': 'It is to be hoped that if Buddhism can be brought back to its early principles and doctrines, it will be simply a kind of abstruse and metaphysical philosophy . . .'[79] This analysis of the Buddhism in front of them into ancient philosophy plus folk superstitions came easily to Protestant fundamentalists who had been used to defining their position vis-à-vis Roman Catholicism. Dharmapāla accepted the dichotomy; but he had also learnt from anti-Christians such as Bradlaugh that Buddhism, since it denied an omnipotent creator God, was rational, in fact not even a 'religion' at all, but a philosophy. I have shown elsewhere[80] that the attempt to translate into Sinhala the English sentence 'Buddhism is not a religion' in a school textbook issued by the government has led to ludicrous self-contradiction.

We find intertwined three characteristics of Protestant Buddhism. It tends to fundamentalism, despising tradition; it claims that Buddhism is 'scientific', 'rational', 'not a religion', etc.; and it depends on English concepts, even when expressed in Sinhala. The fundamentalism comes direct from the Protestant missionaries, the claims of rationalism from their opponents, the English cast of thought from both. The fundamentalism also received an impetus from western scholarship, which began to make the Pali texts more accessible. T.W. Rhys Davids, who had been a colonial administrator in Ceylon, founded the Pali Text Society in London in 1881 and printed the Canon in roman characters before it had been printed in Sinhala characters; moreover, the Pali Text Society began issuing English translations of canonical texts while most of them were unavailable in Sinhala. This makes more understandable the following statement by Mr S.W.R.D. Bandaranaike, who in 1956 was elected Prime Minister as a Sinhalese Buddhist nationalist and whose policy of promoting the use of the Sinhala language soon led to riots. When it was proposed in the Ceylon Parliament in 1944 to make Sinhala the official language, the policy he later espoused, he said:

> My hon. Friend ... thought that the Sinhalese language was necessary from the point of view of a closer study of the Buddha's teaching, culture, doctrine and so on. For that purpose English may be more useful than Sinhalese. At least one would have to know Pali.[81]

Mr Bandaranaike had been brought up as an Anglican and claimed to have first learnt about Buddhism at Oxford.[82]

In traditional Ceylon most of the Canon only existed in Pali. Most of the Buddha's sermons, for example, have been translated into Sinhala only recently, and I am told that the language of the translations is so learned that only those highly educated in Sinhala can understand them. The English-educated middle class will have access to the texts primarily through English translation, the villager through the digests provided in modern educational materials. Thus, while Protestant Buddhism is intimately connected with literacy, most lay Buddhists still have access to most of their scriptures only at second hand and cannot, like Bible-reading Protestants, study them for themselves.

No traditional Buddhist would say (as I believe traditional Roman Catholics have been known to say) that a layman would be ill advised to study the original scriptures by himself; still less would they deny that Buddhism is rational, philosophical, even scientific; but the issues never posed themselves in these terms. Dr G.P. Malalasekera, who was at various times Professor of Pali, High Commissioner for Ceylon in London, and editor of the *Buddhist Encyclopaedia*, wrote:

> The Buddha was the first great scientist to appear among men. The Buddha discovered what scientists have only now discovered, that there is nothing called matter or mind existing separately in this world but they are the result of forces which continually cause them to come into operation and that they dissolved and came into operation again ...[83]

This is not nonsense, in that the Buddha did indeed enunciate a doctrine in roughly these terms. But to call the Buddha the 'first great scientist' is a typical Protestant Buddhist attempt to beat the modern West at its own game. A more extreme case is Professor K.N. Jayatilleke, who during the 1960s was considered by middle-class Sinhalese Buddhists as the foremost Buddhist intellectual of the day. He was the sole Professor of Philosophy at the University of Ceylon and an indefatigable lecturer in both Sinhala and English. He applied his considerable learning, intelligence and expository powers to proving that every major intellectual development in the modern world was anticipated by the Buddha. In the Buddha's sermons, according to Jayatilleke, we can find the theories of Marx, Freud and Wittgenstein; even the discoveries of astro-physics – galactic clusters and the expanding universe. Jayatilleke was also much concerned to prove the theory of rebirth empirically, and held that this had been achieved. For if Buddhism is not a religion founded on faith but a philosophy founded on reason, such scientific procedures are appropriate and even necessary.

Limited scope of Protestant Buddhism

Protestant Buddhism crystallized in the figure of Dharmapāla. For the first half of the twentieth century Ceylon remained under British rule – Independence came in 1948 – and the Sinhalese for the most part remained divided into two classes of very unequal size: a small, urbanized and largely English-educated middle class and a traditional peasantry. To these two classes corresponded the two types of Buddhism I have tried to characterize. The Sangha continued to recruit predominantly from the countryside. Those monks who progressed for their education to one of the Colombo colleges were exposed to the views of such lay intellectuals as Malalasekera and Jayatilleke; but when they returned to their village incumbencies those concerns must have seemed to most of them rarefied and remote. Many took up the traditional life of the village Sangha, their intellectual horizons perhaps having been broadened and their feelings of social responsibility somewhat enhanced. It became normal for the village monk to supervise a village Sunday school, using the course booklets and entering pupils for the examinations of the YMBA; and monks often assumed the presidency of local welfare organizations, Village Development Committees, etc. A minority of them – one would guess mainly those 'younger sons' whose prospect of succeeding to an incumbency was negligible – decided not to fit back into the traditional mould and became salaried schoolteachers or found some other living away from the village; it is a safe assumption that a fair proportion of them ended by reverting to lay status. Some monks interacted with western scholars; during the period of British rule traditional learning flourished in the Sangha, producing many fine scholars.[84] However, the Sangha (in the strict sense – I shall talk of nuns below) found no new organizational forms and underwent no development which might have counterbalanced the rising tide of lay leadership. Since that tide was but dimly perceived as a problem – despite the early protest of Sumangala and his colleagues – the lack of an organized response is not surprising.

CHAPTER EIGHT

Current trends, new problems

In the previous chapter I assigned the rise of a new brand of Buddhism, which I labelled 'Protestant', to two overlapping causes: the influence of the British, especially their Protestant missionaries, and the rise of an urban middle (including professional) class. The British and their missionaries have left, and indeed many Sinhalese Protestant Christians have formally reverted to Buddhism; the middle class, of course, is still there and the cities continue to grow, while the countryside too is being urbanized. One can therefore ask, a whole generation after Independence, which features of Protestant Buddhism seem likely to be of permanent influence and which were more evanescent products of narrow circumstance.

The polemical rhetoric of Dharmapāla has virtually disappeared, now that its targets have retreated over the horizon. A few intellectuals continue to argue that traditional Buddhism is 'corrupt' and one must be guided only by the Canon, and that Buddhism is nothing but true rationalism, science, or what have you; but with the decline of English education in the 1960s and 1970s these issues have become somewhat obsolete, except in very general terms of sloganeering. Sufficient awareness of them to provide a basis for such slogans has been widely diffused by the educational system, especially by such school textbooks as the one mentioned above, which tried to teach six-year-olds that 'the Buddhist religion is not a religion'.

Religious pluralism

What has been irrevocably lost, as I argued in the Introduction, is the perception of the Sāsana as unique and *sui generis*: contact with the wider world, now formalized in the apparatus of government, has lined up Buddhism, Hinduism, Islam and Christianity as the four religions of Sri Lanka, four objects on a par. (That the state assigns Buddhism a 'special place' is irrelevant to this subtler concern.) The recurrent claim that Buddhism is *not* a religion on a par with others but something of a different order, maybe a 'way of life', so that the other religions are or may be compatible with it, is, among other things, an attempt to reclaim Buddhist uniqueness. What is being claimed, usually in a very vague and muddled way, can be expressed in my terms: that the other religions are all right on the communal level, but only the Buddha pointed the true way to salvation. Liberal Buddhists add that you do not have to call yourself a Buddhist to follow the Buddha's way.

The new ethos

Dharmapāla condemned belief in gods, and he and his close followers rejected the traditional communal religion of the Sinhalese. Such radicalism is now virtually unknown. It survives among the middle class and educated as bad conscience, that if they were true Buddhists they 'ought not' to worship the gods for favours or placate demons. It even leads to a good deal of hypocrisy, and uncertainty about what one does 'really' believe in. But the 'systems of patterned interaction with superhuman beings' (see p. 25 above), far from declining, have been acquiring new strength.

What has survived of Protestant Buddhism is its central feature, the emphasis on lay religiosity. The layman should permeate his life with his Buddhism; this means both that he should himself strive for *nibbāna*, without necessarily entering the Sangha to do so, and that he should do what he can to make Buddhism permeate society and the lives of others. This new religious ethos of course fits the new view of Buddhism as a total religious system on a par with Islam or Christianity. Since all share the same religious goal, *nibbāna*, the prime soteriological activity, meditation, is appropriate for all: monk and layman, male and female, young and old.

In an important respect the values of these Protestant Buddhists differ from the 'this-worldy asceticism' of both Weber's Calvinists and the first generation of Buddhists. A strong streak of Dharmapāla's puritanism remains. But the attitude to making money is more negative: there is no norm directing that one should save money – and then invest it profitably. One reason for this, as Bechert has shown,[1] is that in public life Buddhism identifies as anti-capitalist, capitalism having been equated with colonialism. Another, as we shall show below, is that these Buddhists are applying the values of the renouncer to everyday life in the world and so feel guilty about money-making, which is easily stigmatized as 'greed'. This is however not to say, of course, that individual Protestant Buddhists do not closely conform to the Weberian pattern. We find rich, self-made men in the lay Buddhist leadership. But they do not display their wealth as proof of their righteousness; rather they act as if they were atoning by this piety for their excessive worldliness.

Unintended consequences of lay religious activism

I ended the last chapter by saying, perhaps rather provocatively, that lay leadership was not clearly perceived as a problem. The reader may ask why it should be a problem at all. My answer is that the new religiosity entails various unintended consequences for the very content of Buddhism. In particular, lay leadership has the same effect as in Protestant Christianity: sect formation. This has till now gone more or less unnoticed. As we have explained, in traditional Buddhism the Sangha has been the only body capable of forming 'sects', because it is the only formally organized religious institution: the laity have no organization which can split. And the Theravādin Sangha has split over matters of practice, not doctrine; in modern times the main issue that has split the Sangha into separate *nikāya* has been caste. Laymen who consider that the Sangha have no essential role to play in their religious lives are free to go their own way. In recent research in urban Sri Lanka, Obeyesekere and I have found small bodies of Buddhists perfectly analogous to Christian sects. One of them centres on a self-ordained 'monk', others are led by laymen who claim special insight into religious matters. These groups do not consider themselves 'sects' (whatever that might be in Sinhala) or formally define themselves and membership is generally acquired by participation rather than a formal ceremony of initiation. They do not define themselves for the same reason as they are not recognized as distinct bodies: the very idea of a lay Buddhist sect is completely alien. Moreover, none of these bodies has yet devised an institutional framework which may survive the removal of the charismatic founder; they may thus all turn out to be ephemeral. If they are, we are sure that others will take their place.

Naturally, like sects everywhere, these sects claim not to be deviant from the main tradition but on the contrary to be the *true* Buddhists: it is everyone else who is out of step. In particular, the degenerate Sangha have lost the way. So far as I know, these 'true' Buddhists all are tolerant towards other religious traditions, which they claim to be compatible, on a low level, with their own views. They merely claim to overcode other religions (of which they tend to be fairly ignorant), including Buddhism: those are all mere 'religions', which preach the same thing but take you only so far, whereas we have the ultimate Truth. That all religions say much the same thing (if correctly understood) was first preached in Ceylon by the Theosophists; and I have found specifically Theosophical influence still quite strong in the more middle-class sects. But the characterization of one's own religion as *not* a religion but something on a higher plane of generality – an attitude very unlike that of Christian sects – I have shown to be widely characteristic of contemporary Buddhism under modern influence.

Since Obeyesekere and I are about to publish a book on the urban religion of Sinhalese Buddhists, in which some of these sects will be described, I shall say no more of them here. They are in any case quite small bodies of people. Here I shall only comment briefly on the trends in modern Buddhism which find extreme expression in the sects but are quite widespread. In fact, although traditional Buddhism and Protestant Buddhism can always be isolated as pure types, on the ground they are mingling and influencing each other more all the time. It is becoming more and more common to find a distinctly 'Protestant' element in a generally traditional environment (typically a rural village), and the urban, educated and middle-class Buddhist may equally have traditional attitudes and practices. This mingling, like the rest of the religious scene, is not to be explained purely by the interaction of ideologies, but by socio-economic trends. These too are discussed in our forthcoming book; I shall just signalize the most important.

Recent economic and social developments

The greatest change in Sri Lanka since Independence has been demographic. During the Second World War the British, having regard for the safety of their troops, virtually eradicated malaria. This had a dramatic effect on the death rate of the local population. Since Independence the population, which is about two-thirds Sinhalese, has more than doubled. It is now (late 1984) nearing 16 million and rising at $1\frac{3}{4}$ per cent per annum.

This population explosion has almost destroyed the traditional village community. Much of the countryside has become so densely populated that the boundary between one village and the next has no social meaning; it is a line drawn on a map by an administrator. Most Sinhalese villages used to be estates in which land was held by the members of the dominant caste, farmers, on whom the other castes depended for employment. There is now not enough land in these villages for even members of the farmer caste to make a living. Probably the majority of 'peasants' have thus become landless. These poor people have tended to migrate, in three directions.

Firstly, some move to other villages. Rural population density and greatly improved communications (mainly buses) have led to the breakdown of the traditional system of cross-cousin marriage; people now go much further afield for marriage partners, so that marriage no longer reinforces existing or presumptive ties. This is itself both an effect and a further cause of the breakdown of community.

Secondly, the major economic effect of the government has been directed towards opening up new areas to rice cultivation. Large irrigation schemes on the northern and eastern edges of the Sinhalese part of the country have been populated by 'colonies'. The colonists have for the most part been heterogeneous, drawn from those poor constituents who have managed to attract the favour of powerful MPs. In the most recent colonization scheme (1984) the government is trying to avoid this mistake by moving whole communities; even so, the dislocation is immense: shrines and temples cannot be moved, and to the best of my knowledge it is rare for a Buddhist monk to move with the rest of the villagers.

But the largest migration is to the cities, especially Colombo. It is no longer possible to draw a meaningful boundary round either Colombo or Kandy: the urban penumbra continues for many miles into what looks like countryside, and it is common to commute up to 50 miles to a job in the city. Even Colombo dockers may live in apparently agricultural villages. And among the commuters are many who do not have jobs but are looking for ways to make a living. For there has arisen, virtually since Independence, a vast new socio-economic class – not all, of course, either Sinhalese or Buddhist: not so much a proleteriat, neither an industrial workforce nor entirely urban, but a huge number of poor people living in and around the cities and major towns who depend on those towns for their subsistence. It is among such people, some of them geographically uprooted, others merely deprived of their traditional means of life and community support systems, that one would expect to find new religious developments. And we did.

Economic performance in the face of this population crisis has been sadly inadequate. Sri Lanka has so far preserved the forms of parliamentary democracy. But state *dirigisme* has increased: politicans, thinking that they know best, have greatly increased state intervention in the economy. As wealth has failed to increase – sometimes at all, let alone in step with the population – few political leaders have resisted the temptation, at least when in opposition, to divide the population by appeals to envy. Each community, seeing itself grow poorer, has been incited to blame the others and believe them better off. Sinhalese Buddhist nationalism, the lowest common denominator between traditional and Protestant Buddhism, has been nurtured by politicians; the Sinhalese, the majority community, have blamed their economic backwardness on the Tamils. In recent years some of the Tamils, themselves increasingly pauperized, have responded with terrorist violence. In July 1983 this provoked a terrible Sinhalese response. While Buddhist governments may hope to follow in the footsteps of Asoka, they have taken the road of Duṭṭhagāmaṇi, and it is frightening to think where that may lead.

Hinduizing trends

From the political point of view it must seem paradoxical that the religious effect of this sad situation has been what one could well call a wave of Hinduization. We have mentioned above (p. 170) the emotionalism which swept through Hinduism after the middle of the first millenium CE, partly displacing and otherwise oddly complementing the classical religions which sought salvation through the suppression of the emotions. In emotional *bhakti* religiosity, which originated among the Tamils, unreasoning and uncompromising devotion to God was held to be the path to salvation. Hindu *bhaktas* (devotees) have a personal deity (Sanskrit: *iṣṭa-devatā* – literally 'chosen deity') whom they worship for favour which will protect them in this world and take them to heaven in the next.

The traditional Sinhalese pantheon has become quite disordered in the mental world of the new urbanites. Their disorientation in this world is reflected in a cosmology in which power and goodness are no longer correlated and the law of *kamma* seems of remote relevance compared to the special effects which constantly intervene, products of black and white magic, demonic possession or the favour of a guardian deity. In fact, though probably no Buddhist would ever deny the supremacy of the Buddha and his Teaching, many of the poor in this milieu have so little contact with Buddhism as traditionally understood that it does not affect their lives. Their religious concerns are focused on thaumaturgy and their relations with their personal deity.

Traditional gods like Viṣṇu, to whom the *Mahāvaṃsa* attributed the duty of protecting the Sāsana in Ceylon, have lost ground in popularity to hitherto little-regarded gods like Kālī, the terrible goddess whose lolling tongue drips with blood. The newly popular gods share the characteristic of having a terrible aspect, which of course they turn towards the enemies of their devotees; since they punish as well as showing favour, they are of a different moral stamp from the benign Buddhist deities traditionally thought to merit worship: in traditional Buddhist cosmology punishment, which is always ultimately just punishment, is meted out by demons.

The cult of Kālī has for the most part been taken over directly from the Tamils, and so has the firewalking and much else that goes on at Kataragama, the famous shrine to the god of that name in the south-eastern corner of the island. Early in this century, the god's annual festival used to be visited almost entirely by Tamils, some of them making the pilgrimage from the Indian mainland. It is now reliably estimated that during the fortnight of the festival over half a million people, most of them Sinhalese, visit the shrine. Few of these visitors are traditional Buddhist villagers. At this shrine, at Kālī's temple at Munnessarama, and at other shrines to gods which until recently were considered the exclusive cultural property of Tamil Hindus, congregate Sinhala-speaking devotees, nominally Buddhists or even, in a few cases, Roman Catholics, whose ecstatic devotion manifests itself in possession, firewalking, and inflicting on themselves such apparent tortures as hanging themselves up on meathooks – activities in which their guardian deity protects them from pain or permanent damage.

The decline of rationality

These activities are as untraditional for Sinhalese Buddhists as the spirit that informs them. We have stressed in our account of classical Buddhism the importance attached to awareness of one's actions and to calm self-control. Hysterical possession, we remarked, is the polar opposite of this desired condition. Routinized possession has traditionally been practised by certain Sinhalese religious functionaries, but they recognized the supremacy of Buddhist values by not performing in their roles on *poya* days. With this exception, a Sinhalese Buddhist who became possessed was considered to be in the grip of a devil and had to be 'cured' by exorcism. Now, however, all that has changed. When somebody first manifests signs of possession, the initial assumption is still that it is the work of a bad spirit. But frequently the person possessed resists cure and manages to convince those around that the possession is by a good spirit, either a deity or (even more bizarrely, from a traditional point of view) a benign dead relative. Such people, who may be of either sex, may then set up a shrine to their personal deity in their homes and even act as mediums to help others with their problems, either gratis or for a fee.

This cosmology and its attendant practices are less 'rational' than those of traditional Sinhalese Buddhism, in that they do not form a coherent system. In time, greater consistency may well emerge. For the moment, what strikes the observer is the widespread flight from the rational and interest in every form of the occult: palmistry, table-tapping, hypnotism, astrology. Astrology is a pseudo-science traditionally of great importance in Indian culture, traditionally not unknown in Sinhalese culture and considered compatible with Buddhist cosmology. But like all forms of divination it has greatly increased, a product no doubt of the widespread anxiety which there seem to be few rational means to allay. It is noteworthy that again it is Tamils who are generally credited with being the best astrologers. For example, one particularly famous Buddhist monk visits Madras about once a year to consult an astrological bureau there, not only for himself but also on behalf of some of the nation's leaders. Monks are traditionally supposed to take no interest in such matters, but a breach of this principle (it is not a formal rule) was no doubt a common and trivial occurrence. What flagrantly violates tradition is that whereas astrology has traditionally been used only for the present life, this famous monk has used it to find out about his former lives and also about the future after his death.

The crisis of authority

The last few paragraphs have mainly concerned communal religion, not soteriology. One can well argue that the ideas and practices mentioned, while they belong to Buddhists, are not part of their Buddhism. There are, however, important connections. If the traditional authority structure of the pantheon has broken down, this is because society too has no clearly perceived authority structure, and an important aspect of that human anomie is the displacement of the Sangha from the sole and undisputed position of authority in spiritual matters, so far as many contemporary Sinhalese are concerned. Many professionals, intellectuals and businessmen decide for themselves on religious matters, following the advice of a meditation teacher – often a layman – or even an Indian guru: Sai Baba is popular with the middle classes. Nominally, perhaps even stridently, they are Buddhists; but in practice they are following 'the religion of their choice'.

Altered states of consciousness

But the most striking connection between changes in the communal religion and Buddhist soteriology concerns the cultivation of altered states of consciousness. Meditation, as I have shown elsewhere,[2] has become a popular lay leisure activity, mainly among the middle classes. Some of this meditation is expertly taught and supervised, and may well achieve admirable effects on traditional lines. Many people, however, are attempting to learn meditation by themselves or under a teacher whose eccentricity they do not recognize (as in the sects). Our fieldwork leaves no room for doubt that many people who practise meditation are achieving altered states of consciousness. Whether these states are those recommended by the Buddhist tradition it is perhaps impossible for an outsider to judge. Certainly, however, in so far as a meditating monk attained such states, he did so in a rigid institutional framework which guided his reaction to his experience and presumably came to control the experience itself. But many contemporary meditators have no such guidance or control. The results can be bizarre.

We have encountered cases of people who in the context of worshipping gods enter an altered state of consciousness which they interpret as possession, and in the context of doing Buddhist meditation enter an altered state of consciousness which they interpret as a *jhāna*, one of the stages of progress towards complete concentration and equanimity recommended in the Pali Canon and Theravādin tradition. Since possession is total loss of self-awareness and Buddhist meditation is supposed to increase awareness, the two alterations of normal consciousness should be changes in the opposite direction. But the ease with which our informants slip from one to the other leaves us no room for doubt that for them the two states are in fact the same, only their interpretations differing with context. A third interpretation we have encountered of a state which again, in the same way, seems to be interchangeable with *jhāna* is 'hypnosis'. These informants tend to use their power to alter their states of consciousness to effect cures and otherwise help people; they are certainly sincere and well-meaning. However, we deduce that they are interpreting loss of normal awareness, the dissociated state which Freud and Breuer called hysteria, as the goal of Buddhist meditative practices. To interpret impaired awareness as heightened awareness is a dangerous confusion; it bodes ill for the propagation in society of reasonableness and self-control.

Using Buddhism for this world

To use *jhāna* (as subjectively conceived) for 'welfare work' (white magic) is probably still rare. Though we found possession becoming common, to use one's states of altered consciousness for the good of others is the recognized role performance of the religious virtuoso, or the professional. But the urban and suburban middle-class Sinhalese is coming to use meditation as something useful in daily life. A short period of meditation every day, some hold, will enable them to run their lives more efficiently. This message has been preached by such movements as Transcendental Meditation in the West, and no doubt a period of enforced silence and tranquillity is an excellent addition to the daily routine of a harassed businessman or bureaucrat. But to use Buddhist meditation for such a purpose, rather than as an end in itself, is a major innovation. And perhaps a risky one. For Buddhist meditation, which was developed by and for renunciates, cultivates feelings of detachment from the world. People who use it while still involved in family life and economic activity will therefore find themselves torn: making money will appear as 'greed', making love to one's spouse as 'passion'. It seems that lay meditators, followers of the Anagārika, do tend to celibacy, which may be distressing for their spouses.

To use meditation for secular purposes is to try to adapt Buddhist soteriology to life in the word. One could say that it was Dharmāpala's implicit programme to use for communal religion (a concept which of course he did not have) nothing but materials drawn from Buddhism proper. It is in this spirit that modern Sinhalese are Buddhicizing their weddings. The traditional Sinhalese wedding, which has some affinity to non-brahmin south Indian custom, was a secular affair; nothing Buddhist occurred in it, and there were no religious functionaries of any kind. In middle-class weddings it has become customary for girls dressed in white (the colour traditionally associated with mourning) to recite some of the Pali verses of blessing which form part of *pirit* ceremonies. This is a Protestant Buddhist imitation of bridesmaids. Buddhicization has taken another stride in Colombo, where weddings have been held on monastic premises. Moreover, the incumbent has arrived immediately after the ceremony to bless the couple. It is traditional for a bridal couple to visit their local monk at some time before or after their marriage, but this is quite another matter. Tradition is still too strong for a monk, who represents the values opposed to marriage, to officiate at a wedding, but nowadays at fashionable Colombo weddings a Buddhist layman in 'brahmin' garb performs a marriage service allegedly modelled on that of Gotama himself.

Developments in the Sangha

The Sangha as a body has made no planned or even conscious response to these changes. It could not, for it has no central authority. Even the leaders and executive committees of the separate Nikāyas remain concerned only with the purely monastic questions within their traditional jurisdiction.

A development of major significance is that the Sangha, *de facto* though still not *de jure*, is once again an organization of both sexes. Strictly speaking, there are still no 'nuns' in Sri Lanka, as the higher ordination for nuns has not been reintroduced. There are, however, many ladies who wear yellow, shave their heads, and lead cloistered lives observing the same restrictions as if they were nuns. They have taken the Ten Precepts; in the stricter 'convents' also live ladies wearing white who have taken the Eight Precepts, and are the precise equivalent of novices in monasteries. The most important body of such 'nuns' is led by a lady called Sister Sudhammā, who enjoys immense prestige and is in great demand as a preacher. She was launched on her career with help from prominent Protestant Buddhists, but there is nothing particularly untraditional about her views or her movement. She receives hundreds of letters every month from Buddhist women who wish to join one of her convents; she admits applicants only after rigorous screening. Other organizations are not so choosy.

I have suggested in the Introduction that the Order of nuns may soon be formally reconstituted in the West. If a body of educated opinion in Sri Lanka becomes aware that there is nothing inherently Mahāyānist about the *vinaya* of the Mahāyānist nuns of the Far East, the Sangha of nuns may be revived in Sri Lanka, and that would certainly strengthen organized Buddhism. There will be no shortage of postulants. Throughout society women are assuming roles previously reserved for males, not always without male resistance (which may be partly responsible for the failure to ordain proper nuns). It is moreover reasonable to guess that the extinction of the Order of nuns in a society inculcating the value of renunciation left among women an unfulfilled demand.

There have been conspicuously successful developments within the traditional Sangha. Michael Carrithers, in documenting the contemporary hermitage movement,[3] has shown that somewhere in the island the best in Theravādin tradition is preserved as a living reality. I have myself recorded[4] how one monk who has participated in the hermitage movement, the Ven. Pānadurē Ariyadhamma, evolved in the early 1970s a new form of public worship of the Buddha which appealed to enormous numbers of people. It clothed traditional sentiments in modern forms.

It can hardly be coincidental that the Ven. Ariyadhamma is from an urban background, is quite well educated, and became a monk as an adult. I know of no study of modern monastic recruitment, but it is a safe guess that the great majority of monks continue to be recruited when children from a rural background, and therefore also to receive their schooling (unless and until they go to university) in purely monastic institutions. Though these monastic schools incorporate some 'modern' subjects in the curricula, they hardly give the kind of education which will enable their pupils to impress the general public with their intellectual grasp of the modern world. Among those monks and novices who attend university the rate of leaving the Sangha is notoriously high.

The challenge

The traditional Sinhalese system of 'village-dwelling' monks had its defects and dangers for the 'purity' of the Sangha. But it served to bring Buddhist values to village homes. Now that the village community is in irreversible decline, the traditional village incumbent may continue to provide some services as a ritual specialist or a rather amateurish social welfare worker, but he can no longer function as an effective focus of religious life or even, unless he is an exceptional individual, as a symbol of the highest values and spiritual goals. To hold its best-educated young members, the Sangha will have to offer them more interesting careers. The state provides official patronage which should ensure the Sangha's continuance as an autonomous body; but being Established will no more help the Sangha to hold the hearts and minds of the Buddhist public than it ensures the Anglican Church the moral and intellectual leadership of Britain. The Sangha, as some of them realize, will have to learn the use of the mass media so that they can operate on a national rather than a local basis; at the same time, they may have to increase their effective presence in the towns, especially in the slums. The Sinhala service of Radio Ceylon begins its daily programmes with monks chanting *pirit*, so that there are few spots in the Sinhalese parts of the country from which one cannot hear these sacred sounds at 6 a.m. But the noise is deceptive; it can do nothing to counteract secular trends. People can choose their reading matter, tune to another radio station. However, the recent introduction of television has given the Sangha, like everyone else permitted to use it, a potential tool of immense power. Much will depend on whether monks of calibre will come forward to use these new means of communication. But even if the Sangha recruits religious virtuosi who are also gifted communicators, and even if Sinhalese society somehow survives the tensions created by population pressures, lay religiosity is here to stay. The Sangha, being Buddhists, will never become ayatollahs, and the homogeneous Buddhist world of ancient Ceylon will never be recovered.

Works cited

(excluding primary sources in classical languages, for which see *Abbreviations* below)

Adikaram, E.W. (1946), *Early History of Buddhism in Ceylon*, Colombo.

Bareau, André (1983), 'Preface' in Wijayaratna (see below).

Basham, A.L. (1980), 'The Background to the Rise of Buddhism', in A.K. Narain (ed.), *Studies in the History of Buddhism*, Delhi, pp. 13–31.

Bechert, Heinz (1961), 'Aśokas "Schismenedikt" und der Begriff Sanghabheda', *Wiener Zeitschrift für die Kunde Süd- und Ostasiens* V, pp. 18–52.

Bechert, Heinz (1966), *Buddhismus, Staat und Gesellschaft in den Ländern des Theravāda Buddhismus*, vol. I, Frankfurt a M and Berlin.

Bechert, Heinz (1967), *id.*, vol. II, Wiesbaden.

Bechert, Heinz (1973), *id.*, vol. III, Wiesbaden.

Bechert, Heinz (1977a), 'Mahāyāna Literature in Sri Lanka: the Early Phase', in L. Lancaster (ed.), *Prajñāpāramitā and Related Systems. Studies in honour of Edward Conze*, Berkeley, pp. 361–8.

Bechert, Heinz (1977b), 'Mythologie der Singhalesischen Volksreligion', in H.W. Haussig (ed.), *Wörterbuch der Mythologie. I Abteilung: Die Alten Kulturvölker*, Stuttgart, pp. 511–656.

Works cited

Bechert, Heinz (1982a), 'The Importance of Aśoka's so-called Schism Edict', in L.A. Hercus *et al.* (ed.), *Indological and Buddhist Studies: Volume in Honour of Professor J.W. de Jong on his Sixtieth Birthday*, Canberra, pp. 61–8.

Bechert, Heinz (1982b), 'The date of the Buddha reconsidered', *Indologia Taurinensia* 10, pp. 29–36.

Bechert, Heinz and Gombrich, Richard (ed.) (1984) *The World of Buddhism*, London and New York.

Buddhaghosa (1964), *The Path of Purification*, trans. Bhikkhu Ñyāṇamoli, Colombo, 2nd ed.

Bunnag, Jane (1973), *Buddhist monk, Buddhist layman*, Cambridge.

Carrithers, Michael (1983a), *The Forest Monks of Sri Lanka: An Anthropological and Historical Study*, Delhi.

Carrithers, Michael (1983b), *The Buddha*, Oxford and New York.

Collins, Steven (1982), *Selfless Persons*, Cambridge.

Cone, Margaret and Gombrich, Richard F. (1977) *The Perfect Generosity of Prince Vessantara*, Oxford

Coomaraswamy, Ananda K. (1908), *Medieval Sinhalese Art*, Broad Campden, Glos.

Copleston, R.S. (1982), *Buddhism Primitive and Present in Magadha and in Ceylon*, London and New York.

de Jong *see* Jong

De Silva, K.M. (1981), *A History of Sri Lanka*, London, Berkeley and Los Angeles.

Dumont, Louis (1970), 'World Renunciation in Indian Religions', in *Religion/Politics and History in India*, Paris and the Hague, pp. 33–60.

Eggermont, P.H.L. (1956), *The Chronology of the Reign of Asoka Moriya*, Leiden.

Eggermont, P.H.L. (1965–6) 'New Notes on Asoka and his Successors', *Persica* I, 2, pp. 27–71

Frauwallner, Erich (1953), *Geschichte der indischen Philosophie*, vol. I, Salzburg.

Frauwallner, Erich (1956), *The Earliest Vinaya and the Beginnings of Buddhist Literature*, Rome.

Freud, Sigmund and Breuer, Joseph *Studies on Hysteria*, trans. James and Alix Strachey, Harmondsworth (original ed. 1895).

Geertz, Clifford (1968), *Islam Observed*, Chicago and London.

Geertz, Clifford (1975), 'Religion as a Cultural System', in *The Interpretation of Cultures*, London, pp. 87–125.

Geiger, Wilhelm (1912), 'Introduction' to *The Mahāvaṃsa* trans. Geiger, Colombo.

Geiger, Wilhelm (1960), *Culture of Ceylon in Mediaeval Times*, ed. Heinz Bechert, Wiesbaden.

Ghosh, A. (1973), *The City in Early Historical India*, Simla.

Gibbon, Edward (1776–88), *The Decline and Fall of the Roman Empire*, London.

Gokhale, B.G. (1965), 'The Early Buddhist Elite', *Journal of Indian History* XLII part II, pp. 391–402.

Gokhale, B.G. (1980), 'Early Buddhism and the Brahmins', in A.K. Narain (ed.), *Studies in the History of Buddhism*, Delhi, pp. 68–80.

Gombrich, E.H. (1980), 'Four Theories of Artistic Expression', *Architectural Association Quarterly* 12, 4, pp. 14–19.

Gombrich, E.H. (1984), *Tributes*, Oxford.

Gombrich, Richard F. (1966), 'The Consecration of a Buddhist Image', *Journal of Asian Studies* XXVI, 1, pp. 23–36.

Gombrich, Richard F. (1971), *Precept and Practice: Traditional Buddhism in the Rural Highlands of Ceylon*, Oxford.

Gombrich, Richard F. (1980), 'The Significance of Former Buddhas in the Theravādin Tradition', in Somaratna Balasooriya *et al.* (ed.), *Buddhist studies in honour of Walpola Rahula*, London and Bedford, pp. 62–72.

Gombrich, Richard F. (1981), 'A new Theravādin liturgy', *Journal of the Pali Text Society* IX, pp. 47–73.

Gombrich, Richard F. (1983), 'From monastery to meditation centre: lay meditation in modern Sri Lanka', in Philip Denwood and Alexander Piatigorsky (ed.), *Buddhist Studies Ancient and Modern*, London, pp. 20–34.

Gombrich, Richard F. (1984), 'Temporary Ordination in Sri Lanka', *Journal of the International Association of Buddhist Studies* 7, 2, pp. 41–65.

Goody, Jack (ed.) (1968), *Literacy in Traditional Societies*, Cambridge.

Gunawardana, R.A.L.H. (1979), *Robe and Plough: Monasticism and Economic Interest in Early Medieval Sri Lanka*, Tucson.

Heesterman, J.C. (1979), 'Power and Authority in Indian Tradition', in R.J. Moore (ed.), *Tradition and Politics in South Asia*, New Delhi, pp. 60–85.

Jaini, Padmanabh S. (1979), *The Jaina Path of Purification*, Berkeley and Delhi.

Jayatilleke, K.N. (1971), Facets of Buddhist Thought, *The Wheel Publication* no. 162/163/164, Kandy.

Jong, J.W. de (1981), 'Fa-hsien and Buddhist Texts in Ceylon', *Journal of the Pali Text Society* IX, pp. 105–16

Kane, P.V. (1930–62), *History of Dharmaśāstra*, 5 vols, Poona.

Knox, Robert (1956–7), An Historical Relation of Ceylon, ed. S.D. Saparamadu, *Ceylon Historical Journal* VI, 1–4 (original ed. 1681).

Kosambi, D.D. (1965), *The Culture and Civilisation of Ancient India in Historical Outline*, London.

Lamotte, Étienne (1958), *Histoire du Bouddhisme Indien*, Louvain.

Laslett, Peter (1979), *The world we have lost*, London, 2nd ed corrected reprint.

Lévi, Sylvain (1915), 'Sur la récitation primitive des textes bouddhiques', *Journal Asiatique* I, pp. 401–47.

Lévi-Strauss, Claude (1964), *Le cru et le cuit*, Paris.

Loofs, H.H.E. (1979), 'Problems of Continuity between the pre-Buddhist and Buddhist periods in Central Thailand, with special reference to U-Thong', in R.B. Smith and W. Watson (ed.), *Early South East Asia*, Oxford, pp. 342–51.

Lukes, Steven (1973), *Individualism*, Oxford.

Malalgoda, Kitsiri (1976), *Buddhism in Sinhalese Society 1750–1900*, Berkeley.

Malamoud, Charles (1981), 'Inde védique. Religion et mythologie', in *Dictionnaire des Mythologies*, Flammarion, Paris.

Maleipan, Veerapan (1979), 'The Excavation at Sab Champa', in R.B. Smith and W. Watson (ed.), *Early South East Asia*, Oxford, pp. 337–41.

McNeill, William H. (1979), *Plagues and Peoples*, Harmondsworth (original ed. 1976).

Mendis, G.C. (1947), 'The Chronology of the early Pali chronicles', *University of Ceylon Review* 5, 1, pp. 39–54.

Nikam, N.A. and McKeon, Richard (ed. and trans.) (1959), *The Edicts of Asoka*, Chicago.

Norman, K.R. (1975), 'Aśoka and Capital Punishment', *Journal of the Royal Asiatic Society* no. 1, pp. 16–24.

Norman, K.R. (1982), 'The Four Noble Truths: a problem of Pāli syntax', in L.A. Hercus *et al.* (ed.), *Indological and Buddhist Studies: Volume in Honour of*

Professor J.W. de Jong on his Sixtieth Birthday, Canberra, pp. 377–91.

Obeyesekere, Gananath (1970), 'Religious Symbolism and Political Change in Ceylon', *Modern Ceylon Studies*, 1, 1, pp. 43–63.

Popper, Karl R. (1974), 'Towards a rational theory of tradition', in *Conjectures and Refutations*, 5th ed, London (paper originally published 1949).

Popper, Karl R. and Eccles, John C. (1977), *The Self and its Brain*, Berlin.

Rahula, Walpola (1956), *History of Buddhism in Ceylon: the Anuradhapura Period*, Colombo.

Rahula, Walpola (1967), *What the Buddha taught*, 2nd ed, Bedford.

Rhys Davids, T.W. (1887), *Buddhism*, London (original ed. 1877).

Rhys Davids, T.W. (1896), 'Introduction' to *The Yogāvacara's Manual* ed. T.W. Rhys Davids, London.

Rhys Davids, T.W. and Oldenberg, H. (1881), 'Introduction' to *Vinaya Texts Part I, Sacred Books of the East* XIII, Oxford.

Saddhatissa, H. (1970), *Buddhist Ethics*, London.

Sarkisyanz, E. (1965), *Buddhist Backgrounds of the Burmese Revolution*, The Hague.

Schofield, R.S. (1973), 'Dimensions of Illiteracy, 1750–1850', *Explorations in Economic History* 10, 4, pp. 437–54.

Seneviratne, H.L. (1978), *Rituals of the Kandyan State*, Cambridge.

Sharma, R.S. (1983), *Material Culture and Social Formations in Ancient India*, Delhi.

Spiro, Melford E. (1970), *Buddhism and Society: A Great Tradition and its Burmese Vicissitudes*, New York.

Thapar, Romila (1966), *A History of India*, vol. 1, Harmondsworth.

Thomas, Keith (1971), *Religion and the Decline of Magic*, London.

Wasson, R. Gordon (1968), *Soma: divine mushroom of immortality*, The Hague.

Weber, Max (1958), *The Religion of India*, trans. and ed. Hans H. Gerth and Don Martindale, New York (original ed. 1921).

Welch, Holmes (1967), *The Practice of Chinese Buddhism, 1900–1950*, Cambridge, Mass.

Wijayaratna, Mohan (1983), *Le moine bouddhique selon les textes du Theravâda*, Paris.

Abbreviations and primary sources

References to Pali texts in the list below are to the original, but that does not make them useless to the reader who knows no Pali. The references are to the Pali Text Society editions, and almost all English translations give the pagination of those editions. Translations of the Sanskrit and Prakrit texts too will invariably use the systems of reference used below. All the texts cited are Pali except those marked with an asterisk, which are Sanskrit, or with a dagger, which are Prakrit.

In the references to chapter 4, the Pali words not found in this list are monastic rules of the *pātimokkha* (see p. 92).

Abbreviations for names of texts

AN	*Aṅguttara Nikāya*
BA.Up.	*Bṛhad Āraṇyaka Upaniṣad**
B.Dhs.	*Baudhāyana Dharmasūtra**
Car.S.	*Caraka Saṃhitā**
Ch.Up.	*Chāndogya Upaniṣad**
Dhp.	*Dhammapada*
DN	*Dīgha Nikāya*
Dv.	*Dīpavaṃsa*
G.Dhs.	*Gautama Dharmasūtra**
J	*Jātaka*
Mhv.	*Mahāvaṃsa*

Mil.	*Milindapañha*	
MN	*Majjhima Nikāya*	
Pap.s.	*Papañca-sūdanī*	
PE	Pillar Edict†	} of Asoka
RE	Rock Edict†	
Sam.p.	*Samanta-pāsādikā*	
SN	*Saṃyutta Nikāya*	
Snip.	*Sutta-nipāta*	
Sum.v.	*Sumaṅgala-vilāsinī*	
Thīg.	*Therī-gāthā*	
Utt.	*Uttarādhyayana Sūtra*†	
V.nid.	*Vinaya-nidāna*	
Vin.	*Vinaya*	
Vism.	*Visuddhi-magga*	
Yāska	Yāska, *Nirukta**	

Other abbreviations used below

Id.	same work as in previous reference
Ibid.	same reference as the previous one

References

Chapter 1 Introduction

1 Gibbon chap. XV.
2 Rhys Davids 1887, p. 3.
3 Popper and Eccles, chap. P1.
4 Quoted E.H. Gombrich 1984, pp. 167–8.
5 E.H. Gombrich 1980, pp. 18–19.
6 Popper p. 129.
7 Popper p. 124.
8 *Ibid.*
9 Popper p. 123.
10 *Vin.* I, 21.
11 Bechert and Gombrich, pp. 77–80.
12 Carrithers 1983b.
13 Rhys Davids 1887, p. 3.
14 R.F. Gombrich 1971, p. 46.
15 Rhys Davids 1887, p. 7.
16 R.F. Gombrich 1971, p. 11.
17 Geertz 1968, p. 97.
18 *DN* I, 60 ff.
19 *MN* I, 134–5.

Chapter 2 Gotama Buddha's problem situation

1 *DN* II, 100 and 151.

2 Bechert 1982b.
3 See also Geertz 1975, especially pp. 93–4, 114.
4 Wasson.
5 Lévi-Strauss.
6 *Ch.Up.* I, 9.
7 Malamoud p. 3.
8 *BA.Up.* IV, 4, 6.
9 Dumont.
10 *DN* II, 73–7.
11 Weber p. 204.
12 Kosambi p. 89.
13 Sharma p. 93.
14 *Id.* p. 94.
15 Ghosh p. 7.
16 *Id.* p. 30.
17 *Id.* p. 9.
18 Sharma p. 98.
19 *Id.* p. 103.
20 *Id.* p. 100.
21 Ghosh pp. 20–2
22 *Id.* p. 30.
23 *Id.* p. 14.
24 *Id.* p. 71.
25 *B.Dhs.* quoted Sharma p. 124.
26 Basham p. 25 fn. 8.
27 Ghosh p. 14.
28 Thapar p. 63.
29 Goody p. 2.
30 Ghosh pp. 25–6.
31 *Id.* p. 68.
32 *Id.* p. 70.
33 *Id.* p. 64.
34 Sharma p. 123.
35 *DN* II, 146.
36 Ghosh p. 16.
37 *AN* I, 213 = *AN* IV, 252.
38 Heesterman p. 66.
39 *B. Dhs.* I, 10, 31.
40 *G. Dhs.* XVI, 46.
41 *B. Dhs.* II, 6, 33.
42 Gokhale 1965 and 1980.
43 Professor S. Nagaraju, personal communication.
44 *MN* I, 387.

45 Ghosh p. 37.
46 McNeill p. 91.
47 *Id.* p. 86.
48 *Id.* chap. 2, pp. 40–77.
49 *Car.S.*, *Vimānasthāna* III, 20.
50 Frauwallner 1953, p. 184.

Chapter 3 The Buddha's Dhamma

1 *Vin.* I, 10.
2 *MN* I, 246.
3 Norman 1982.
4 E.g. *AN* IV, 249.
5 Carrithers 1983a, p. 101.
6 E.g. *DN* I, 238–40.
7 *Vin.* I, 1.
8 *Vin.* I, 34.
9 *Vin.* I, 13.
10 *DN* II, 290ff.
11 *Vism.* IX, p. 321.
12 *Snip.* I, 8 = verses 143–52.
13 *AN* IV 241 = *DN* III, 218.
14 *Ch.Up.* VI, 8ff.
15 *DN* I, 52.
16 *AN* III, 415.
17 *Snip.* verse 136.
18 *AN* IV, 202.
19 *J* VI, 1–30 = story 538.
20 *SN* III, 120.
21 *DN* II, 154.
22 Yāska, I, 1, *passim*.
23 *Vin.* II, 139.
24 *Vin.* II, 108; Lévi.
25 *AN* I, 188–93.
26 Personal communication.
27 Lukes p. 94.
28 Basham p. 17.
29 *Mil.* p. 264.
30 *AN* IV, 211.
31 *MN* III, 261.
32 *DN* III, 191.
33 *AN* IV, 203.
34 *Ch.Up.* VI, 13.

35 *SN* IV, 314–6.
36 *Vin.* I, 152.
37 *MN* II, 149.
38 *MN* II, 148; *DN* III, 81–2.
39 *MN* II, 84–6.
40 Saddhatissa, especially chap. 6.
41 *DN* II, 85–6.
42 *SN* I, 86.
43 *AN* III, 45–6.
44 *AN* III, 76–8.
45 *DN* III, 180–93.
46 *AN* IV, 269.
47 *AN* IV, 43–5.
48 *AN* II, 69–70.
49 *MN* II, 197–9.
50 *Mil.* pp. 121–3.
51 *Vin.* I, 73–4.
52 *SN* I, 75–6
53 *Utt.* XII.
54 Cf. also *Vin.* I, 122.
55 *DN* I, 7.
56 *Dhp.* 129.
57 *DN* III, 58–79.
58 *DN* I, 127–49.
59 *DN* I, 135.
60 *DN* III, 61.
61 *DN* III, 80–98.

Chapter 4 The Sangha's discipline

1 *DN*, II, 100.
2 Carrithers 1983a, p. 281.
3 *Id.* p. 43.
4 Wijayaratna p. 143.
5 *Vin.* III, 21 etc.
6 Bareau p. 10.
7 Frauwallner 1956, p. 3 and chap. 4.
8 See also Frauwallner 1956, chap. 5.
9 Rhys Davids and Oldenberg pp. ix-xxxiv.
10 *Id.*, p. xxxiii.
11 For details see Rhys Davids and Oldenberg pp. xv-xix.
12 *Nissaggiya pācittiya* 10, *Vin.* III, 219–23.
13 Wijayaratna p. 15.

14 *SN* III, 283; *SN* IV, 35–7.
15 Wijayaratna p. 59.
16 *Vin*. I, 58.
17 *Vin*. II, 197.
18 *MN* III, 40–2.
19 Collins pp. 167–76.
20 *Vin*. I, 137.
21 *DN* I, 5.
22 *Vin*. III, 42.
23 *Vin*. I, 39.
24 Wijayaratna p. 40.
25 *Vin*. II, 146.
26 E.g. *Vin*. III, 155.
27 *Vin*. III, 169–70.
28 Wijayaratna p. 49.
29 E.g. *Vin*. II, 175–7; *Vin*. III, 158.
30 *Vin*. IV, 296.
31 *AN* III, 258.
32 *Vin*. I, 139.
33 Welch pp. 10–6.
34 Bunnag pp. 91, 96.
35 Carrithers 1983a, p. 43.
36 *Id*. pp. 56–7, 121.
37 *Vin*. IV, 278.
38 *Vin*. II, 122.
39 *Vin*. I, 305.
40 *Vin*. IV, 91.
41 *Vin*. III, 212.
42 *Vin*. I, 280.
43 *Ibid*.
44 *Vin*. I, 287.
45 Wijayaratna p. 51.
46 *Vin*. I, 294.
47 *Vin*. I, 288.
48 *Vin*. I, 298.
49 Wijayaratna p. 62.
50 *Vin*. II, 136.
51 *Vin*. I, 288.
52 *SN* II, 221.
53 *Vin*. I, 297.
54 *Vin*. I, 283–5.
55 *Vin*. I, 253ff.
56 *Vin*. I, 187.

57 *Vin.* II, 130.
58 *Vin.* II, 112–4.
59 *Vin.* I, 90.
60 *MN* I, 473.
61 Carrithers 1983a, p. 285.
62 *Vin.* I, 199.
63 *Vin.* IV, 90.
64 *Pāṭidesanīya* 39, *Sekhiya* 37, etc.
65 *Vin.* II, 197.
66 *Vin.* I, 218–20.
67 *Vin.* I, 238.
68 *Vin.* II, 215–7.
69 *Vin.* I, 223.
70 *Vin.* II, 197.
71 E.g. *Vin.* I, 38.
72 *Vin.* III, 158.
73 *Vin.* IV, 66.
74 *Vin.* I, 211.
75 *Vin.* I, 212.
76 *Vin.* I, 207.
77 *Nissaggiya pācittiya* 18.
78 *Nissaggiya pācittiya* 20.
79 *Vin.* II, 294ff.
80 *Vin.* III, 238.
81 *Vin.* I, 245.
82 *Vin.* I, 211.
83 See also *Sam.p* VI, 1238.
84 *Pācittiya* 10.
85 *Pācittiya* 8.
86 *Vin.* II, 112; Wijayaratna p.143; Ven. W. Rahula, personal communication.
87 *Vin.* III, 109.
88 *Vin.* IV, 211–22.
89 Wijayaratna pp. 116–19 and references there cited.
90 *Vin.* IV, 134–5.
91 *SN* I, 86.
92 *AN* I, 1–2.
93 *SN* IV, 110–1.
94 *Vin.* III, 158.
95 *AN* III, 78.
96 *Thīg.* passim.
97 *Vin.* II, 255.
98 *Vin.* I, 49 para. 20.
99 *Vin.* I, 46 para. 10.

100 *Vin.* I, 79.
101 *Vin.* I, 83.
102 *Vin.* I, 82.
103 *Vin.* I, 83–4.
104 *Vin.* I, 93.
105 See R.F. Gombrich 1984, p. 42.
106 *Vin.* I, 60.
107 *Vin.* I, 58.
108 *Vin.* I, 197.
109 *Vin.* I, 56.
110 *Vin.* I, 93.
111 *Vin.* I, 91.
112 *Vin.* I, 104.
113 *Vin.* I, 102–3.
114 *Vin.* I, 112–3.
115 *Vin.* I, 101.
116 *Vin.* I, 115.
117 *Vin.* II, 236–7.
118 *Vin.* I, 125–6; *Vin.* II, 240–1.
119 *Vin.* I, 124.
120 *DN* II, 76.
121 *Vin.* I, 120.
122 *Vin.* I, 106.
123 *Ibid.*
124 *Pap.s.* I, 115.
125 Bechert 1961, pp. 30–1 and 1982a, p. 64.
126 *Snip.* verse 231.
127 Frauwallner 1956, chap. 1.
128 Bechert 1977a, p. 362.
129 *Pācittiya* 68.
130 Carrithers 1983a, p. 251.
131 *DN* II, 73–7.
132 Carrithers 1983a, p. 252.
133 *Vin.* I, 158, 351.
134 *Vin.* I, 159.
135 *Ibid.*
136 *Vin.* I, 351.
137 *Dhp.* 382.
138 Carrithers 1983a, p. 51.
139 *Id.* p. 292.
140 Jaini pp. 4, 35–6, 42.
141 *MN* I, 12.
142 *Vin.* II, 125.

143 *Vin.* I, 73–4.
144 *Vin.* I, 76.
145 *DN* I, 60.
146 *Vin.* I, 138.

Chapter 5 The accommodation between Buddhism and society in ancient India

1 *DN* II, 100.
2 *DN* II, 154.
3 R.F. Gombrich 1980.
4 Cone and Gombrich.
5 *DN* II, 142.
6 *DN* II, 166.
7 *DN* II, 160.
8 R.F. Gombrich 1971, chap. 3.
9 *Id.* chap. 5.
10 *DN* II, 88.
11 *Vin.* I, 223.
12 Carrithers 1983a, pp. 50–1.
13 Eggermont 1956 and 1965–6.
14 RE XIII.
15 Minor RE I.
16 Barabar inscription.
17 RE XII
18 PE IV; Norman 1975.
19 PE V.
20 RE I.
21 RE II.
22 RE XIII.
23 RE VIII.
24 RE V; PE VII.
25 Kalinga Separate Edict I.
26 RE IX.
27 Saddhatissa p. 143.
28 Nikam and McKeon.
29 RE III.
30 RE VI.
31 PE VII.
32 Rummindei inscription.
33 Nigalisagar inscription.
34 Bhabra inscription.
35 Kosam, Sāñci and Sārnāth.

36 RE XIII.
37 RE V.
38 *Mhv.*, mainly chap. V.
39 *Mhv.* V, 63.
40 *Mhv.* V, 273.
41 Rahula 1956, pp.73 fn, 86.
42 Sarkisyanz pp. 33–6, 66–7, 93–4, 97.
43 Bechert 1967, pp. 143, 168.
44 *Id.*, p. 253.
45 Professor T. Ling, personal communication.
46 Rahula 1956, p. 5fn.
47 Bechert 1966, p. 128.
48 *Id.*, 74.
49 *V. nid.* para. 64.
50 *V. nid.* para. 71.
51 Lamotte p. 333.
52 *Id.* pp. 320–39.
53 Frauwallner 1956, pp. 12–23.
54 *V. nid.* paras. 73–5; *Mhv.* XIII.
55 *Dv.* XII, 5ff.

Chapter 6 The Buddhist tradition in Sri Lanka

1 Loofs p. 349.
2 Dr. Janice Stargardt, personal communication.
3 Loofs; Maleipan.
4 *Mhv.* VII, 4.
5 Rahula 1956, p. 111.
6 *Id.* p. xx.
7 *Id.* pp. xxii–xxiii.
8 *Mhv.* XXV, 1.
9 *Mhv.* XXV, 4.
10 *Mhv.* XXV, 108–11.
11 *Mhv.* LXXVIII, 6.
12 *Mhv.* LXXXII, 19ff.
13 R.F. Gombrich 1971, pp. 257–8.
14 *Mhv.* LXXXIV, 9–10.
15 Gunawardana pp. 262–77.
16 Rahula 1956, pp.65–6; Gunawardana pp. 45, 47–8.
17 R.F. Gombrich 1971, especially chap. 4.
18 See however Rahula 1956, p. 237 fn2.
19 Bechert 1977b, pp. 602–3.
20 Rahula 1956, p. 71.

21 *Id.* pp. 108–10; Gunawardana pp. 219–21.
22 R.F. Gombrich 1971, pp. 113–40.
23 Seneviratne chap. 3.
24 R.F. Gombrich 1971, p. 113; Rahula 1956, pp. 121–5.
25 R.F. Gombrich 1966.
26 R.F. Gombrich 1971, pp. 201–6 and references there cited.
27 *Mhv.* XIII, 18–20.
28 *Mhv.* XIV, 23.
29 *Mhv.* XIV, 53.
30 *Mhv.* XIV, 65.
31 *Mhv.* XV, 26.
32 *Mhv.* XV, 181.
33 *Mhv.* XVII, 2–3.
34 *V. nid.* para. 105.
35 *V. nid.* para. 106.
36 Rahula 1956, p. 54.
37 Thomas pp. 73, 163–7.
38 *Mhv.* XXXIII, 100–1.
39 Quoted Rahula 1956, p. 158.
40 *Id.* pp. 159–60.
41 *Sum. v.* I, 1.
42 Adikaram chap. 3.
43 *Id.*, especially pp. 10–23, 87.
44 *Sam. p.* I, 2.
45 *Mhv.* XXXVII, 175.
46 Cf. R.F. Gombrich 1971, pp. 85–91.
47 *Vism.* I, p. 38.
48 Coomaraswamy p. 168.
49 *DN* I, 5 ff.
50 Rahula 1956, p. 108; see also Gunawardana p. 43.
51 *Mhv.* LXI, 58–61.
52 Rahula 1956, p. 196.
53 Bechert fn to Geiger 1960, p. 206 para. 198.
54 Rahula 1956, pp. 83–4.
55 *Id.* p. 94.
56 *Mhv.* LXXVIII, 30.
57 *Mhv.* LXXIII, 21–2.
58 *Mhv.* LXXVIII, 25–6.
59 Bechert 1966, p. 265.
60 Bechert 1967, p. 185.
61 Bunnag pp. 73–6.
62 Geiger 1960, para. 197.
63 *Mhv.* XXXVII, 148.

64 *Mhv*. XXXVII, 112–71.
65 *Mhv*. XXXVII, 145.
66 *Mhv*. XXXVII, 109.
67 Geiger 1960, para. 203.
68 Rahula 1956, p. 62.
69 *Mhv*. XXXIII, 50.
70 *Mhv*. XXXIII, 82.
71 Gunawardana p. 59.
72 Rahula 1956, p. 147.
73 *Id*. p. 146.
74 *Id*. p. 148.
75 *Id*. p. 149.
76 *Id*. p. 148.
77 *Mhv*. XXXIII, 49.
78 Gunawardana p. 68.
79 *Id*. p. 57.
80 *Id*. pp. 77–8.
81 Rahula 1956, p. 145.
82 Gunawardana p. 77.
83 *Sam. p*. III, 679, trans. Gunawardana p. 58.
84 Rahula 1956, p. 139.
85 De Silva pp. 83–4.
86 Spiro, p. 284.
87 Bechert 1967, p. 26.
88 *Mhv*. LXI, 54–8.
89 Gunawardana pp. 91–4.
90 Rahula 1956, p. 136.
91 *Id*. p. 137.
92 *Ibid*.
93 Gunawardana pp. 84–5.
94 Rahula 1956. p. 135 fn. 1.
95 Gunawardana p. 82.
96 R.F. Gombrich 1971, p. 307.
97 *Id*. p. 308.
98 *Mhv*. LXXVIII, 3–4.
99 Rahula 1956, pp. 67, 104–5.
100 *Id*. p. 68.
101 *Mhv*. LX, 4–8.
102 Gunawardana pp. 273–4.
103 *Id*. p. 272.
104 *Id*. p. 276.
105 *Id*. p. 280; see also de Jong p. 113 and fn. 20.
106 Gunawardana p. 39.

107 Carrithers 1983a.
108 *Id.*, especially p. 223.
109 R.F. Gombrich 1971, pp. 285–6.
110 Rahula 1956, p. 221.
111 *Id.* p. 229.
112 *Id.* pp. 148–9.
113 Kane II, pp. 869–70.
114 Rahula 1956, p. 148.
115 Cone and Gombrich.
116 Rahula 1956, p. 271.
117 *Ibid.*
118 *Id.* p. 262.
119 *Id.* p. 148.
120 R.F. Gombrich 1971, chap. 6.
121 Knox p. 102.

Chapter 7 Protestant Buddhism

1 Malalgoda pp. 65–6.
2 De Silva p. 296.
3 Copleston p. 434.
4 Bechert 1966, p. 221.
5 Copleston p. 461.
6 Malalgoda pp. 91, 97.
7 *Id.* p. 98.
8 *Id.* pp. 98–100.
9 *Id.* p. 101.
10 Quoted *id.* p. 109.
11 *Id.* p. 114.
12 *Id.* p. 122.
13 *Id.* pp. 115ff.
14 *Id.* pp. 123–4.
15 Bechert 1966, p. 260.
16 Malalgoda p. 125.
17 *Id.* p. 120.
18 *Id.* p. 235.
19 *Id.* p. 192.
20 *Id.* pp. 207–8.
21 Copleston p. 7.
22 Above facts from Malalgoda pp. 193–6.
23 *Id.* p. 209.
24 *Id.* pp. 199–200.
25 Quoted *id.* pp. 222–3.

26 *Id.* p. 223.
27 *Id.* p. 197.
28 Quoted *id.* p. 201.
29 *Id.* p. 202.
30 *Id.* p. 203.
31 Quoted *id.* pp. 204–5.
32 *Id.* p. 205.
33 *Id.* p. 210.
34 *Id.* p. 211.
35 *Id.* p. 212.
36 Quoted *id.* p. 227.
37 Quoted *id.* p. 213.
38 Quoted *id.* p. 231.
39 *Id.* pp. 216–8.
40 *Id.* p. 219.
41 *Id.* p. 208 fn. 49.
42 *Id.* pp. 220–2.
43 *Id.* pp. 224–5.
44 *Id.* p. 232 fn. 1.
45 *Id.* p. 226.
46 *Id.* p. 230.
47 *Id.* p. 229.
48 Quoted *id.* p. 229 fn. 107.
49 Quoted *id.* p. 228.
50 Jayatilleke pp. 1–16.
51 *Id.* pp. 62–75.
52 Quoted Bechert 1966, p. 67.
53 Quoted Malalgoda p. 176 fn. 9.
54 Schofield p. 446.
55 Malalgoda pp. 180, 240.
56 *Id.* pp. 239–40.
57 *Id.* pp. 241, 248.
58 *Id.* p. 188.
59 Quoted *id.* p. 230.
60 Quoted *id.* p. 231.
61 *Id.* pp. 242–6.
62 Bechert 1966, p. 100.
63 Malalgoda pp. 244–51.
64 *Id.* p. 250.
65 Bechert 1966, p. 52.
66 *Id.* p. 237.
67 *Id.*, especially chaps. 25 (d), 26.
68 Malalgoda p. 248.

69 Biographical data on Dharmapāla from Bechert 1966, pp. 47–51; interpretation from Obeyesekere.
70 Malalgoda p. 253.
71 *Id.* p. 255.
72 Quoted Obeyesekere p. 54.
73 Reproduced Bechert 1973, pp. 422–39.
74 Quoted Bechert 1966, pp. 26–7.
75 Rhys Davids 1896, p. V.
76 R.F. Gombrich 1983, pp. 21–3.
77 Laslett p. 176.
78 Quoted Obeyesekere p. 57.
79 Quoted Malalgoda p. 257.
80 R.F. Gombrich 1971, pp. 62–3.
81 Quoted Bechert 1966, p. 310.
82 *Id.* pp. 360–1.
83 Quoted *id.* p. 63.
84 Malalgoda p. 175.

Chapter 8 Current trends, new problems

1 Bechert 1966, especially chaps. 17, 22.
2 R.F. Gombrich 1983.
3 Carrithers 1983a.
4 R.F. Gombrich 1981.

Index

Foreign terms are explained where they first occur in the text.